Literary Bristol
Writers and the City

Redcliffe Press/The Regional History Centre,
University of the West of England, Bristol

'Bristol is still the most beautiful big city of England'

John Betjeman in 'Bristol: An Unspoiled City' (1937)

In memory of St Matthias
and all who worked and studied there
including Boris, the well-loved campus cat

Opposite
Portrait of Ann Yearsley, 1787 by Joseph Grozer after a mezzotint by Sarah Shiells
(BMAG M3108). *Bristol's Museums, Galleries & Archives*

Literary Bristol

Writers and the City

Redcliffe Press/The Regional History Centre,
University of the West of England, Bristol

Editor Marie Mulvey-Roberts

First published in 2015 by Redcliffe Press Ltd.,
81g Pembroke Road, Bristol BS8 3EA

www.redcliffepress.co.uk
info@redcliffepress.co.uk

 RedcliffePress

 @RedcliffePress

© the contributors

ISBN 978-1-908326-73-7

British Library Cataloguing-in-Publication Data
A catalogue record for this book is available from the British Library

Design and typesetting by Stephen Morris www.stephen-morris.co.uk
Garamond 12/12
Printed and bound by Hobbs The Printers, Totton

Contents

Acknowledgments

For this protracted love-letter to Bristol, where I have lived for over two decades, I contrived to edit some chapters in relevant parts of the city, as an especially apt homage to writer and place. I would like to thank Steve Poole for his generous help with research and for including this book in the Regional History Centre series. At Redcliffe Press, enormous thanks are due to John Sansom and Clara Hudson for their help and encouragement and to Stephen Morris for his much-appreciated patience and calm efficiency. My appreciation goes to my English Literature colleagues at the University of the West of England for their support and participation. I am grateful to Bristol's Museums, Galleries and Archives, especially Julia Carver, for kind permissions regarding the reproduction of images. Thanks are due to Jenny DiPlacidi, Linda Dryden, Dawn Dyer at the Bristol Central Reference Library, the librarians at Bristol University Library, particularly Michael Richardson and Jamie Carstairs, and Ellen Reed at the University of the West of England, Bristol, as well as to Tom Abba, Peter Fleming, Caroline Franklin, Alex Gilkison, Sue Hardiman, David Hopkinson, Robin Jarvis, Andrew Kelly, Melanie Kelly, Hannah Lyons, Peter Malpass, Helen McConnell, Christine O'Brien, Martin Sampson, Sue Tate and most especially Nigel Biggs, Madge Dresser, Roger Evans, Marion Glastonbury and Maria Santamaria.

Marie Mulvey-Roberts, September 2015

Literary Bristol

Marie Mulvey-Roberts

Bristol deserves panegyric instead of Satire. I know no mercantile place so literary.[1]

Robert Southey

The very finest powers of intellect, and the proudest specimens of mental labour, have frequently appeared in the more contracted circles of provincial society. Bristol and Bath have each sent forth their sons and daughters of genius.[2]

Mary Robinson

While Bristol has been renowned as a city of churches and recognised as a thriving commercial port, insufficient attention has been paid to its literary importance, even though more writers are connected to this 'Venice of the West' than almost any other city in England, apart from London. The project, 'Mapping Literary Bristol', started at the University of the West of England, has traced the city's associations with over a hundred significant writers, past and present. Besides those of local interest, many are internationally important, and the numbers keep on growing. This book takes the reader on an armchair tour of Bristol, linking writer and place from the late eighteenth century up to the present day. With its rich maritime legacy, it should come as no great surprise that this city of writers is tied to the literature of seafaring, as in the well-loved novels, *Robinson Crusoe* (1719), *Gulliver's Travels* (1726) and *Treasure Island* (1883). Bristol's literary heritage is also built on the major Romantic poets, William Wordsworth and Samuel Taylor Coleridge, whose lesser-known counterparts include local poets, Robert Southey, Hannah More, Ann Yearsley and Robert Lovell.

The earliest Romantic poet in English is widely regarded to be Thomas Chatterton, born near St Mary Redcliffe church. Bristol was also the birthplace of Wordsworth's and Coleridge's *Lyrical Ballads* (1798), whose preface is the veritable manifesto for the Romantic Movement. The poems were originally printed by the Bristol bookseller and poet Joseph Cottle.[3] His fellow-poet Southey hailed from Bristol and was the first to record the children's story *The Three Bears* (1837) (*colour plate 1*). He not only pioneered the revival of the Gothic ballad[4] but was also the earliest writer to refer to a vampire in an English poem and to use the word '*zombi*' [sic], a connection continuing to this day, since Bristol has the oldest zombie walk in England.[5]

These and other Gothic firsts are discussed in chapter 1, which refers to several early women novelists residing in the city, who helped pioneer and popularise the Gothic novel. Among them are the landmark writers, Sophia Lee and Jane Porter. With its dissenting tradition, Bristol was also an inspirational centre for a number of radical women writers from the eighteenth century through to the Victorian age, who made significant contributions to social and political causes. They include Mary Robinson, who was born in Bristol, Mary Hays who lived there and Mary Wollstonecraft, the pioneer for women's rights and author of *A Vindication of the Rights of Woman* (1792), who wrote her first novel *Mary* (1787) during a visit. Later radicals include the educationalist and social reformer, Mary Carpenter, the social theorist Harriet Martineau and Emma Martin, who succeeded Mary Wollstonecraft as the movement's leading feminist.[6] A woman writer from Bristol, who made inroads into travel writing, was Anna Maria Falconbridge. Born in All Saints Lane, she was the first English woman to produce an eye-witness narrative account of her travels in Africa. At the age of nineteen, she married a slave-ship surgeon, turned abolitionist and, in 1794, published her experiences of Sierra Leone in a series of letters, in which she wrote about the slave trade. As Madge Dresser indicates, her views anticipated certain colonial paternalistic attitudes.[7]

The following century saw literary innovation of a different kind. The leading Victorian poets Arthur Quiller-Couch and John Addington Symonds were respectively a pupil and a teacher at Clifton College. It was there that Symonds, who had fallen in love with a chorister at Bristol Cathedral, cultivated a relationship with a schoolboy Norman Moore. His book, *A Problem with Greek Ethics*, an eulogy to 'Greek love' or pederasty, was written in 1873, though not published until 1883, and is the first extensive historical and literary study of homosexuality written in English. It appears to be the first published work in English to use the term 'homosexual'.[8] His daughter Margaret, who was aware of her father's studies in this area from the age of six, is thought to have been the object of Virginia Woolf's first passion. Katherine Bradly and her niece Edith Cooper were lesbian lovers and poets, who lived at Stoke Bishop, a suburb of north-west Bristol. They both attended classes at University College, Bristol. Publishing poems and verse dramas under the name 'Michael Field', they kept their identity hidden until it became public knowledge, not long after it was revealed to their friend Robert Browning. They were not the only aunt and niece with Bristol connections who were publishing poetry. The acclaimed Scottish poet Carolina Oliphant, Lady Nairne, whose songs were second in popularity only to Robert Burns, spent around six months in Clifton. She had come to visit her favourite niece Caroline Oliphant the Younger, who started writing poetry when she was thirteen and was acclaimed by some as 'a Girl Chatterton'.[9] Unlike her male name-sake, she was well-connected having friendships with distinguished *literati* and had been given the opportunity to travel extensively around Europe. Oliphant came closer to Chatterton in death, for she too died tragically young. Her death in 1831, at the age of twenty four, took place at 10 St Vincent's Parade, Hotwells (now 386 Hotwells Road) and she was buried in the churchyard of Clifton Parish Church.

As well as poets, Bristol has been associated with eminent dramatists, such as Tom Stoppard and Sarah Kane. In the middle of the twentieth century, the city became a powerhouse for the formation of national drama and is where Harold Pinter's first play was performed. More recent years have seen the emergence of some significant playwrights including A.C.H. Smith, a successful novelist and screen-writer, and Sheila Yeger, who has also written extensively for theatre, radio and television. Sheila Hannon is another figure who has contributed to the flourishing life of dramatic art in Bristol through her theatre company, Show of Strength. Bristol is also connected to some of Britain's most important novelists, who include Iris Murdoch and Barbara Pym. Angela Carter, one of the finest authors of the twentieth century, lived in Clifton where she wrote her first three novels, which are set in the city. The author of Harry Potter, the best-selling children's book series of all time, is J.K. Rowling, who was born in Yate and went to live in Winterbourne, within the Bristol environs. Harry Potter's surname and aspects of his character were inspired by a childhood friend in Winterbourne. This was where the young Rowling and her sister Dianne played witches and wizards with their neighbours, the Potter children.[10] The first writer to win the prestigious Orange Prize for Fiction was Helen Dunmore, a poet and novelist, who lives in Bristol. Despite these impressive connections and achievements, the extent of the city's literary heritage has not yet been fully appreciated, which has been the driving force for this book.[11]

The following chapters focus on writers who lived in Bristol and whose work engages with the city. These contributions started out as presentations for the 'Writing the West' conference organised by the Regional History Centre, University of the West of England, Bristol, held at the museum of local history, the M Shed on the city's waterfront. Much of the research already published on literary Bristol focuses on the Romantic poets, as in *English Romantic Writers and the West Country* (2010), which has a section on Bristol, and *Thomas Chatterton's Bristol: From Gothic to Romantic* (2005).[12] *Literary Bristol,* however, covers a broader range of writers, periods and genres in order to showcase the achievements of this writing city over a longer period of time.

Literary connections with Bristol may be traced back to two anonymous early fifteenth-century poems, whose author has been identified by Peter Fleming as Bristolian.[13] The title of a poem written around the middle of the century, 'The Childe of Bristow', refers to the Old English name for Bristol and tells of a local young man, who becomes a merchant.[14] The following century, John Browne published *The Merchants Avizo* (1589), a guide for apprentice merchants trading with Spain and Portugal. This manual combines practical advice with moral exhortation and ends with a fictional narration of a philosopher counselling his son from his death bed. The work is dedicated to Thomas Aldworth of Small Street and through him reaches out to the merchants of the city.[15] Bristol's ruling elite was the mercantile class and the city prospered as a commercial centre mainly due to its location on the river Avon. Appropriately as a conduit of trade, the river flows right into the heart of the city which, in 1739, prompted Alexander Pope to observe that, 'as far as you can see, hundreds of ships, their Masts as thick as they can stand by one another, which is the oddest and most surprising sight imaginable'.[16] This eighteenth-century spectacle is re-created in the historical novel, *A Respectable Trade* (1995) by Philippa Gregory, who was brought up and educated in Bristol. She writes: 'The town centre itself was crammed on the banks of the river with masts of sailing ships overtopping the chimneys, and the prows of the boats almost knocking on the doors', a time when Bristol 'was all port and no town, quaysides and no pavements. Every other street towards the town centre was a bridge with a river running beneath it'.[17]

As a port, Bristol has always been a place of departure and arrival, not merely of goods and people but also of ideas. This dynamo of exchange has seen writers come and go. One of Bristol's most famous departures was that of Thomas Chatterton, the teenage poet who went to London to make his mark as a writer. He never returned, ending his life in a garret from an overdose of arsenic. Conversely, Bristol has attracted arrivals due to its architectural splendour, commercial prosperity and natural beauty, most notably that of the Avon Gorge.[18] A lure for those seeking relaxation or cure for ailments was the warm milky-white spring water arising from St Vincent's Rocks in the Avon Gorge. The Hot Well which helped give the area lying directly south of Clifton its name, Hotwells, was at the height of its popularity between 1760 and 1800.[19] William Whitehead wrote a florid encomium to the spring, *An Hymn to the Nymph of Bristol Spring* (1751), which begins:

> Nymph of the Fount! from whose auspicious Urn,
> Flows health, flows strength, and Beauty's roseate
> Which warms the virgin's cheek, thy gifts I sing!
> Whether inclining from thy rocky couch
> Thou hear'st attentive [...].
>
> *Avonia* hear'st thou, from the neighb'ring stream
> So call'd; or *Bristoduna*; or the sound
> Well-known, *Vincentia*? Sithence from thy rock
> The Hermit pour'd his Orisons of old,
> And dying, to thy fount bequeath'd his Name.[20]

At the end of the poem, the Bristol nymph is depicted in a drawing as a barebreasted woman reclining against an urn gushing water, representing the Hot Well. Whitehead transforms 'Bristol' into '*Bristoduna*' and the River Avon into '*Avonia*'. By saturating the poem in classicism, he pays tribute to the upperclass clientele, who graced its waters. This gentrified gathering ground saw a fair influx of writers. Among them was Mary Wollstonecraft who, as mentioned earlier, wrote her first novel *Mary* whilst there and started work on another called *The Cave of Fancy*, which was never completed. At that time, Wollstonecraft was employed as a governess for the Kingsborough family, who came to take the waters. In 1784, the youthful Wollstonecraft met the elderly Dr Samuel Johnson, a close friend of Hester Lynch Thrale, the diarist and author, who ended her days on Sion Hill, overlooking the Avon Gorge. In turn Thrale was a friend to the young Frances Burney, the diarist and author, who visited the Hot Well with her father in 1767 and walked down the rocky zigzag path from Clifton Hill to Hotwell House, in which the spring was contained (*figures 1 and 2*).[21]

This is the setting for her enduringly popular novel *Evelina* (1778), where she describes the place as 'a most delightful spot; the prospect is beautiful, the air pure, and the weather very favourable to invalids.'[22] A few years earlier, this was where the novelist and ex-naval surgeon Tobias Smollett set the opening chapters of his most well-known novel, *The Expedition of Humphrey Clinker* (1771), in which Lydia Melford, while visiting Hotwell House, describes how 'the ships and boats going up and down the river, close under the windows of the Pump-room, afford such an enchanting variety of Moving Pictures.'[23] The novel contains satirical observations of English life and manners gleaned from spa towns.

Smollett was an important influence on Charles Dickens, whose character Mr Winkle, from his comic novel *Pickwick Papers* (1836), travels from Bath to Bristol. On arriving, 'Having inspected the docks and shipping, and viewed the cathedral, he inquired his way to Clifton, and being directed thither, took the route which was pointed out to him. But, as the pavements of Bristol are not the widest or cleanest upon earth, so its streets are not altogether the straightest or least intricate', Mr Winkle finds himself 'being greatly puzzled by their manifold windings and twistings'.[24] Dickens came to Bristol to give readings from his novels at the Victoria Rooms in Bristol in 1851, a venue for many other readers and performers, including the sensationalist novelist Wilkie Collins, Oscar Wilde and the actress Sarah Bernhardt. A city of actors and acting, Bristol is steeped in theatrical tradition. The novelist Elizabeth Inchbald of *A Simple Story* (1791) fame was also an actress who made her stage debut in Bristol playing Cordelia to her husband's King Lear and becoming Britain's first female professional theatre critic. The dramatist Richard Brinsley Sheridan also visited the city but, in 1792, he was involved in the melancholy task of accompanying his wife to Hotwells, as she was suffering from consumption. Although the Bristol waters were believed by some to bring about a cure, she did not survive the visit. Her husband, the well known Irish playwright wrote some of the leading plays of his day including the Restoration comedies *The Rivals* (1775) and *School for Scandal* (1777).

At the time of Sheridan's visit, the English-born novelist, Maria Edgeworth (*figure 3*), who had spent most of her life in Ireland, was living in Clifton with her family from 1791-3. Edgeworth's experiences of the South West region may have impacted upon her novels *Castle Rackrent* (1800) and *The Absentee* (1812).[25] Here, she satirises absentee Irish landlords who left their estates in chaos, choosing to spend their time in places like Bristol and Bath, which boasted fashionable spas. In one of her *Moral Tales* (1801), Edgeworth conveys the hustle and bustle of Bristol through her heroine Angelina who,

1 Samuel Jackson, *The Old Hotwell House, Bristol*, early nineteenth-century lithograph. Some of the 200 slippery steps leading down to the Hotwell House from Clifton are visible on the right-hand side (BMAG M923). *Bristol's Museums, Galleries & Archives*

2 George Holmes, *The Hotwell House seen from the Rocks at Clifton* (1815). This view conveys just how steep the ascent and descent must have been for walkers (BMAG M3397). *Bristol's Museums, Galleries & Archives*

after disembarking at the quay, walks to the Bush Inn in Corn Street where, 'she was now surprised to find herself jostled in the streets by passengers, who were all full of their own affairs hurrying different ways'.[26] It was a busy part of town with stage-coaches leaving and arriving at regular interviews to and from various parts of the country.

In 1794 Maria's sister Anna married the physician Thomas Beddoes and nearly a decade later their son, the poet Thomas Lovell Beddoes, was born at Rodney Place, Clifton. Thomas Beddoes senior developed some of the 'rational toys' for children, found in Edgeworth's *Practical Education* (1798).[27] It was rumoured that he brought corpses home to dissect on the carpet in his parlour. Beddoes was renowned for experiments in treating diseases through

Mrs Maria Edgeworth.

3 This portrait of an unknown woman, engraved as Maria Edgeworth by F. Mackenzie, after William Marshall Craig, is a line and stipple engraving published 1 November 1808, from the Fry Portrait Collection. *University of Bristol Library, Special Collections*

the inhalation of different gases at the Pneumatic Institute, which he founded in 1799 at Dowry Square in Hotwells. Richard Polwhele's poem, 'The Pneumatic Revellers' (1800), comically records Dr Beddoes observing the effects of gas on some experimental subjects:

> When I tried it, at first, on a learned society,
> Their giddiness seem'd to betray inebriety,
> Like grave mandarins, their heads nodding together;
> But afterwards each was as light as a feather:
> And they, ev'ryone, cried, 'twas a pleasure extatic;
> To drink deeper draughts of the mighty pneumatic.

As if by the wand of a wizard entranc'd,
How wildly they shouted, and gambol'd, and danc'd![28]

Coleridge was one of the revellers who attended 'laughing gas parties', where nitrous oxide or 'laughing gas' was inhaled, thereby marking the start of recreational drug-taking. (Its continuation in Bristol is the subject of Melvin Burgess's novel, *Junk* (1996), set in the 1980s in the areas of St Pauls, Stokes Croft and Montpelier.) By contrast, Coleridge's addiction to opium, through the use of laudanum, had started as pain-relief rather than for pleasure or experimentation. He tried keeping his habit discreet, but it came to light when the autobiographical *Confessions of an English Opium Eater* (1821) was published. The author was his close friend Thomas De Quincey, who was a visitor to Bristol. A walk taken with Coleridge's son Hartley in Leigh Woods had inadvertently involved, 'endangering their necks on the tangled paths.'[29] De Quincey made a literary connection with Bristol in his satiric essay, *On Murder Considered as one of the Fine Arts* (1827), in which he describes the killing of a lady and her servant girl at their home in College Green. He commented upon the audacity of the criminal in carrying out the murder at noon in such a large city.

A contemporary of De Quincey was the writer Frances (Fanny) Trollope and mother of the famous Victorian novelist Anthony Trollope, who spent her early years up to adulthood in Bristol. Her maternal grandfather was a respected apothecary residing in Queen Square and her paternal grandfather was a Bristol saddler and distiller. Fanny Trollope's father was the Reverend William Milton, an absentee vicar from his parish in Hampshire, who supplemented his income by undertaking duties at St Michael's Church in Bristol and as a curate at Almondsbury. During his twenty seven-year absence, he lived firstly in the village of Stapleton, where it was believed Fanny was born in 1779, before moving to Clifton. His real vocation appears to be that of inventor and he came up with an idea in 1791 for a tidal bypass, which led to the New Cut being dug from Totterdown to Rownham in Hotwells (*figure 4*).[30] The Bristol harbour used to have one of the most variable tides in the world, causing water levels to drop by as much as 40 feet or 13 metres This decrease could damage the hulls and cargo of moored ships when beached twice a day, unless their keels and method of securing storage were 'shipshape and [in] Bristol fashion'. The New Cut helped towards the construction of the floating harbour under the supervision of the engineer William Jessop, which provided a deep-water anchorage for vessels. In 1800 the Reverend Milton

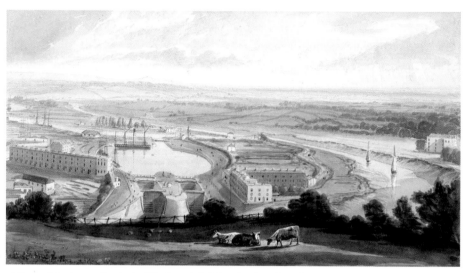

4 Samuel Jackson, *Cumberland Basin and the New Cut from Rownham*, c. 1825. This was the fruition of an idea that had originated with William Milton, the father of author Frances (Fanny) Trollope, the mother of the Victorian novelist Anthony Trollope (BMAG M970), *Bristol's Museums, Galleries & Archives*

left Bristol to return to his parish, taking his family with him.

His daughter went on to become a writer and drew on Clifton locations in her novel *The Widow Barnaby* in 1839. She is most remembered for her satiric *Domestic Manners of the Americans* (1832). For this, she drew on her travels in the United States, which included a trip to Nashoba, a plantation set up by her friend Frances Wight for the purpose of transforming slaves into Enlightenment citizens. Fanny Trollope was dismayed by the desolation of the setting, which was effectively a fever-ridden swamp, and left after only ten days fearful for her health and that of her children. The vision of Americans 'with one hand hoisting the cap of liberty, and with the other flogging their slaves'[31] prompted her to write what many consider to be the first anti-slavery novel in English, *The Life and Adventures of Jonathan Jefferson Whitlaw* (1836), in which she exposes the hypocrisy of those profiting from the slave trade. Her contact with Bristol is a possible factor in having helped plant the seeds of her indignation against slavery. It seems likely that the novel was an influence on the powerful abolitionist novel *Uncle Tom's Cabin* (1852) by Harriet Beecher Stowe. Another radical social commentator and novelist was Harriet Martineau who, before becoming a writer, spent a formative time in Bristol studying utilitarianism. She went on to introduce British readers to the struggle for abolition in the United States, well after its abolition in

Britain.[32] A much later author who makes overt links between the city and slavery is Marguerite Steen, whose historical novel set in Bristol was a bestseller on both sides of the Atlantic.[33] Forming part of a shipping saga, *The Sun is My Undoing* (1941) deals with the city's involvement in the slave trade and demonstrates how slavery degraded its Bristol slave-owners.

Bristol's unsavoury connection with the slave trade is explored in Marie Mulvey-Roberts's chapter on Gothic Bristol. Here Mary Shelley's *Frankenstein* (1818) is discussed as a novel dealing with the monstrosity and controversies surrounding slavery. During a debate in Parliament on the emancipation of slaves, Frankenstein's creature was compared to a slave as a warning against immediate emancipation. Indeed Mary Shelley may also have shared the widely-held fear that emancipating slaves too quickly could lead to bloody retribution. Having stayed in Bristol the year before starting work on the novel, she would have been aware of the city's involvement with slavery. Around that time, local newspapers regularly itemised the amounts of sugar and tobacco imported from plantations in the West Indies to Bristol, which had helped fuel the city's commercial success. Mary and her future husband Percy Bysshe Shelley had taken part in the anti-sugar boycott. For Mary Shelley, Bristol held family associations relating to birth and bereavement, which have relevance for *Frankenstein*. As Mulvey-Roberts also points out, the city's Gothic legacy forged links between architecture and authors. These include Jane Austen and the Blaise Castle Gothic folly, built from the profits from slavery; Thomas Chatterton and St Mary Redcliffe church and Mary Robinson and Bristol cathedral. Robinson, who produced a volume of poetry in reply to Wordsworth and Coleridge's *Lyrical Ballads* (1798), was an exponent of the Gothic ballad, along with Southey. Robinson's interest in vampires would be prescient for Bristol, which has historical connections with the most well-known literary blood-sucker, Count Dracula. Yet as this chapter indicates, Bristol's association with Gothic terror goes beyond the imagination to the real-life horrors of slavery.

Writers condemning the transatlantic slave trade include the Bristol poets Southey, More, Yearsley and Coleridge, who declared: 'Slavery is an Abomination to every feeling of the Head and Heart'.[34] In his 'Fears in Solitude' (1798), Coleridge asks:

> [...] my countrymen! have we gone forth
> And borne to distant tribes slavery and pangs,
> And deadlier far, our vices, whose deep taint

With slow perdition murders the whole man,
His body and his soul![35]

In 1792, while a student at Cambridge University, Coleridge (*colour plate 6*) won a medal for his poem, 'A Greek Ode on the Slave Trade'. Three years later, he gave a lecture on the subject at the Assembly Coffee-House on the quay in Bristol for an admittance of one shilling. The event had been prompted by the 'falling off of zeal in the friends of the Abolition'.[36] It was part of a series of lectures intending to fund a scheme, devised by Coleridge and his fellow-poet Southey, to found an idealistic community in Pennsylvania. Slavery was so taken for granted that Coleridge felt the need to point out in a letter to fellow abolitionist Southey of the inequity in taking on field slaves, while they themselves would be occupied pursuing philosophical ideas. Even though that collective venture never materialised, the two poets did collaborate on the slave trade lecture and made use of the Bristol Library Society.[37] Towards the end of the lecture, Coleridge argued that if those who regarded themselves as 'Christians' abstained from sugar and rum, which were being imported into Bristol, and was 'Food [...] sweetened with the Blood of the Murdered', this boycott would be sufficient to 'demolish the Whole of the Trade'.[38] In *The Watchman*, a short-lived journal he founded in Bristol, Coleridge published an essay against the slave trade where he pointed out that Europeans had exploited nine million slaves and that for every one procured, at least ten are slaughtered. 'Who are these kidnappers, and assassins?' he asked, a question which hardly failed to point a finger at Bristol.[39] In another journal, the *Edinburgh Review*, Coleridge reviewed Thomas Clarkson's *History of the Abolition of the Slave Trade* (1808), the year after the slave trade was abolished. Coleridge was a great admirer of Clarkson, whom he knew, and whose research into the sailors on slavers from Bristol had played such an important role in providing William Wilberforce with ammunition for eventually bringing about abolition.

As Robin Jarvis indicates in his chapter on Bristol's Romantic poets, Coleridge had a rather fraught relationship with Bristol, owing to his preoccupation with the slave trade and advocacy of the radical redistribution of property. This was not helped by Coleridge glorying in the fact that he was *not* a Bristolian, as when 'recollecting that there was not virtue enough in [Bristol] to tear the cloak of authority from the limbs of murder, I should blush for my birth-place.'[40] Through his poetry, he responded to the natural beauty of Bristol's surrounding scenery even though, as Jarvis points out, his main focus was elsewhere. After leaving Cambridge in 1795, Coleridge moved into College Street, near the cathedral, with his friend Southey. Later that year, both men married the Bristol Fricker sisters at St Mary Redcliffe church within less than a month of each other. Southey was born in Bristol and, as Jarvis demonstrates, his poetry displays a more concrete and committed engagement with the landscapes, legends, and regional history of the West Country than can be said of either Wordsworth or Coleridge, despite their longstanding identification with the almost oxymoronic concept of 'Romantic Bristol'. Jarvis conveys the extent of Southey's role in 'writing the West' through an exploration of his minor and occasional poetry of the 1790s. Of particular interest is a sub-genre of poetry especially favoured by Southey known as the 'inscription'. The genealogy has been traced back to a form of prosopopeia in which the inscription becomes the voice of the *genius loci* (spirit of the place) by calling to the passer-by. Southey's early inscriptions and other lyric poems bring to life obscure corners of the West Country, imbuing them for the reader with personal, historical, and political meanings. In 1813 Southey became Poet Laureate until his death in 1843 and is listed by Joseph Cottle as one of several pre-eminent figures from Bristol:

> It is a singular coincidence, reflecting great credit on Bristol, that, – the King's Poet, the King's Painter, the King's Physician, the King's Musician, and the Champion of England, should all, at the same time, have been bristol men! namely Robert Southey; Sir Thomas Lawrence; Dr Henry Southey; Charles Wesley; and the – Game Chicken! [41]

The mention of poultry is an allusion to Henry Pearce, the English boxing champion. Besides being a poet, Southey was also a historian, biographer, essayist and dramatist, who wrote a three-act drama with Coleridge and Lovell entitled *The Fall of Robespierre* (1794). This play was dedicated to Hannah More (*figure 5*), who would have responded with disapprobation since she was averse to revolutionaries.

Playwright, poet, moral campaigner, evangelical Christian and education-alist, More has been seen as one of the most influential women of her age. Born in Fishponds, she ran a school with her sisters at 43 Park Street[42] and went on to set up schools for the poor in Cheddar and its surroundings in 1789, with the aim of teaching labourers to read the Bible and accept their lowly place in the social order. Her conservative attitudes towards class tempered her approach to patronage, as in the case of tradeswoman poet

MISS HANNAH MOORE.

Published by Alexr Hogg at the Kings Arms Nº 16 Paternoster Row Nov.1.1796.

Lowry sculp.

5 Portrait of Hannah More from the Fry Portrait Collection. *University of Bristol Library, Special Collections*

Ann Yearsley (*frontispiece*). By acting as a patron for a woman who had fallen on hard times (*figure 6*), More's actions would have been welcome in Bristol by helping to mitigate the civic guilt felt over the neglect of Chatterton.[43] But Yearsley was uncomfortable with More's patronising attitude and willingness to market her as a poor Bristol milkwoman. According to Andrews, sobriquets relating to occupation were part of a pattern applicable to lower-class poets. Examples may be found around the country as in the case of John Clare who became 'the Northamptonshire peasant', Robert Burns, 'the Ayrshire Ploughman' and Robert Bloomfield, from rural Suffolk, who was known as 'the Farmer's boy'. As Kerri Andrews explains in chapter three entitled: 'In her place: Ann Yearsley or "The Bristol milkwoman"', such poets

Mifs More *presenting the* Briftol Milkwoman *to* Mrs Montague.

6 *Miss More presenting the Bristol Milkwoman to Mrs Montague* [sic]. Here Hannah More is introducing Ann Yearsley to Elizabeth Montagu, the leader of the Bluestocking Circle. *University of Bristol Library, Special Collections*

would find, along with Yearsley, that being identified through location and occupation significantly shaped how their works were read. Whilst their locale was undoubtedly important to these poets, their literary appendages invited them to be viewed as 'natural geniuses', who were fixed to a particular location. Andrews pays close attention to the ways in which Yearsley explores ideas of place, from her description of her own home in 'Clifton Hill' (published as part of *Poems on Several Occasions* (1785)), to her engagement with Bristol's involvement in slavery in *On the Inhumanity of the Slave Trade* (1788), and her critique of Bristol's governing classes in 'Bristol Elegy' (1796). Andrews examines the ways in which Yearsley seeks to understand her own place, not just in terms of physical spaces but also in regards to her role as a lower-class poet from Bristol, eager to secure for herself a place in literary culture.

Yearsley, who ran a circulating library at the Colonnade, Hotwells from about 1793, may not have been entirely happy to have found herself included in a book published after her death by Southey entitled *The Lives and Works of the Uneducated Poets* (1831). Here she is placed in the company of Bristol pipe-maker poet, John Frederick Bryant and the shoe-maker poet, James Woodhouse from the village of Rowley, near Birmingham. Another shoe-maker poet, this time from Bristol, is John Gregory. Born the same year in which Southey's book was published, Gregory found inspiration from the work of another poet of humble origin, Chatterton. This is the subject of chapter 4 written by John Goodridge, who discusses Gregory's sequence of four sonnets celebrating St Mary Redcliffe church which had inspired Chatterton's mock-medieval 'Rowley' poems. According to Goodridge, Gregory demanded that the church's doors be flung open to re-admit the spirit of the poet, whose statue had been exiled on unhallowed ground. This reflected the ambivalent local feeling about this perceived 'forger' and 'suicide', which continues to this day. Gregory's later poem 'Concerning Chatterton' (1908) forms a sequel to the sonnets, bringing the Chatterton statue imaginatively to life so that, as Goodridge explains, the earlier poet can make his own posthumous 'wail' for fairer treatment from his erstwhile community. These poems articulate the desire to re-socialise and re-localise Chatterton's spirit and art. As a radical socialist and a Christian, Gregory saw the church, with its elaborate peal of bells and aesthetically pleasing medieval craftsmanship, as a place that could inspire those in humble life. Goodridge demonstrates how Gregory was able to reinstate Chatterton's lonely art into the joyfully socialised world of his own political and social milieu. As well as a poet, shoemaker and singer-musician, Gregory was a pioneering figure in the development of an independent working-class movement in Bristol and a passionate speaker against capital punishment and war. His call for Chatterton's readmission into Bristol culture was fired by his campaigning instincts and has relevance for today. Since the original memorial to Chatterton has long fallen into disrepair, it is fitting that a new bronze statue was erected in Bristol's Millennium Square to mark the year 2000 (*colour plate 2*).

Writers not so posthumously fortunate, who have been allowed to fall into obscurity, include the prolific Emma Marshall. Popular during her life-time, especially as a children's author, she is all but forgotten today. Before moving to Bristol, she married a banker, with whom she had nine children. The collapse of her husband's bank in 1879 put a strain on the family finances and must have spurred her into producing an astonishing 200 novels and tales. Marshall wrote historical novels, some of which have Bristol settings including, *The Bristol Bells* (1892) about Thomas Chatterton, *In Colston's Days* (1884) and *Bristol's Diamonds or The Hot Wells of the Year 1773* (1888), which refers to the crystals once studding the Avon Gorge, now denuded owing to their collectability.

Another woman novelist, who was also a Clifton resident, is E.H. Young (1880-1949), the subject of chapter 5 by Kathy Mezei and Chiara Briganti. Young was the author of eleven novels and two children's books and became the winner of the James Tait Black Prize for *Miss Mole* (1930), her most acclaimed novel. Young's later novel *William* was selected as one of the first ten paperbacks to be published by Penguin in 1935. Penguin's founder Allen Lane, who was educated at Bristol Grammar school, went on to join the publishing company The Bodley Head. The story goes that after visiting Agatha Christie in Devon, he found that he had nothing worth reading during his return by train, so he came up with the idea of making cheap paperbacks available at railway stations, which could be purchased from vending machines. The proposal met with resistance from 'respectable publishers' trading in hard-back books, who were inclined to dismiss paperbacks as 'dirty rubbish'.[44] But Lane persisted with his idea and the venture proved hugely successful. It is a tribute to Young's popularity that her novel was published alongside Ernest Hemingway's *A Farewell to Arms* (1929) and the detective fiction of Dorothy L. Sayers. As Mezei and Briganti reveal, many of her novels have evocative settings in Bristol and Clifton, fictionalised as Radstowe and Upper Radstowe, while the streets, houses, and social negotiations of middle-class Bristol play a crucial role in her subtle renditions of family life and personal relationships. With a wry touch and ironic tone, Young observes the foibles, deceptions and affections of husbands and wives, children and parents, brothers and sisters, and lovers. After briefly presenting Young's biography, Mezei and Briganti discuss her novels, *Miss Mole, William, and Chatterton Square* (1947), in which Bristol and its landmarks (Brunel Bridge, the docks, Hotwells and the Avon Gorge) play a crucial role.

Young was a keen rock-climber, as is contemporary poet, Libby Houston, who can count among her ancestors, Southey and Clarkson. While carrying out her duties to help preserve rare flora in a site of special scientific interest, she can sometimes be seen rock-climbing on the Avon Gorge, where she discovered a new species of the whitebeam tree now named after her. Houston's poem to the Clifton Suspension Bridge, 'Bridge', was performed on BBC Radio 4 in 2006, interwoven with the voices of Bristolians using the bridge.[45] From rock to stone, the poet Alyson Hallett, who was the Visiting Writer at the University of the West of England, Bristol in 2001, launched a project that year called 'The Migration Habits of Stones', which involves moving stones around the world in an ongoing conversation with the land. The first of her travelling stones was a piece of slate re-located from North Wales to Leigh Woods in Bristol, a process she writes about in her first collection of poems, *The Stone Library* (2007). For this she ventures beyond the urban environment to demonstrate the intimate connection between nature, person and place.[46]

The last three chapters of this book deal with twentieth-century writers. In her chapter on drama in Bristol during the 1950s and 1960s, Dawn Fowler considers the integral role that Bristol played in the discovery and nurturing of some of the most important and critically acclaimed British dramatists of the twentieth century. She analyses the work of Bristol-based dramatist Charles Wood and explores the emergence of subversive themes, inventive language and radical politics. As Fowler explains, the mid-1950s onwards is considered a decisive milestone in British theatre with the premiere of John Osborne's *Look Back in Anger* in 1956 at the Royal Court often cited as marking the era of the 'Angry Young Man' and the beginning of 'kitchen-sink drama', with the vast majority of critical attention on this period focusing on London theatres. Bristol was, in fact, the venue for the premiere of Harold Pinter's first play *The Room* in 1957 and where Alfred Fagon, Tom Stoppard, Charles Wood and Peter Nichols began their writing careers, as well as a host of actors, producers and directors, all of whom made a vital contribution to British cultural output nationally and internationally. This chapter charts the emergence of a generation of writers who would prove to be a dynamic influence over British theatre, film and television writing and asks what the cultural climate in Bristol was at the time, which precipitated this surge of subversive creativity.

Zoe Brennan also looks at Bristol during the 1960s in the following chapter on Angela Carter, the author of the 'Bristol Trilogy', which focuses on the dark underside of the lives led by the city's bohemian youth. Through her ex-husband, Paul Carter, she became involved in the Bristol folk-scene. Paul was a lecturer at Bristol polytechnic and later became a colleague of Mulvey-Roberts who took the opportunity to ask him about Carter and her work. He insisted that the best of her work were these three novels set in Bristol.[47] As Brennan points out, while Carter insisted that the trilogy's locations were authentic, she managed to transform them into a Gothic cityscape in which her beats and hippies play out their intense and destructive relationships. Brennan argues that through her writing, Carter was subversive both in her refusal to laud countercultural norms and by challenging the London-centric bias of urban Gothic. Her chapter explores Carter's use of various Bristol settings, from the once decaying streets of Clifton through to the 'Bali Hai' bar of the 'Mecca Centre' on Frogmore Street. The bar was part of a Bristol pleasure palace, the lavish 'Grand Locarno' ballroom with its revolving stage and star-studded ceiling, which was demolished in 1998. The gypsy caravan and Irish Elk in the city's museum featuring in the Bristol trilogy can still be seen today and are artefacts worthy of a literary pilgrimage (*colour plate 3*).

In the final chapter, on the late Bristol-based author Diana Wynne Jones, Catherine Butler explores the idea of literary pilgrimage. This can be realised imaginatively, as well as in actuality. As revealed by the fiction of E.H. Young, another way of re-visiting Bristol is through memory. The city can also exist as a place of the imagination, as in Eugene Byrne's *Things Unborn* (2001). Partly set in Bristol, the novel deals with a parallel universe in which the dead are resurrected. The gap between reality and representation may also be addressed through the notion of the virtual city, whose story can be told through technology. Butler refers to a 'locative' experiential story set in Bristol, the immersive *These Pages Fall Like Ash: A Volume of Circumstance*, which uses a digital platform.[48] It works as a city within a city, locating streets which border two worlds. As Butler indicates, the idea of a parallel city co-existing with the real is fundamental to the approach taken by Jones in her fantasy and science-fiction novels for children and adults, which draw frequently on the topography of Bristol and the surrounding area, allowing one to enter a different and uncanny dimension. Novels discussed include: *A Tale of Time City* (1987), *Fire and Hemlock* (1985) and *Archer's Goon* (1984). The chapter uses a selection from Jones's work to produce a taxonomy of the ways in which she involves place in her fiction. Some of the obstacles to using knowledge of place in critical accounts of texts under discussion pay special attention to the dangers of opaque, idiosyncratic or exclusive readings. Butler proposes a new way of framing such questions under the rubric of 'intertopicality', a word coined by analogy with intertextuality. As she points out, the world itself can be seen as a text, while intertopicality invokes a reader's physical experience of a place through reading, whether or not it be actual or imaginary, while intertextuality is the never-ending conversation which literature has with itself.

Contributors to this book engage in a dialogue with previous writers through which they construct a bridge across time linking past and present. The old name for Bristol means 'place by the bridge' and Richard Coates, who is a specialist in place names, has suggested that it denoted a meeting-place.[49] Certainly the city has been renowned as a location for a number of memorable literary meetings. Wordsworth and Coleridge are said to have first met at John Pinney's house at 7 Great George Street Bristol (*figure 7*). Another significant literary meeting allegedly taking place in the city was between Daniel Defoe and Alexander Selkirk, a shipwrecked sailor, who was rescued by a Bristol ship. His story provided Defoe with the basis for his novel *Robinson Crusoe*. The Llandoger Trow in King Street is frequently cited as their meeting place, but other venues have been suggested including The Star in Cock and Bottle Lane, destroyed during the Blitz of 1940 in the area now known as Castle Green.[50] The Llandoger Trow is also thought to have been the model for The Admiral Benbow inn, situated on the road to Bristol in Robert Louis Stevenson's classic adventure *Treasure Island*. The Spyglass Inn owned by his most enduring fictional character, Long John Silver, is set in Bristol. It is believed that the inn was based on what is now the popular restaurant and pub The Hole in the Wall, near the quay-side, which in bygone days was a tavern for seafaring men. A small room off the bar parlour provided a convenient look-out for press-gangs.[51] The Bristol docks are assumed to have provided overall inspiration for Stevenson's novel, which was serialised in 1882. Yet links between Stevenson's novel and any actual Bristol location cannot be verified. Stevenson most probably passed through the city in March of 1865 and 1866 en route with his family to Torquay. Evidence that he stayed in Bristol appears in a fragile notebook held at the Huntington Library in California, though no dates are supplied.[52] Stevenson's ghostly presence in the city lives on through his characters. *Treasure Island* was selected in 2003 as the first novel in the citywide Great Bristol Reading Adventure.[53] Thousands of free copies were distributed to schools, libraries and to members of the public. Stevenson's reason for choosing this city as a setting might have been because of literary associations drawn from seafaring fiction invoking the Bristol of popular imagination, but it could also have been due to the influence of his friend, the Bristol writer John Addington Symonds and resident of Clifton Hill House, whom he met in Switzerland three years before the book was published. The urge to pin writers down to a first-hand experience of a place in their writing is understandable, whilst unfounded assumptions can give rise to literary folklore.

Indeed doubt has even been cast on the claim that Wordsworth and

7 The Georgian House Museum, 7 Great George Street, Bristol. Built for John Pinney, the sugar merchant, this house is where Wordsworth and Coleridge are reputed to have met. *Photograph: Marie Mulvey-Roberts*

Coleridge first met in Bristol. Furthermore, there is no evidence that Defoe and Selkirk had ever encountered each other in the city, or elsewhere.[54] The iconic suicide of Chatterton, immortalised in the pre-Raphaelite painting by Henry Wallis (*colour plate 4*), may only be indicative of Romantic myth-making. Nick Groom presents the more likely and less sanitised alternative that Chatterton, who was living above a brothel at the time, accidently overdosed while trying to cure himself of a venereal disease contracted from a sexual relationship with a prostitute.[55] In this place of transport and transition, apocryphal tales persist. Yet their durability helps shape a civic cultural tradition.

Bristol has not only attracted literary legend but also nurtured, as well as neglected, more than its fair share of writers and inspired symbolic as well as actual literary locations.. The city is a place of aspiration both culturally and comercially, from where creative imaginations soar and seek out new horizons. In view of this, it is appropriate that Jonathan Swift chose Bristol as the port from where his fictional character Gulliver set sail for 'real' places, ending up in fantastical locations, including a land of giants, a floating island and a dystopia of talking horses. As such, these fictive voyages provide an apt metaphor for how the city functions as a portal for creativity. On the water-front next to the Arnolfini, with its art gallery and book-shop, a rugged larger-than-life sculpture of the Venetian merchant John Cabot looks out to sea in the direction of Newfoundland. In 1497 Cabot set sail from Bristol to open up new trade routes with India, China and the Spice Islands but actually arrived in North America. His vessel was the small Tudor ship, the *Matthew*, whose replica also crossed the Atlantic and is frequently seen as a floating peripatetic 'land-mark' within the shifting maritime cityscape. Cabot's fictional biography is told by the Newfoundland writer Lillian Bouzane in her historical novel, *In The Hands of the Living God* (1999). His transfixed seated figure serves as a fitting reminder of how writers seek out new worlds of the imagination (*colour plate 5*). This 'city built on water' has been imprinted with a creative energy that not only preserves but also replenishes its literary traditions.[56] Mapping literary Bristol enables us to appreciate more fully the various ways in which this West Country city serves as a living testimony to the importance of the relationship between writing and place and how it continues to provide inspiration for creative writers today.

Gothic Bristol: City of Darkness and Light

Marie Mulvey-Roberts

BRISTOL no more a vulgar sound we hear,
But soft BRISTOLIA soothes the list'ning ear;
Or if perchance, the gothic word we trace,
'Tis dubb'd 'Majestic' and assumes a grace.[1]

Robert Lovell

Gothic genius improved every fiction which it adopted. Like torchlight
in a cathedral, its strong lights and shades, made every thing terrible, and
as if it were living.[2]

Robert Southey

Because of its links with Romanticism, Bristol has been referred to as a
'Romantic City', yet it could just as easily be identified with the Gothic.[3] Over
the centuries, Bristol has been the matrix for a significant number of Gothic
innovations, inspirational settings and associations with writers from late
eighteenth-century Gothic fiction through to Mary Shelley's *Frankenstein*
(1818), Bram Stoker's *Dracula* (1897) and beyond.[4] Bristol's dark legacy of the
slave trade makes it a city of darkness as well as light, a binary opposition
that is particularly conducive to the Gothic as a mode of cultural and even
civic expression.

One of the pre-eminent Gothic novelists associated with Bristol, Angela
Carter, in her novel, *The Infernal Desire Machines of Doctor Hoffman* (1972), writes:

> Consider the nature of a city. It is a vast repository of time, the discarded
> times of all the men and women who have lived, worked, dreamed and
> died in the streets which grow like a wilfully organic thing, unfurl like
> the petals of a mired rose and yet lack evanescence so entirely that they
> preserve the past in haphazard layers, so this alley is old while the avenue
> that runs beside it is newly built but nevertheless has been built over the
> deep-down, dead-in-the-ground relics of the older, perhaps the original,
> huddle of alleys which germinated the entire quarter.[5]

The city is a time-machine containing memories, inscriptions and creations from different eras. Carter had spent the decade before writing the book in Bristol and it is likely that its darker aspects relating to commerce, piracy and slavery are evoked in her description of a dystopian city 'built on a tidal river', which 'throve on business':

> It was prosperous. It was thickly, obtusely masculine. Some cities are women and must be loved; others are men and can only be admired or bargained with and my city settled serge-clad buttocks at vulgar ease as if in a leather armchair. His pockets were stuffed with money and his belly with rich food. Historically, he had taken a circuitous path to arrive at such smug, impenetrable, bourgeois affluence; he started life a slaver, a pimp, a gun-runner, a murderer and a pirate.[6]

While studying English at Bristol University, Carter specialised in medieval literature, the period in which the Gothic style originated. Bristol Cathedral is one of the earliest and largest examples in Europe of the German Gothic hall-church style. Overlooking College Green, it is situated near the bottom of Park Street, whose steep incline rises to the top of a hill surmounted by a more modern and secular Gothic cathedral devoted, this time, to learning. This is Bristol University's Wills Memorial Tower which, at 215 feet high, is said to be the last great neo-Gothic building constructed in England. But neither building matches the Gothic splendour of St Mary Redcliffe church. Built from the twelfth to the fifteenth century, this is said to have been described as, 'the fairest, goodliest and most famous parish church in England'.[7] A link between writers and Gothic edifices in Bristol is forged by poet and literary 'forger' Thomas Chatterton with St Mary Redcliffe, the novelist and poet Mary Robinson to the city's cathedral and Jane Austen's literary connections with Blaise Castle.

Horace Walpole, reputed to be the founder of the Gothic novel, instigated a new fashion for Gothic in architecture and literature. Leading the way was his *The Castle of Otranto* (1764) inspired by his Twickenham home, Strawberry Hill, which he transformed into his 'little Gothic Castle'.[8] For the first edition of the novel, Walpole masquerades as the translator of a sixteenth-century Italian text written by a church canon, Onuphrio Muralto, though by the second edition he reveals his true identity. In view of this duplicity, it is ironic that he rebuffed the struggling young Bristol poet Thomas Chatterton who, having secretly adopted the persona of Thomas Rowley, a fifteenth-century

Bristol priest, sent him his fake antiquarian Gothic poems. While it appears that Walpole was initially duped into believing that they were genuine, he later became suspicious and non-compliant with the poet's requests for assistance. Not responding well to rejection by this prospective patron and owner of a printing press, Chatterton damned Walpole in the following verse:

> Say, didst thou never practise such deceit?
> Who wrote *Otranto*? [...]
>
> Had I the gifts of wealth and luxury shar'd,
> Not poor and mean, *Walpole*! thou hadst not dar'd
> Thus to insult. But I shall live and stand
> By *Rowley's* side, when thou art dead and damn'd.[9]

But it turned out to be Walpole who would outlive the seventeen-year-old Chatterton and be blamed for his tragically premature death in London in 1770, far from the Gothic inspiration of St Mary Redcliffe (*colour plate 4*). The effect of reading Chatterton's archaic writing, as in his *A Discorse on Brystowe* (the old name for Bristol), where he fictionalises the building of the church using apocryphal dates in his invented Rowleyan language: 'The inhabiters of Rudcleve ybuilden a Churche of Woden Warke casen with a sable Stone and A.D. 644 did the same dedycate to Oure Ladie and Sayncte Warreburgus', transports us, according to Alistair Heys, into 'an adolescent's English Gothic dream world.'[10] The co-ordinates for a Gothic reading of the city are put in place by Chatterton mythologising Bristol as 'Brightstowe' ('place of bright-ness'), a variation on his medieval 'Bristowe', a city of light,[11] and subsequent re-configuration of his birth place as an enclave of darkness, reflected in his bitter valediction to Bristol:

> Farewell, Bristolia's dingy piles of brick,
> Lovers of Mammon, worshippers of Trick!
> Ye spurn'd the boy who gave you antique lays,
> And paid for learning with your empty praise. [...]
> Have mercy, Heaven! when here I cease to live,
> And this last act of wretchedness forgive.[12]

Nick Groom doubts this to be an authentic attribution, but what is genuine was the poet's antipathy to Bristol. Even though Chatterton was bitterly critical of the mercantile character of Bristol, he did not baulk from commercial exploitation himself, selling his fraudulent manuscripts to wealthy patrons, such as the antiquarian William Barrett.

More prosaically and pedagogically, Gothic literature and architecture were brought together for English literature students at the University of the West of England, Bristol in Fishponds at St Matthias. This is one of the finest Gothic Revivalist buildings in Bristol, whose links with higher education continued for 160 years until 2014. Originally the building was used by the Gloucester and Bristol Diocesan Training Institution for School Mistresses. The Bristol-born John Norton, the architect of Tyntesfield, another Gothic Revival house not far from the city, was associated with its design. Extensions in the Gothic style were constructed in 1903 by William Venn Gough, who designed Cabot Tower on Brandon Hill (*chapter 7, figure 4*) which also has Victorian Gothic features.[13] In 1852, the very same year in which St Matthias was built, John Ruskin published the second volume of his *Stones of Venice* containing the essay 'The Nature of Gothic', described by Kenneth Clark as 'one of the noblest things, written in the nineteenth century'.[14] Norton was a follower of the Victorian architect Augustus Pugin, for whom the Gothic style was not simply fashion, but fundamental to a moral, spiritual and political revival. It was the labour unrest during the 1830s, the worst of which took place in Bristol, which prompted Pugin to diagnose a strong dose of social reform through Gothic architecture. This was needed, in his view, to restore the supposed stability and spirituality of medievalism. In his first book *Contrasts* (1836), Pugin includes figures in his plates to impart political messages for which Bristol provided a moral topography (*figure 1*). Here he depicts an orderly dignified procession with respectful kneeling devotees outside St Mary Redcliffe church. As Rosemary Hill points out: 'In choosing Bristol Pugin evoked another contrast, fresh in most minds, with the city's recent past, the anticlerical riots, the Bishop's palace in flames' (*colour plate 7*).[15] These riots of 1831 had been triggered by the House of Lords' rejection of the Second Reform Bill, which would have given Bristol greater representation in the House of Commons. Several people died in the fires and there is a moment of Gothic horror witnessed by the Victorian novelist, Charles Kingsley on seeing a piece of charred human flesh attached to a red petticoat.[16] The nationalism of Pugin's moral vision extended to the Houses of Parliament. After being destroyed in a fire of 1834, they were re-built in the Perpendicular Gothic style. There can be no better acknowledgement of Gothic as a national style, an alignment going back to the previous century.

REDCLIFFE CHVRCH BRISTOL

1 Augustus Pugin, a drawing of St Mary Redcliffe church in Bristol in *Contrasts* (1836).
University of Bristol Library, Special Collections

The Bristol riots played a key role in cementing Pugin's vision of architecture and morality in the context of the Victorian Gothic Revival. Indeed didacticism was a concept also embraced by Gothic novelists. In his celebration of the variety intrinsic to the Gothic aesthetic, Pugin's successor Ruskin draws comparisons between books and buildings as purveyors of taste, enjoyment and morality.

> To repeat itself is no more a characteristic of genius in marble than it is of genius in print; and that we may, without offending any laws of good taste, require of an architect, as we do of a novelist, that he should be not only correct, but entertaining.[17]

Female Gothic Pioneers

Early women writers associated with Bristol, whose entertaining and edifying fiction helped popularise the Gothic, have not received adequate local recognition. Amongst them was Mary Robinson, celebrated for her accomplishments as a novelist, actress, radical female polemicist and poet, who was also reviled for her scandalous life (*colour plate 8*). In her memoirs, she describes her birth in Bristol at Minster House near the bottom of Park Street in the language of a Gothic novel. The event took place 'during a tempestuous night, on the 27 November 1758' and was the worst storm her mother ever remembered: 'The wind whistled round the dark pinnacles of the minster tower, and the rain beat in torrents against the casements of her chamber.'[18] Brought up under the Gothic shadow of Bristol Cathedral, Robinson inhabited what 'no doubt' must have been the 'awe-inspiring' remains of an Augustan monastery with 'the mouldering arches of the cloisters; dark [and] Gothic'.[19] Later in life, she recollected listening to the 'long-remembered' pipe organ 'flinging its loud peal through the Gothic structure' and how, as a child, she liked to sit beneath the brass eagle lectern.[20] For Robinson, Gothic Bristol was not only a site of memory but also a place of historic imaginings. She begins her memoirs by recalling the destruction of the Minster when Bristol was besieged by Royalists during the Civil War, which had taken place a century earlier. Despite never having experienced the original building first hand, she still responds to it in her mind's eye as a 'beautiful Gothic structure, which at this moment fills the contemplative mind with melancholy awe'.[21] Recollections of the sublime Gothic interior of Westminster Abbey had much the same effect in transporting her to a more spiritual realm:

> I have often remained in the gloomy chapels of that sublime fabric, till I became as it were an inhabitant of another world. The dim light of the Gothic windows, the vibration of my footsteps along the lofty aisles, the

train of reflections that the scene inspired, were all suited to the temper of my soul: and the melancholy propensities of my earliest infancy seemed to revive with an instinctive energy, which rendered them the leading characteristics of my existence.[22]

From her early years in Bristol, Robinson acquired a Gothic sensibility which found expression through her writing. On learning to read, her great delight was to memorise the epitaphs and inscriptions on monuments in the cathedral. For Robinson, Bristol and the Gothic merged together. As she notes in her memoirs:

> *Bristol!* Why does my pen seem suddenly arrested while I write the word?
> I know not why, but an undefinable melancholy always follows the idea
> of my native birth-place. I instantly beheld the Gothic structure, the lonely
> cloisters, the lofty aisles, of the antique minster.[23]

Appropriately, Robinson's fictional debut was a Gothic novel. It would be the first of several.[24] *Vancenza: or the Dangers of Credulity* (1792) is a grim warning of the dangers of incest. The plot centres on a heroine, who dies just before her wedding, on realising that she is about to marry her half-brother. *Vancenza* made literary history as the first novel by a woman to sell out on its first day of publication and prompted one reviewer to declare her Britain's greatest female writer.[25] Known as 'Perdita', after one of her most celebrated theatrical roles, Mary Robinson courted notoriety as the mistress of the Prince of Wales. Part of the interest in her novel was for readers to detect the thinly veiled allusions to this love-affair with the future King George IV, which had taken place during the early 1780s. In addition to this overnight success as an author, Robinson was acclaimed 'the English Sappho' for her verse, a title inspired by her sonnet sequence 'Sappho and Phaon' (1796). She succeeded the Bristol-born poet Robert Southey (who became Poet Laureate), as poetry editor for the *Morning Post*, where her poetry was published. In addition, she introduced a new type of lyric, which apparently influenced another future Poet Laureate, Alfred Tennyson. Robinson received more acclaim as a poet in her day than Wordsworth.[26] Her *Lyrical Tales* (1800) was a reply to his *Lyrical Ballads*, for which she also used the same Bristol printer as did Wordsworth and Coleridge.[27] In this collection of verse, Robinson employs the conventions of the Gothic, as in 'Golfre: A Gothic Swiss Tale, in 5 Parts', which has been seen as a response to Coleridge's *The Rime of the Ancient Mariner* (1798).[28]

The poem tells the tale of the wicked Baron Golfre, who seizes a peasant maiden for his bride. Fiends, demonic whirlwind and a murderous wolf set the scene for his grisly end:

> The rosy dawn's returning light
> Display'd his corse, – a dreadful sight,
> Black, wither'd, smear'd with gore!
>
> High on a gibbet, near the wood –
> His mangled limbs were hung.[29]

Robinson's use of the Gothic is markedly different to how it was applied by Wordsworth and Coleridge. She deploys its imagery and themes to throw light on inequalities for women within existing power relations and to this end, produced a treatise protesting against the subordination of women.[30] In her memoirs, Robinson portrays herself as a victim along the lines of a Gothic heroine. From early on, coercion, seduction and abandonment were familiar motifs in her turbulent life. When her mother was abandoned by her father for his mistress, the family were obliged to leave their comfortable home on Clifton Hill. Later in life, Robinson was spurned by the Prince of Wales. Since the social disgrace of being a royal mistress put an end to her career on the stage, Robinson fell into serious debt. Desperate for money, she threatened to publicise the Prince's love letters unless she received monetary compensation. Eventually she managed to gain an annuity of £500, though the Prince was often dilatory in making payment. Yet it was to him she turned when plagued by illness and convinced that she had not much longer to live. After many years of absence, Robinson 'wept with melancholy pleasure' at the thought of returning to Bristol to die and 'terminating her sorrows on the spot which gave her birth'.[31] At the same time, her physician Dr Henry Vaughan prescribed a visit to the Hot Wells as the last resort in trying to slow down her rapid decline. Not having sufficient funds for the journey, she appealed in vain for assistance from her former royal lover insisting: 'Without your aid I cannot make trial of the Bristol waters, the *only* remedy that presents to me any hope of preserving my existence.'[32] For many years, Mary Robinson had been suffering from a mysterious illness, involving paralysis and rheumatic fever. While this may have been caused by an infection contracted during a miscarriage, a more likely cause was gonococcal arthritis, a complication arising from the sexually transmitted infection of

2 Portrait of Jane Porter
by Samuel Freeman,
after George Henry
Harlow, engraved after
1811.
*Fry Portrait Collection,
University of Bristol
Library, Special
Collections*

Drawn by Harlow.   Engraved by Freeman.

Miss Jane Porter.

gonorrhoea. There was more than one candidate from whom Robinson could have contracted the disease. The gambler and womaniser Banastre Tarleton had seduced her on a bet and started a fifteen-year relationship, finally abandoning her in 1798. Two years later, he became the Member of Parliament for Liverpool which, by the 1730s, had overtaken Bristol as Britain's second biggest slave-trading port after London. Tarleton was well-known for opposing William Wilberforce's abolition of slavery. Robinson, however, was against the trade and attacked the institution of slavery in writings from the 1770s to the 1790s, taking up the female point of view in poems such as 'The Negro Girl' (1800).[33] Robinson, whose ancestral roots were in Ireland, may also have been aware of Bristol's involvement in an earlier slave trade involving the transportation of large numbers of Irish men, women and children to the American and Caribbean colonies during the seventeenth century.[34] Bristol's unsavoury role in slavery was part of 'the air of this bad world' which Robinson first inhaled when she was born 'within a few short paces' of the city's cathedral, while her time spent inside its Gothic walls may have increased her susceptibility to 'the progressive evils of a too acute sensibility.' [35]

As a melancholic, a condition which she Gothicises in her poems 'Ode to Melancholy' (1789) and 'Ode to Despair (1806), Robinson had an affinity with friend and fellow-Gothic novelist Jane Porter, nicknamed *La Penserosa* on account of her gloomy disposition, who lived in Portland Square with her novelist sister Anna Maria (*figure 2*). Porter pioneered a new form of the nationalist tale involving the politicisation of the Gothic romance, with its use of landscape and the sublime.[36] Her most well-known example is the novel, *The Scottish Chiefs* (1810) telling the story of William Wallace, the historical inaccuracy of which matches Mel Gibson's rendition of his life in the film *Braveheart* (1995). It has not been adequately acknowledged that Porter's *Thaddeus of Warsaw* (1803) is one of the earliest examples of the historical novel which she helped popularise. The genre was continued by family friend, Sir Walter Scott, who mistakenly is widely regarded as its inventor. Porter was not the only female writer, who had lived in both Edinburgh and Bristol and whose literary contribution was confused with that of Scott. Carolina Oliphant, Lady Nairne who moved from Edinburgh to live in Clifton for a brief period in 1830 wrote some anonymous songs and poems, which were wrongly ascribed to Scott, as well as to Robert Burns and James Hogg.[37]

Another Bristol woman writer who, like Porter, combined the historical novel with the Gothic genre, was Sophia Lee (*figure 3*). She lived in Clifton with her younger sister Harriet Lee, who wrote one of the earliest Gothic dramas *The Mysterious Marriage; or the Heirship of Roselva* (1798), which London theatres refused to stage. The sisters co-authored a series of thematically-linked short stories *Canterbury Tales* (1797-1805), based on German sources, which dealt with Gothic themes. After the death of her father, the actor and theatre manager John Lee, Harriet helped her sister run a successful school at Belvedere House in Bath. It was financed from the proceeds of Sophia's successful comedy, *The Chapter of Accidents* (1780), performed at the Haymarket Theatre in London.[38] Eventually, the sisters retired to Hatfield Place near Bath. It was there in 1805 that their youngest sister Anna hanged herself. The shock-waves of the tragedy brought them eventually to Clifton, where they spent many years and where Sophia, the more famous of the two sisters, died in the arms of Harriet at 11, Vyvyan Terrace (*figure 4*) on 13 March 1824.[39]

3 Portrait of Sophia Lee by William Ridley, after Sir Thomas Lawrence stipple engraving, published by Thomas Bellamy in the *Monthly Mirror*, 1 August 1797. *University of Bristol Library, Special Collections*

Sophia was the author of the best-selling Gothic novel *The Recess* (1783-5) about the fictional twin daughters of Mary Queen of Scots forced to live in an underground recess to avoid threatening the legitimacy of Queen Elizabeth. With its themes of madness, mystery and imprisonment, the novel pioneered female Gothic writing by setting a trend in sentimental Gothic writing and contributed to the eighteenth-century cult of sensibility. *The Recess* was also satirised as a warning against the dangers of reading. One account tells of how a reader was so deeply affected by reading the novel that she was obliged to take to her bed for three days to recover:

> From the moment I first opened it, till the last sorrowful scene which closes the overwhelming narration of miseries, I quitted not the book. As I read, I felt all the pains of suspense at my heart, and I know not a term which can convey to you an idea how infinitely I felt myself interested through the whole: I was frequently affected even beyond the power of weeping, and scarcely could prevail on my aunt, with all my entreaties, to let me read the last volume; but persuading her that I should, perhaps, be less affected when alone, I had all the luxury of weeping over it by myself.[40]

Similarly, Mary Robinson's *Vancenza* was found by the *English Review* to be 'an elegant and affecting little tale' which would send readers 'weeping to their beds.'[41] The Gothic reader of excessive sensibility is gently mocked in Jane

4 Vyvyan Terrace, Clifton. This was the house where Sophia Lee died on 13 March 1824. *Photo: Marie Mulvey-Roberts*

Austen's *Northanger Abbey* (1818), in which the heroine Catherine Moreland proves herself so highly impressionable when reading novels of terror and horror that she fancies herself a Gothic heroine. This sets up false expectations, some of which lead to Blaise Castle, near Bristol, where Catherine expects to find a piece of Gothic antiquity. In fairness to her, she is misled by John Thorpe, who informs her that it was the oldest castle in the land and proposes a coach ride to Clifton and then on to Blaise. As it transpires, the expedition is aborted for practical reasons. Had Catherine arrived, she would have been disappointed at discovering a modern Georgian house of that name and a sham Gothic castle of 1766 as inauthentic as the Lover's Leap and Robber's Cave, which were the inventions of its owner.

A more obscure Austen novel with a Bristol setting is *Lesley Castle*, which also subverts Gothic expectations. This unfinished comic epistolary novel was written supposedly in 1792 when Austen was just sixteen years of age. It is known that she stayed in Clifton in 1806 but, in view of her references to Bristol in this juvenile work, it is possible that she made an earlier unrecorded visit. The castle itself is situated in the 'northern extremities' of Scotland and it is likely that Austen derived the name 'Northanger Abbey' from this northerly location.[42] Lesley Castle would have presented to Catherine Moreland 'all the horrors that a building such as "what one reads about" may produce'.[43] The main plot involves the death of a bridegroom in a riding accident shortly before his wedding. His untimely death might have been inspired by Walpole's *The Castle of Otranto*, where the bridegroom Conrad is killed just before the marriage ceremony. According to her biographer David Nokes, Austen was 'an avid connoisseur of Gothic shockers like *The Castle of Otranto*'.[44] In *Lesley Castle*, her bridegroom's death is quite tame compared to that of Conrad who is crushed to death by a mysterious giant helmet. Austen's grief-stricken bride is taken to Bristol for medicinal purposes by Miss Charlotte Lutterell, who complains: 'Eloisa's indisposition has brought us to Bristol at so unfashionable a season of the year, that we have actually seen but one genteel family since we came.'[45] She goes on to observe that 'Poor Eloisa is still so very indifferent both in Health & Spirits, that I very much fear, the air of the Bristol-downs, healthy as it is, has not been able to drive poor Henry from her remembrance.'[46]

Lesley Castle was written not long after Ann Radcliffe published her Gothic romances, *A Sicilian Romance* (1790) and *The Romance of the Forest* (1791). In *Northanger Abbey*, Austen pays tribute to Radcliffe, who was known as the Great Enchantress. She married William Radcliffe in neighbouring Bath, where her father had a Wedgwood showroom. In the posthumous essay 'On the Supernatural in Poetry' (1826), Radcliffe discusses her use of terror, a crucial element of her fiction. Her psychological approach is more typical of women writers compared to the sensationalism and visceral horror of the more masculine approach to Gothic writing, exemplified by Matthew Lewis in his lurid novel, *The Monk* (1796). Radcliffe drew on a key work of aesthetics written by Edmund Burke, the MP for Bristol from 1774-80, whose statue in contemplative pose was erected in the city centre (*colour plate 9*).[47] In his *Philosophical Enquiry into the Origin of our Ideas on the Sublime and the Beautiful* (1757), Burke identifies terror as a source of the sublime, making much of the awe inspired by nature, which became so characteristic of Radcliffean Gothic. Lee's novel *The Recess* provides another source of the sublime, only this time through history rather than nature. According to Patricia Meyer Spacks: 'Sublimity in this novel finds realization in history, history conceived as a concatenation of irresistible but incomprehensible forces. Obscure, terrible, all-powerful, unmindful of individuals, it possesses all the qualifications of the sublime.'[48]

Robert Southey's Gothic verse

The evocation of history found in Gothic fiction manifested in poetry, through the return to an earlier poetic form. This was the ballad, associated with oral traditions and whose revival was central to Romanticism, as testified by *Lyrical Ballads* (1798). The authors Wordsworth and Coleridge are said to have first met at the Georgian House in Great George Street, Bristol. Across from the centre in the Old City is Wine Street, the birthplace of another Romantic poet, Robert Southey (*colour plate 10*) whose father owned a draper's shop there. The house was destroyed in the Blitz (*figure 5*). Southey's Gothic resonances are recognised by his editor Geoffrey Grigson, for whom he 'dreams and half-fools with the rotting dead and the skeleton and the skull.'[49] Indeed Southey supplied Bristol with more than one Gothic first. His 'The King of the Crocodiles' (1799) has been seen as a grotesque poem anticipating Lewis Carroll's nonsense verse,[50] while Southey has been credited with pioneering the Gothic ballad.[51] As Caroline Franklin observes, his originality also lay in a comparativist approach to superstition, myth and folklore, along with a distinctive replication of authentic folk-tradition.[52] Fellow-Bristolian Thomas Chatterton had also set out to recreate poetry from a bygone age. Franklin notes: 'Southey created, through the sheer excess of satanic Gothic, a visual cartoon of the medieval church on the verge of the Reformation.'[53] One of Southey's most notable examples is 'Cornelius Agrippa's Bloody Book' (1799) written in 1798 at his home in Westbury-on-Trym.[54] It tells of a young man, who reads a forbidden book belonging to the magician Agrippa, made out of dead man's skin and written in blood. Southey's own favourite ballad, 'The Old Woman of Berkeley' (1798), was based on a supernatural legend of an old woman from Berkeley Castle in Thornbury, near Bristol (*figure 6*). The ballad was published in Matthew Lewis's *Tales of Wonder* (1801), where eight of Southey's ballads appeared. Southey later expressed dissatisfaction with some of his early 'Balladings', referring to them as 'cask droppings – and cheese parings & candle ends.'[55] He withdrew all his poems from a planned second edition of *Tales of Wonder* (1801). There appears to have been some dispute over Lewis identifying Southey as the author of ballads, which had originally been published anonymously, as well as over the issue of permissions.[56] Wordsworth pointed out that when the anthology was first published, it was mockingly re-named *Tales of Plunder* because there was so little that was new in the volume.[57]

Southey experimented with other literary forms for his Gothic verse as in 'An Ode to Horror' (1791) written in Bristol:

> DARK HORROR! hear my call!
> Stern Genius, hear from thy retreat

5 The pump on Wine Street, Bristol where Robert Southey was born, which appears in Charles Bird, *Picturesque Old Bristol* (1886). The feelings connected with this place were so deeply rooted in him that he believed that they would be the last to survive before his death (BRL BNL10F). *Bristol's Museums, Galleries & Archives*

> On some old sepulchre's moss-canker'd seat,
> Beneath the Abbey's ivied wall
> That trembles o'er its shade;
> Where wrapt in midnight gloom, alone [...].[58]

Following his invocation of horror, Southey uses the Gothic conventions of an aged mossy tomb, ivy-covered abbey wall and 'midnight gloom'. He was influenced by the pre-Romantic school of graveyard poets, as well as by Thomas Chatterton's Gothic manuscripts, whose work he and Cottle helped publish to provide financial assistance for his surviving sister. For the final stanza, Southey invokes a real-life horror which has particular resonance for Bristol – slavery.

> HORROR! I call thee yet once more!
> Bear me to that accursed shore,
> Where round the stake the impaled Negro writhes.
> Assume thy sacred terrors then! dispense

6 'A ballad shewing how an old
woman rode double and who rode
double and who rode before her'
to illustrate the Gothic ballad,
'The Old Woman of Berkeley'
from *Poems* (1797-99) by Robert
Southey, engraved for the poet by
James Wathen taken from a
medieval woodcut from the
Nuremberg Chronicle (1494) in
which the story is related. *Bristol
Reference Library. Photo: Marie
Mulvey-Roberts*

The blasting gales of Pestilence!
Arouse the race of Afric! holy Power;
Lead them to vengeance![59]

Southey's achievement, as Franklin explains, was 'to transform the Gothic
sublime from individual sensation into social consciousness'.[60] He also transports horror from the realm of imaginative convention into real-life, invoking
it for the purposes of bringing about radical change. The discourse of horror
is employed in another anti-slavery poem, which echoes an episode involving
Captain John Kimber, whose ship *Recovery* was owned by Bristol merchants.
He was accused by Wilberforce of causing the death of an African girl on
board ship. For refusing to eat, she was beaten with a whip while suspended
by her ankle (*colour plate 11*). In 1792, Captain Kimber was arrested in Bristol,
put on trial in London and later acquitted. Several years later in a letter to
John May for 26 September 1798, Southey explains how a sailor in Bristol
recounted a similar incident, which he turned into verse.

The Captain made me tie her up
 And flog while he stood by,
And then he curs'd me if I staid
 My hand to hear her cry.

She groan'd, she shriek'd – I could not spare
 For the Captain he stood by –
Dear God! that I might rest one night
 From that poor woman's cry!

She twisted from the blows – her blood
 Her mangled flesh I see –
And still the Captain would not spare –
 Oh he was worse than me![61]

The oral testimony was transcribed by the mother of Joseph Cottle, Southey's Bristol publisher, who also wrote against the slave trade. Other poets in support of abolition included Coleridge and Hannah More, as well as her former pupil Mary Robinson,[62] while her protégé Ann Yearsley produced a particularly searing indictment of the city:

BRISTOL, thine heart hath throbb'd to glory. – Slaves,
E'en Christian slaves, have shook their chains, and gaz'd
With wonder and amazement on thee.[63]

The relationship between Bristol and slavery haunts the parish register of the Church of St Augustine the Less, once situated by the cathedral, which contains the baptismal record of an African, significantly named 'Bristol'.[64] Much of the wealth of the city was built on the proceeds of slavery. Towards the end of the nineteenth century, an anonymous commentator claimed: 'There is not a brick in the city but what is cemented with the blood of a slave'.[65]

While only a minority of Bristolians were directly involved with the slave-trade, the city has been tainted by an almost endemic ruthless commercialism, prompting Southey to remark: 'The people of Bristol seem to sell every thing that can be sold' and with a wry nod towards the Burkean sublime, he asserts: 'they are selling the sublime and beautiful by the boat-load!'[66] Appearing in the *Bristol Weekly Intelligencer* for 1752 is the following Gothic ditty making a similar point.

> The World's A Citty [sic] full of Crooked Streets
> And Death the Market Place Where All Men Meets.
> If Life was Merchandize that men could buy
> The Rich would always live, the Poor alone would Die.[67]

In view of the example set by the privileged mercantile class, it is tempting to detect moral condemnation in Walpole's description of Bristol as 'the dirtiest great shop I ever saw'.[68] Ostensibly, he was referring to the grubbiness of the city, which is also conveyed in Robert Lovell's 'Bristol: A Satire' (1794):

> In mingled heaps here mud and misery lie,
> Here vice and folly rear their standard high;
> Here sweating dustman, sweating dustman meets,
> But all their efforts ne'r can cleanse their streets.[69]

His brother-in-law Southey imparts an equally damning description of urban dirt and deprivation in his *Letters from England*, describing the approach of his Spanish Catholic narrator to the city:

> Bristol was presently in sight, – a huge city [...] black towers of many glass-houses rolling up black smoke. We entered through a gate of modern and mean architecture into a street which displayed as much filth, and as much poverty, as I have seen in any English town.[70]

Conversely cleanliness and prosperity were associated with the Hot Wells, whose warm spring attracted visitors for its health-giving properties.[71] But even this glimmer of light cast a pall of darkness over the city, since 'Hotwells cases' provided 'a genteelism for a corpse'[72] while, according to Southey, it gave Bristolians the opportunity to trade in death:

> I tasted their famous medicinal water which rises at the foot of these rocks; it is tepid, and so completely without any medicinal flavour, as to be excellent water. [...] Several unhappy patients, who had been sent here to die at a distance from home, were crawling out upon the parade as if to take their last gasp of sunshine. It was shocking to see them, and it is shocking to see how thoroughly the people here regard death as a matter of trade. The same persons who keep the hotels furnish the funerals; entertain patients when they are living, and then, that they may accommodate them

all through, bury them when they die. [...] You will think it scarcely possible that this scene of disease and death should be a place of amusement, where idlers of fashion resort to spend the summer, mingle in the pump-room and in the walks with the dying, and have their card-parties and dances within the hearing of every passing bell.[73]

A row of houses where the sick lodged became known as 'Death Row', while the association with the dead and dying contributed to the very demise of the spa itself.

City of the Undead

This Gothicisation of the Hot Wells is in keeping with the Gothic's preoccupation with death, particularly since Southey represents the citizens of Bristol as almost vampiric in their mercenary exploitation of the sick, the dying and the dead. Certainly he had a well-attested interest in vampires, having taken his place in literary history for making the first reference to a vampire in an English poem, *Thalaba the Destroyer* (1801). The Bristol publisher Cottle had been involved with another poem, which contained elements of vampirism. This was Coleridge's *Christabel* (1797-1800), which had originally been destined for inclusion in the second edition of *Lyrical Ballads* in 1800. Coleridge was related to Southey through marriage, as each had married a Fricker sister from Bristol, while the third had married Robert Lovell. Not only were these poets highly significant for the Romantic movement, but they also made major contributions to the development of Gothic verse. An important predecessor was the German writer Gottfried August Bürger. His poem 'Lenore' (1773) was translated into English by William Taylor, who met Southey in 1798. The poem describes how a maiden is spirited away by her dead lover on horseback. There are similarities to Southey's 'The Old Woman of Berkeley', who takes to the saddle with the devil. However, these poems are more in the tradition of the demon lover than the vampire. Southey followed the lead of Goethe, who had composed the vampire poem 'The Bride of Corinth' (1797), which combines the eroticism of traditional ballads of the revenant with the folklore of the vampire. Southey's poem tells of how Thalaba's bride Oneiza dies and turns into a vampire corpse, who is staked to death by a lance. Neither she nor the bride of Corinth drink blood. Early literary vampires were often revived not by blood but by moonlight. Southey's quasi-vampire, the old woman of Berkeley, prefers imbibing breath rather than blood:

I have suck'd the breath of sleeping babes,
The fiends have been my slaves:
I have nointed myself with infants' fat,
And feasted on rifled graves.

And the Fiend will fetch me now in fire,
  My witchcrafts to atone;
And I, who have rifled the dead man's grave,
  Shall never have rest in my own.

Bless, I intreat, my winding sheet,
My children, I beg of you!
And with holy water sprinkle my shroud,
And sprinkle my coffin too.[74]

In the end, the old woman, vampire-like, rises from her grave. The similarity between the burial of a vampire and a servant girl, hanged by her cruel master and wrongly declared a suicide in Bedminster, is evident from a poem Southey wrote in 1798:

They laid her where four roads meet,
Beneath this very place,
The earth upon her corpse was prest,
This post is driven into her breast [...].[75]

Southey's interest in vampires connects to the eighteenth-century vampire craze in Europe, which had enthralled the Enlightenment mind. Empirical investigations involved exhuming the bodies of those believed to be 'undead'. One case Southey mentions concerned a man called Arnold Paul who, as the living dead, was said to be terrorising his village in Hungary. The villagers put an end to his depredations by opening up his grave and impaling his body with a stake. Reports of such cases were made in English newspapers, in which the earliest use of the English word 'vampire' dates back to 1732. Southey compiled detailed notes on these reports and appended them to *Thalaba the Destroyer* (Book Eight). John Polidori refers to the same material in the introduction to his novella, *The Vampyre* (1819), which is the first fictional work in English on vampirism. It seems likely that he obtained the information directly from the notes accompanying Southey's poem, which he acknowledges in his introduction. Since Polidori's vampire story is partly set in Greece, the material on Greek vampires in Southey's appendix may have captured his interest.

Southey's poem marks the start of the career of the literary vampire in English literature, a lineage culminating in Bram Stoker's *Dracula*. Here we have another link with Bristol since, according to Stoker's biographer, Barbara Belford, the model and inspiration for Count Dracula was the great Victorian actor, Henry Irving, who is linked to the city. At no 1, Ashley Road in Montpelier may be found a plaque stating that he had lived there. It is not clear how long Irving was actually there, since his family sent him to Cornwell to live with his aunt, as they feared that the industrial air of the city might harm his delicate health. For many years, Stoker served as Irving's manager at the Lyceum Theatre in London. He had hoped to persuade the celebrated actor to play the title role in a stage version of *Dracula*, but Irving's response to the suggestion was 'Dreadful!'[76] Born John Henry Brodribb, he adopted the stage name Irving from the Irvingite sect that took its name from their founder Edward Irving. The church, St Mary-on-the-Quay, which his mother attended, had been designed for the Irvingites, who claimed to be members of the 'Catholic Apostolic Church'. The building, which used to be on the quay-side before it was built over, is still in use as a church and situated nowadays on the city centre.

The Bristol connection with vampires was continued in the 1930s by Sydney Horler, who was educated at Redcliffe School and Colston's School in Bristol and then worked as a journalist with the local *Western Daily Press* and Allied Newspapers from 1905 to 1911. He wrote 157 crime novels and became a best-selling author. It was common for his publisher to write on his dust-jackets: 'Horler for excitement'.[77] Despite having sold two million copies of his books, he is regarded as one of the worst writers of the thriller genre. His secret service agents are bombastic manly chaps with names like Bunny Chipstead and Tiger Standish, described on the dust jacket as 'suave and ruthless'. They appear in novels with titles like *Tiger Standish Does his Stuff* (1941). Horler's villains sport such names as 'the Master of Venom' and include a blood-sucking, man-eating bush. Horler's decline as a popular author was not merely because of the absurdity of his plots and predictable charac-ters but also because his writing is littered with racism, homophobia and an unfashionable high-mindedness. For example, his gentleman thief known as 'Nighthawk', would only steal jewels from women he regarded as sexually immoral, scrawling the word 'wanton' on their pillowcases and writing insults on their mirrors with their own lipsticks.[78] On one occasion, Horler started a riot at Wimbledon over a woman wearing shorts.

In several works he draws on vampires and his novel *The Vampire* (1935) is clearly indebted to Stoker. In an open letter to his friend, John C. Woodiwiss, to whom the book is dedicated, Horler explains that 'it would be necessary more or less to use the same materials as Bram Stoker had done – and that, as I was bound to obey the rules set by the authorities on the subject, I must necessarily follow in the footsteps of the author of the greatest story of horror that has ever been written.' After being given an outline of the plot, Woodiwiss reassured him that 'no fair-minded person will be able to say either that you have "borrowed" anything from Bram Stoker or that you have failed for lack of originality'.[79] Notwithstanding this endorsement, Horler seems to have transposed Stoker's *fin de siècle* novel into the 1930s, culminating in an attempted human sacrifice, as part of a Black Mass, conducted by a devil-worshipping sect. His vampire protagonist Baron Ziska rents Pit House from a 'hideous-looking dwarf', the Hungarian Count Szilagyi.[80] Even though Count Dracula is Transylvanian, his ethnicity is that of a native Szekely, whose name Horler has adapted for that of his dwarf. The surname of his female villain, the *femme fatale* Helena von Alsing, is a variation on the name of Professor Van Helsing, Stoker's Dutch medical expert, who is brought in by his former tutee Dr John Seward to advise on the treatment of Lucy Westenra, Dracula's victim. She hunts for children on Hampstead Heath, which Horler transposes to Wimbledon Common. In his *The Vampire*, the eminent Viennese neurologist Professor Paul Metternich steps in to assist Dr Martin Kent, who is treating Sonia Rodney, the daughter of Sir Norman Rodney, a consulting physician, who is under the mesmeric control of Baron Ziska. After Metternich pierces Baron Ziska with a sword, he 'crumbled into dust',[81] just like Count Dracula. Horler also published a short story called 'The Vampire' in a collection called *The Screaming Skull and Other Stories* (1930), in which the narrator decides to write a tale about a vampire called *The Curse of Doone*. Two years earlier, Horler published a novel with the same title, which evokes Richard Doddridge Blackmore's West Country romance, *Lorna Doone* (1869) set in Exmoor. The narrator, after outlining the plot to his friend, a Catholic priest notes: 'Bram Stoker stirred the public imagination with his "Dracula" – one of the most horrible and yet fascinating books ever written – and I am hoping that the public will extend to me the customary "author's license".'[82] Unexpectedly the priest replies by confessing that he believes in vampires and had even encountered one in the West Country, 75 miles from a big city, which happens to be the approximate distance between Bristol and Exmoor.

Vampire connections with Bristol continued into Hammer Horror Films in *Taste the Blood of Dracula* (1969) and *Countess Dracula* (1971), directed by Peter Sasdy, who studied drama at Bristol University. More recently Toby Whithouse's supernatural TV drama *Being Human*, first broadcast in 2008, had its first two series filmed in Bristol where it portrayed a vampire, a werewolf and a ghost sharing a house in Windsor Terrace, Totterdown.[83] The vampire and the werewolf worked in a hospital, where, as a place of blood and death, rich pickings were to be found. Much of the filming took place in South Bristol and locations included Victoria Park and the General Hospital in Guinea Street, which housed a vampire's lair. The award-winning series, on which Bristol writer Lucy Catherine worked, was a beguiling mixture of humour, the horrors of everyday life and supernatural menace. *Being Human* acquired a cult following and spawned a version for American television, only this time set in Boston.

Frankenstein and the 'workshop of filthy creation'

Another perennially popular Gothic novel, besides *Dracula*, with several overlooked links with Bristol is *Frankenstein*. Mary Shelley (*colour plate 12*) stayed in Clifton the year before she started work on the novel, most probably during the month of July and a few days in August of 1815.[84] At the time of her stay, Mary was desperately missing Percy Bysshe Shelley, the father of the child she was carrying. Even though he had gone away to find a home for them, she may have felt abandoned by him, like the monster she would create, who is deserted by Victor Frankensten, a character who shares a number of characteristics with Shelley.[85] In a letter written from Clifton on 27 July, Mary complained: 'Indeed, my love, I cannot bear to remain so long without you [...] for I am quite sick of passing day after day in this hopeless way.'[86] She was particularly distressed that they would be apart the following day, the anniversary of their elopement to the Continent. They had been accompanied there by her step-sister Claire Clairmont, who was born in Brislington, an area in south east Bristol, and who was clearly attracted to Shelley. According to Edward Silsbee, a retired sea captain who wrote down Claire's recollections of events decades later, Shelley had been the love of her life.[87] Her mother noted that Mary's jealousy of Claire had driven her daughter away to Lynmouth.[88] Mary would later deny rumours of an affair, but they persisted and it has even been suggested that at the time she was in Bristol, Claire was pregnant with Shelley's child.[89] Indeed, the contemporary writer Thomas

Hogg joked about 'Shelley and his two wives'.[90] In a recently excavated journal, Claire proclaimed how 'free love' had turned both Shelley and her other lover Lord Byron into 'monsters'.[91] In view of this, Mary's enquiry to Shelley in her letter from Clifton: 'Pray is Clary with you?'[92] may well have been a loaded question.

It is not known while she was there whether Mary sought the distraction of other company. Two Clifton residents with whom she had a family connection were the novelists Sophia and Harriet Lee, described as charming by the perceptive Hester Lynch Thrale, whose final days were spent in a house near to the Avon Gorge.[93] A year after the death of her mother Mary Wollstonecraft, Mary Shelley's father, the philosopher and novelist William Godwin, proposed marriage to Harriet, but she turned him down, partly because of his disdain towards her intellectually and lack of respect for her religious convictions. In spite of this, Harriet wanted to continue the friendship. It is possible that Mary Shelley might have welcomed the prospect of visiting a nearby fellow-writer. But as she was pregnant and unmarried and Harriet was a spinster and devout member of the Church of England, this was probably enough to deter her from transgressing social propriety. The child was born in January the following year and named William. This was the name given to Victor Frankenstein's little brother who, rather disturbingly, becomes the monster's first victim. The murder of his fictional name-sake proved to be a grim omen of young William's death in Italy from fever at the age of three, the year after *Frankenstein* was published, where he is described as 'Poor William! he was our darling and our pride!'[94]

Another tragic family death with Bristol connections was the suicide of Mary's half-sister Fanny Godwin in October 1816. Travelling between London and Swansea, she stayed overnight in the city. Her biographer Janet Todd suggests that Fanny would have opted for accommodation at the Bush Tavern in Corn Street, since this was a prominent coaching inn with connections to South Wales.[95] The tavern was also on the route from London, a journey which would have taken around sixteen hours.[96] Had Fanny spent the time during this long carriage ride deciding whether or not to end her life? An advertisement from October 1816 reveals that the Cambrian Post-Coach travelled to Swansea from the Bush Tavern and directly to the hotel where her body would be found (*figure 7*).[97] As she was short of money, its announcement of 'Reduced Fares' would have been an added incentive particularly since post-coach was the most expensive mode of transport because of its speed and security. In the same street as the Bush Tavern was the

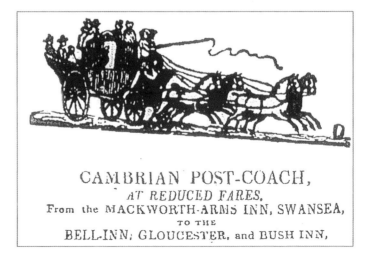

7 An advertisement for the Cambrian Post-Coach on which Fanny Godwin made her final journey from Bristol to Swansea where she died at The Mackworth Arms Inn

chemist and druggist shop, Hassall & Williams, where Todd proposes she purchased the laudanum which killed her. A popular potion was 'Sydenham's Laudanum', made up of 'strained opium mixed with cinnamon, cloves, saffron and canary wine. An ounce cost 8d.'[98] Fanny's knowledge of doses might have been acquired from acquaintances who were addicts. Two of these with Bristol links were Coleridge, whose drug habit she had mentioned to Shelley, and Robinson, the long-time friend of her mother Mary Wollstonecraft, who had dictated her poem 'The Maniac' (1793) in a 'frenzied delirium after swallowing eighty drops of laudanum to dull the pain of her rheumatism'.[99] Her biographer Byrne claims that she anticipated the Romantic tradition of opium-inspired poetry, associated mainly with Coleridge, who was a great admirer of her poetry.[100]

During her brief stay in Bristol, Fanny posted two letters about her intention to commit suicide. One sent to her step-father William Godwin at Skinner Street, London declared that she was 'disgusted with life', which seemed to imply that he and her step-mother, Mary Jane Clairmont were to blame.[101] The other letter went to Shelley in Bath where he was living with Mary and announced that she would be dead by the time he received it. Why she directed this message to him is a mystery only deepened by his insistence: 'It is not my fault – it is not to be attributed to me'.[102] These words were written on the back of a poem he wrote after her death entitled 'On Fanny Godwin', where Shelley seems to blame himself for not picking up the signals of her distress during their final meeting, which Todd speculates might have taken place in Bath, immediately prior to her arrival in Bristol.

Her voice did quiver as we parted,
Yet knew I not that heart was broken
From which it came – and I departed –
Heeding not the words then spoken.
Misery – oh misery.[103]

As soon as he read Fanny's disturbing last letter, in a state of shock, Shelley 'jumped up thrust his hand in [his] hair' and announced: 'I must be off', planning to intercept her at Bristol.[104] But once he had managed to work out her final destination through 'post horses', it was too late. It is possible that he arrived in time to find Fanny's dead body and tamper with the suicide note by tearing off the name to prevent it from being identified in order to protect the family from scandal and infamy. Fearing adverse publicity and blame, Godwin confided to Shelley: 'What I have most of all in horror is the public papers; & I thank you for your caution as it might act on this.'[105] In her letter to Shelley, Fanny requested that he bury her body. But her last wish was denied. The corpse was never claimed, most probably out of deference to Godwin's directive to his future son-in-law: 'Go not to Swansea, disturb not the silent dead' and his insistence:

Do nothing to destroy the obscurity she so much desired, that now rests upon the event. It was, as I said, her last wish. It was the motive that led her from London to Bristol & from Bristol to Swansea.[106]

The dead remaining not so silent was the nameless creature put together from cadavers in Mary Shelley's novel. This living composite of death would beget other deaths. Following the murder of little William was the death of Justine Moritz, who was wrongly blamed for the killing and judicially executed. Having been adopted by the Frankenstein family, she had taken on the role of a servant even though she was treated, to a certain extent, as a member of the family. Her interstitial status was similar to that of Fanny, the family drudge, and whose illegitimacy made her an outsider. In her suicide note, Fanny insisted, 'that the best thing I could do was to put an end to the existence of a being whose birth was unfortunate', referring to herself as 'a creature'.[107] It was a term which her mother, Wollstonecraft used during her pregnancy when referring to her unborn child. Rather poignantly, the daughter would die wearing her mother's corsets inscribed with the initials 'MW'. Mary Shelley uses the word 'creature' numerous times in *Frankenstein* to describe the unloved and parentless being which Victor created. 'Misery has come home'[108] was the response to Justine's death by Victor's fiancée Elizabeth Lavenza, who would soon become another of the monster's victims.

Robert Southey's verse, including 'Thalaba the Destroyer' and 'Cornelius Agrippa's Bloody Book' (1799), was read by Mary Shelley before starting work on *Frankenstein*.[109] Marilyn Butler has noted parallels between his poem about Agrippa, which is a retelling of 'The Sorcerer's Apprentice', and Mary Shelley's novel.[110] Certainly Agrippa is a source of inspiration for her scientist hero. It is possible that she also read Southey's 'The Surgeon's Warning' written in 1796 about a surgeon who, like Victor Frankenstein, rifles graves in order to carry out anatomical dissection. A book Mary Shelley was known to have been reading at the time of writing *Frankenstein* was Bryan Edward's history of the West Indies, containing accounts of slave riots in St Domingue, Jamaica and elsewhere. This is a subject explored in Sophia Lee's *The Recess*, a novel said to have influenced *Frankenstein*.[111] One of the two heroines, Matilda, is kidnapped and forcibly taken to Jamaica where she spends eight years. It is a plight not dissimilar to that of a slave, especially when she finds herself in the middle of a slave rebellion. *Frankenstein* can be read as an allegory of the slave trade and the contentious road towards emancipation. The novel is impregnated with the language of slavery, particularly that of a master-slave discourse. The creature's impassioned speech to his maker revealing his human sensibility is evocative of the abolitionist's slogan: 'Am I not a Man and a Brother?' Mary Shelley might have come across ex-slaves in Bristol working in the docks or in domestic service.[112] The wealth derived from slavery helped finance the elegant Georgian residences in Clifton where Mary Shelley would have stayed, finding herself amongst the highest concentration of retired plantation owners outside of London.[113]

The slave trade had been abolished only eight years earlier in 1807. From then on, the campaign shifted towards the emancipation of slaves, but was thwarted by delaying tactics. In Parliament in 1824, the year after the first theatrical version of *Frankenstein,* Foreign Secretary George Canning used the Frankenstein monster as a warning against the dangers of emancipating slaves too quickly saying: 'To turn him loose in the manhood of his physical strength, in the maturity of his physical passion, but in the infancy of his uninstructed reason, would be to raise up a creature resembling the splendid fiction of a recent romance.'[114] In the novel, the creature behaves in ways resembling those of a rebellious slave. He goes on the run from his master, burns down a cottage and carries out murder and mayhem. Since Mary Shelley

8 The Blaise
Castle Folly
(photo c.1930).
*Bristol's
Museums,
Galleries &
Archives*

did not appear to question Canning's politicised use of her novel and even expressed pleasure at his praise in 'honourable terms',[115] it seems likely that she shared his anxiety. While Mary and Percy certainly supported the abolition of slavery and joined the sugar boycott, like the ameliorists, they may not have embraced the cause for immediate emancipation, fearing mass insurrection. Canning complies with this agenda by warning of the dangers in emancipating slaves too rapidly by comparing the possible consequences to an unleashing of the Frankenstein monster. Mary Shelley was aware of such concerns through reading the work of Edwards, who describes in harrowing detail the enormous death toll for blacks and whites brought about by the rebellion of slaves and Maroons. She had been reading this book, first published in 1793, around the time of her visit to Bristol, the year before starting to write *Frankenstein*. There is no doubt that the brutalising and evil effects of slavery were known to her, which may be why she might have feared that the immediate emancipation of slaves could lead to insurrection born out of revenge.[116] In view of this, might the city's involvement with the slave trade have been a cradle of inspiration for her novel, the urban equivalent of Victor Frankenstein's 'workshop of filthy creation'?[117]

The final novel in the triumvirate of canonical Gothic novels, along with *Frankenstein* and *Dracula*, is Robert Louis Stevenson's *The Strange Case of Dr Jekyll and Mr Hyde* (1886). Even though Bristol does not appear in the novel, a connection is made by Jeanette Winterson in her adaptation, *Lighthousekeeping* (2004). Here she tells of a nineteenth-century Scottish minister, Babel Dark, who lives with his mistress in Bristol. Like Dr Jekyll, he lives a double life, this time as Mr Lux, a name that was derived from the Latin for 'light'. Pew, the blind keeper of the lighthouse, claims that he was the model for Stevenson's Dr Jekyll and Mr Hyde. The double life of Reverend Babel Dark and Mr Lux provides us with a fitting metaphor for Bristol as a city of darkness and light. Paradox is inlaid within the very foundations of a city, whose positioning as a centre of commerce gave rise to prosperity and helped shape its mercantile character and yet, as we have seen, the pursuit of material gain and pleasure ran parallel with a much darker side.

A Gothic building, which charts Bristol's changing involvement in slavery is the Blaise Castle folly[118] built in 1766 by Thomas Farr, who made his fortune from the transatlantic sugar trade (*figure 8*). One of several reasons for constructing this triangular prospect tower, it was said, was so that he could watch his ships sailing back to Bristol up the River Avon.[119] On seeing a 'shining vision' is how local poet Henry Jones eulogised the tower in his poem *Clifton* (1767), where he was unable to resist the pun on 'sudden blaze':

> Here Farr, with inbred rapture may resort
> And see his ships glad sailing into port.[120]

By the time Austen was writing *Northanger Abbey* in 1797-8, which brought the Gothic folly to national attention, the estate had been sold to the Quaker John Scandrett Harford, whose business interests linked him to the slave trade.[121] On the novel's publication in 1818, it had already been inherited by his son, the friend and biographer of Wilberforce, who turned the Blaise estate into a centre for the abolitionist movement.[122] The Gothic style had most probably been adopted by Thomas Farr as a symbol of British patriotism. As we have seen, Pugin insisted that the true Gothic style was needed to imbue cities like Bristol with the requisite moral and spiritual values. Throughout the history of literature and architecture, the Gothic has served as a versatile mode of representation.

The Victorian Revival, which saw the rise of many Gothic buildings in Bristol, went into decline as the twentieth century crept closer. Its death knell would be sounded by West Country author Thomas Hardy. In his anti-Gothic novel, *Jude the Obscure* (1895), Sue Bridehead resists Jude's invitation to visit Fonthill Abbey, built by the Gothic novelist William Beckford.[123] She makes her feelings explicit by declaring: 'I hate Gothic!'[124] Even Ruskin would turn on the Gothic Revival, describing it as the Frankenstein monster he had

9 Thomas Telford's design for the Clifton Suspension Bridge with Gothic towers (1830), later superseded by Isambard Kingdom Brunel's design (BMAG M1034). *Bristol's Museums, Galleries & Archives*

helped create.[125] This verdict has come a long way from the view of the so-called father of the Gothic novel, Walpole, who insisted: 'one only wants passions to feel Gothic.'[126] Gothic writing continues in Bristol as demonstrated by Helen Dunmore, whose Gothic novel, *A Spell of Winter* (1995), was the winner of the first Orange Prize For Fiction.[127] With its legacies of darkness, this West Country capital surely qualifies in taking its place as a truly Gothic city.

Bristol's Romantic Poets:
Robert Southey and Samuel Taylor Coleridge

Robin Jarvis

In June 1794 Samuel Taylor Coleridge (*colour plate 6*) passed through Oxford on his way into Wales to begin an ambitious walking tour with a fellow Cambridge undergraduate, Joseph Hucks. There he met Bristol-born Robert Southey (*colour plate 10*), who was completing his second year at Balliol College. The two students, who shared literary aspirations, radical politics, youthful idealism, and totally uncertain futures, hit it off immediately: Southey found Coleridge to be 'of most uncommon merit – of the strongest genius the clearest judgment & the best heart', while Coleridge was equally enamoured of the 'sturdy Republican' Southey, whom he viewed as 'a Nightingale among Owls'.[1] Together they began formulating a utopian transatlantic emigration scheme which would see twelve couples settling on the banks of the Susquehannah in Pennsylvania, dividing equally both the labour involved in clearing and cultivating the land and the produce of that labour; the rest of the settlers' time would be devoted to recreation, intellectual self-cultivation, and the education of their children. Discussion of this experimental 'Pantisocracy' (as Coleridge playfully dubbed the scheme: it means 'equal power to all') continued via letter after Coleridge had finally departed on his tour and resumed when he unexpectedly turned up in Bristol in early August. Before long, four of the potential emigrants were all married, or engaged, or romantically attached to one of four sisters of the middle-class Fricker family, and the prospective Pantisocratic community appeared to be taking shape. By the end of January 1795 Coleridge had abandoned his degree and moved into lodgings with Southey in College Street, Bristol, close to the Cathedral (*figure 1*). Over the next nine months they read, studied, and wrote poetry; ventured into lecturing and political journalism as they made their mark as public intellectuals; went on several long walking tours and explored the environs of Bristol, and argued interminably over Pantisocracy as the scheme mutated and eventually collapsed under the weight of practical difficulties as

1 Thomas Rowbotham, *The Cathedral, College Green and College Street*, 1827 (BMAG M2538). *Bristol's Museums, Galleries & Archives*

well as temperamental and ideological differences. In the end they separated in an atmosphere of bitterness and mutual recrimination, with Southey accusing Coleridge of behaving 'wickedly towards me' and Coleridge accusing Southey of falling in love 'with that low, dirty, gutter-grubbing Trull, WORLDLY PRUDENCE'.[2] By the end of the year Coleridge had married and moved to Clevedon (then just a seaside village ten miles to the west of Bristol) and Southey was on his way to Portugal with his uncle, who wanted to remove him from bad influences. As it turned out, Coleridge moved back to Bristol early the following year and the city would continue to be the centre of Southey's existence well into the next decade, but their friendship would take a long time to heal. The big differences between their periods of residence in Bristol and their personal histories of association with the city are reflected in the degree to which their poetry engages with the local area.

Coleridge: 'Bristowa's citizen'

Coleridge makes few direct references to Bristol in his poetry of the mid-1790s. Perhaps the best-known is the passage in his conversation poem, 'Reflections on Having Left a Place of Retirement' (1796), which describes a stereotypical Bristolian passing by his 'pretty Cot' on the coast:

> Once I saw
> (Hallowing his Sabbath-day by quietness)
> A wealthy son of Commerce saunter by,
> Bristowa's citizen: Methought, it calm'd

> His thirst of idle gold, and made him muse
> With wiser feelings: for he paus'd, and look'd
> With a pleas'd sadness, and gaz'd all around,
> Then eyed our cottage, and gaz'd round again,
> And sigh'd, and said, *it was a blessed place.*[3]

The passer-by is seduced by the charms of nature to forget – at least for a while on his Sunday constitutional – the urgency of getting and spending and tune in to the same 'inobtrusive song of HAPPINESS' (23) that the speaker enjoys in his 'VALLEY of SECLUSION' (9). His acknowledgement of '*a blessed place*' suggests the stirrings of a more spiritual response, and this theme is picked up in the next section, where Coleridge describes climbing a 'stony Mount' (27). (On a biographical reading, this could be Wain's Hill or Church Hill, close to his cottage at 'the western extremity' of Clevedon,[4] or possibly Dial Hill.) He surveys an ever-widening 'goodly scene' of 'sunny fields' and winding river, the Bristol Channel dotted with 'Islands and white Sails', and 'cloud-like Hills' beyond, all of which appears like a natural 'Temple' in which he senses the presence of God (29, 31, 35-36, 39). In this panorama Bristol is removed to a comfortable distance and is dreamily represented by no more than a 'faint City-spire' (35),[5] a detail that blends with the poet's religious interpretation of the more pastoral elements of the scene.

In the next verse paragraph, somewhat abruptly, the speaker reports that he was 'constrain'd to quit' (44) this idyllic environment, electing some form of Christian activism in preference to a self-indulgent enjoyment of 'delicious solitude' (58). This abandonment of his place of retirement translates biographically as Coleridge's departure from Clevedon; if Joseph Cottle is to be believed, however, the latter move resulted not solely or largely from a practical commitment to address social ills but from what we might nowadays term lifestyle considerations:

> The place was too far from Bristol. It was difficult of access to friends; and the neighbours were a little too tattling and inquisitive. And then again, Mr Coleridge could not well dispense with his literary associates, and particularly with his access to that fine institution, the Bristol City Library [. . .] so that his friends urged him to return once more to the place he had left; which he did, forsaking, with reluctance, his rose-bound cottage, and taking up his abode on Redcliff-hill.[6]

As Tom Mayberry suggests, the reality underlying Coleridge's rhetorical re-embrace of public life in this poem was his discovery 'that neither natural beauty nor loving domesticity could replace his need for intellectual stimula-tion'[7] – even if that meant moving into cramped accommodation in his mother-in-law's house.

The negative image of Bristol – as personified by a seemingly typical citizen – conveyed by Coleridge's 'Reflections' was not unrepresentative of contemporary attitudes. Bristol's self-image as England's second trading city after London, together with its deep involvement in the transatlantic slave trade, underwrote a body of opinion that saw it as a place full of grubby manufacturers, unprincipled merchants and swindling shopkeepers, where commercial interests outweighed all others. This stock characterisation of the city received ample expression in topographical and tour literature of the late eighteenth and early nineteenth centuries. Richard Warner, the author of numerous narrative excursions in the region, shunned Bristol as a 'town of speculation' and saw it as a 'faded beauty' deploring its decreasing share of the African trade as a result of competition from Liverpool.[8] Edward Davies struck a similar note in his topographical poem, 'Blaise Castle' (1783). Whereas the tower on Blaise Hill had been constructed to obtain a view of the shipping in the Severn and Avon, reflecting the priorities of the wealthy sugar-merchant, Thomas Farr, who had bought the estate in 1762, Davies chose instead to launch an attack on the 'lust of trade' which kept nations at war and praised the picturesque charms of Blaise (then well outside and to the north of Bristol) as a 'Garden of Delight' far removed from the taint of commerce. But if Coleridge required a direct textual influence for his conde-scending attitude to Bristolians in 'Reflections', he needed to look no further than his new acquaintance Robert Lovell, a Bristol-born friend of Southey's from a wealthy Quaker family and another of the prospective Pantisocrats. Lovell's *Bristol: A Satire*, published in 1794, was unrelenting in its criticism of the author's native city, distinguished by its 'black clouds of smoke' and the 'muddy stream' on which it sits.[9] Lovell's Bristol is ruled by Dullness and Avarice, a satirical royal couple underlining the link between the accumulation of wealth and indifference towards the arts and culture. Lovell loses no opportunity to point out the moral and intellectual consequences of Bristol's commercial mindset:

> Trade, mighty trade, here holds resistless sway,
> And drives the nobler cares of *mind* away.

> To this sole object every effort tends,
> And virtue dies and *pliant* honor bends;
> No soft humanities are cherish'd here,
> No sympathetic feeling prompts the tear
> No mild urbanity attracts the sight,
> No arts of skill or elegant delight. (200-7)

Bristol's neglect of its 'ill-starred' youthful genius, Thomas Chatterton, is added to the charge sheet, and the poem ends with caustic lines on the city's involvement in the slave trade ('Slaves torn and mangled, cultivate the sweet, / That trade may thrive, and luxury may eat' (282-3)) and its brutal suppression of the Bristol Bridge riot in 1793. Bristolians are viewed as unconcerned with freedom, either their own or anyone else's, so long as they can carry on lining their pockets. In the light of such a damning critique, Coleridge might be thought to have given his impressionable passing merchant in 'Reflections' a relatively easy ride.

Although the perception that Bristol was defined by its preoccupation with trade and making money was widespread, the authors of local tours and guidebooks did their best to offer a more flattering portrait. J. C. Ibbetson's *Picturesque Guide* to Bath and Bristol was one of many that countered the image of Bristol as a West Country Babylon and marshalled evidence that culture and commerce were not incompatible:

> The idea of total occupation in trade, which must strike every mind, on beholding a city, in which from twenty to thirty sugar-houses, and abundance of sulphur, turpentine, vitriol, and coal-works, brass and iron foundries, distilleries, glass-houses, and manufactories of woollen stuffs, and china, are almost incessantly at work, is agreeably corrected by the great encouragement and success literature, and the polite arts, meet with in this emporium of the west, and the very liberal urbanity with which persons of all nations are encouraged to settle here.[10]

Elsewhere, Ibbetson rehearses what seems to have been a popular comparison – present in guidebooks from at least the 1750s onwards – of Bristol with Rome, the Avon substituting for the Tiber. Although he defends this analogy purely on grounds of physical geography, it seems to offer silent support for his defence of Bristol as a provincial capital of culture. By the time John Evans published his *Picture of Bristol* in 1814, it was possible to produce a roll-call of local literary legends to amplify the swelling theme. Evans cites the work of Chatterton, Ann Yearsley, and Mary Robinson before concluding:

> [I]n the present age Bristol has produced talents which will bear a comparison with the most splendid period of the ages that are gone. The productions of Southey, of Coleridge, of Cottle, and of Hannah More, have given it celebrity in the world of letters; the public libraries, the book societies, and the numerous and valuable private collections which at present exist among us, are sufficient indications that a taste for literature is by no means incompatible with that attention to commerce, by which Bristol is supposed to be principally distinguished.[11]

Local publisher Joseph Cottle himself claimed, later in life, that during the period of Coleridge's residence in Bristol 'so many men of genius were there congregated, as to justify the designation, "The Augustan Age of Bristol".'[12] Despite the fact that, in the Romantic period, Rome symbolised imperial decadence as well as republican virtue and was often the subject of moralising historical interpretations,[13] there is no trace of irony in the way partisan commentators invoke the power and prestige of classical Rome to bolster the reputation of Bristol. As Richard Cronin notes, 'It was a city in which civic pride ran deep', and Cottle looked back fondly on his own role in fostering a 'school of poets' united by a 'defiant provincialism' and sturdy Nonconformist values.[14] In his eyes, Bristol was the Rome of western England, the 1790s were its Augustan age, and Coleridge was its Virgil or Horace. It is ironic that Coleridge, who did little more than recycle negative stereotypes of Bristol in those few poems, such as 'Reflections', that take note of the city, should have become central to the case for its cultural pre-eminence.

Many of Coleridge's best-known poems, including poems written in his Nether Stowey period such as 'Frost at Midnight' (1798) and 'This Lime-Tree Bower My Prison' (1797), engage with contemporary aesthetic theories of the sublime and the beautiful and with the cult of the picturesque, so it may seem odd that he wrote so little in this mode about the striking natural scenery of Bristol and the surrounding area. However, this is only surprising when one forgets that his Bristol years were, as Peter Kitson reminds us, Coleridge's 'most active and ardent Dissenting days', when he was establishing his position as a journalist and public speaker and throwing his energies into pamphlets and lectures 'against the war with revolutionary France, established religion, and the transatlantic slave trade'.[15] Preoccupied with 'Mobs and Mayors, Blockheads and Brickbats, Placards and Press gangs [. . .] leagued in horrible Conspiracy' against him,[16] it is perhaps unremarkable that he found little time to write poems about local places and landscapes, despite exploring the locality in a series of walking tours.

Those excursions did leave their mark on at least one notable minor poem, his sixteen-line sonnet 'Composed while Climbing the Left Ascent of Brockley Coomb, in the County of Somerset', written in May 1795 and published in *Poems* (1796):

> With many a pause and oft-reverted eye
> I climb the Coomb's ascent: sweet songsters near
> Warble in shade their wild-wood melody:
> Far off th' unvarying Cuckoo soothes my ear.
> Up scour the startling stragglers of the Flock
> That on green plots o'er precipices brouze:
> From the forc'd fissures of the naked rock
> The Yew tree bursts! Beneath it's dark green boughs
> (Mid which the May-thorn blends it's blossoms white)
> Where broad smooth stones jut out in mossy seats,
> I rest.—And now have gain'd the topmost site.
> Ah! What a luxury of landscape meets
> My gaze! Proud Towers, and Cots more dear to me,
> Elm shadow'd Fields, and prospect-bounding Sea!
> Deep sighs my lonely heart: I drop the tear:
> Enchanting spot! O were my SARA here![17]

Brockley Combe (in its modern spelling), now around five to six miles from Bristol but more like twice that distance in Coleridge's time owing to the city's subsequent expansion, was a well-established destination for the picturesque tourist by the time of his visit. Shiercliff's *Bristol and Hotwell Guide* (1789) states that the Combe 'is much frequented, and admired for the romantic beauty which nature here displays', and describes the hills on either side of the road as 'cloathed with a variety of stately trees, that tower and overhang each other in the most pleasing and picturesque manner'.[18] George Heath's *New History, Survey and Description of the City and Suburbs of Bristol* (1794) describes the location in similar (perhaps borrowed) language. The most extravagantly lyrical account comes a little later in Evans's *Picture of Bristol* (1814):

> One side of the Coombe is a lofty mass of limestone rock; yet this rock
> is so profusely ornamented with vegetation, as to resemble a garden fantas-
> tically suspended in the air. [. . .] The rays of the Sun broke in through
> several openings amongst the trees, and cast upon the variegated foliage,
> on the ground, on the broken masses of stone, and on whatever object
> they chanced to fall, a beautifully transparent golden light, which the
> painter knows how to appreciate in nature, perhaps better than any other
> man, and to appropriate to the purposes of art.[19]

The key elements in these descriptions – variety, roughness ('broken masses
of stone'), partial concealment ('openings amongst the trees'), *chiaroscuro* –
are all hallmarks of the picturesque style. The final sentence of the above
quotation exemplifies the central paradox of the picturesque – that artistic
representations or constructions (as with the eighteenth-century landscape
garden) are only valued in so far as they appear to owe more to nature than
to art: in picturesque theory, that is, nature is the real artist, and all the painter
or gardener can do is help her along and correct some of her mistakes.

Coleridge's poem also presents a typical assembly of picturesque objects
and effects. The 'green plots' intermingled with sharp 'precipices', the intricate
entanglement of white hawthorn blossom with the 'dark green boughs' of
the yew trees, and the encrustations of moss altering the texture of otherwise
flat, 'smooth stones', offer a characteristically rich and visually involving scene.
Irregularity, another keyword of the picturesque, is embodied in the very form
of this elongated sixteen-line sonnet. On the other hand, Coleridge's reference to yew-trees bursting 'From the forc'd fissures of the naked rock' shows
him bringing a more exact eye to his description, since thick-rooted yews
emerging from rocky outcrops are a well-known and striking feature of this
limestone valley (*colour plate 13*). The poem is also clearly written from the
angled perspective of one who has ascended the valley on foot and welcomes
the 'rest' that the very early caesura in line 11 dramatically reinforces for the
reader. Coleridge's Brockley is given a sentimental inflection by the desire
expressed in the concluding lines to share its delights with the woman he
loves, further differentiating his poem from the picturesque norm. And a final
interesting feature of the poem is the speaker's revelling in a 'luxury of
landscape' when he reaches the highest point. 'Luxury' had many negative
connotations in Coleridge's time, including that of an indulgent, expensive
lifestyle made possible by great social inequality; it is a term that is never far
away in contemporary accounts of the Bristol area. Although the word seems

to be used here in a positive way (perhaps in the sense of 'refined and intense enjoyment' [*OED* 4]), the reference to 'Proud Towers' in the next line reminds us of Coleridge's radical politics in the mid-1790s and it is not inconceivable that he has allowed his social and moral distaste for Bristol to infect his delight in this rural paradise on the city's doorstep.

Coleridge, then, was not unresponsive to his natural surroundings in his Bristol years, as shown by 'Brockley Coomb', by the well-known 'Eolian Harp' (1795) from his honeymoon period at Clevedon, or by his beautiful 'Ode to Sara, Written at Shurton Bars, near Bridgewater, in Answer to a Letter from Bristol' (1795). Another interesting case is his 'Monody on the Death of Chatterton' (1794), a poem that in one version or another dates back to Coleridge's schooldays, but which was revised in the autumn of 1794 (following his arrival in Bristol) to include lines imagining its subject roving the wooded sides of 'Avon's rocky steep' where 'the screaming sea-gulls soar', while taking note of the 'slow-sequester'd tide'.[20] Nevertheless, it is undeniable that in his Bristol period Coleridge's main attentions were elsewhere, as he rose to local prominence as a political figure and sought a national audience for his work. The nature of his preoccupations at this time – including opposition to the war on France and the transatlantic slave trade, and support for civil liberties and a radical redistribution of property – were guaranteed to bring him into disfavour with the Bristol establishment and make him susceptible to hostile generalisations about the city, especially when these were given eloquent reinforcement by key figures in his West Country coterie such as Robert Lovell.

Southey: Inscribing the West

To the general public, Robert Southey is much less well-known than Coleridge. Even to students of Romantic literature, he is usually little more than the shadowy 'third man' of the so-called Lake School of English poetry, or the butt of poetic gibes from a younger generation of writers – notably Byron – who deplored his conversion from youthful republican to militant middle-aged Tory. Although scholarly interest in Southey has increased significantly in recent years, his rehabilitation has been hindered by the fact that many of his attitudes have proved obnoxious to modern sensibilities, his causes have mostly been rejected by posterity, and the quality of his poetry deemed insufficient to atone for his ideological errors. As David Simpson has observed, the Romantic landscape has changed profoundly over the last thirty years, but Southey 'fits comfortably in neither the old canon nor any of the new countercanons'; indeed, 'We have yet to devise a category into which he might fit at all'.[21]

Among the categories in which Southey sits rather awkwardly is arguably that of Lake poet. It is true that, in September 1803, Southey and his wife moved to Keswick in the northern Lake District (sharing a large residence with Coleridge and his family) and stayed there for the rest of his life. But Southey, an incomer to the Northwest, had his roots in a very different corner of the country. Born in his father's draper's shop in Wine Street, Bristol (*figure 2*), in August 1774, his paternal and maternal grandparents came from long-established Somerset families. His early childhood and education involved continual relocation between Bristol, Bath, and outlying areas, and this peripatetic existence set the pattern for the first thirty years of his life. His centre of gravity during this period was undoubtedly Bristol, where he inhabited a series of temporary lodgings in College Street, Kingsdown, Westbury-on-Trym, and Stokes Croft. It was here that his friendship and creative collaboration with Coleridge were, as we have seen, at their most intense and productive, here that his literary career was launched with the encouragement and support of provincial publishers, and from here that he set off on numerous excursions and walking tours around the West Country – the places, landscapes, myths, and history of which furnished material for much of his early shorter poetry. As Mark Storey says, 'Bristol was the place he regarded as home, and he found it hard to contemplate leaving the area.'[22] Nevertheless, following the death of his only child in 1803, and of his mother the previous year, he *did* leave, claiming that the place was 'haunted' and that he wished 'never to see it again'.[23]

In fact, Bristol had been haunted from the beginning of Southey's poetic career. In one of his earliest surviving poems, the speaker is accosted at sunset by the ghost of Chatterton in the precincts of St Mary Redcliffe (*figure 3*) – the splendid Gothic church that stood over the road from the house where Chatterton was born, and lies at the heart of the Chatterton legend. The 'indignant form' proceeds to berate his place of birth for having slighted his poetic reputation and condemned his family to hardship and neglect:

> Ungrateful city – why am I forgot?
> Why why is poverty my parents lot?
> Forgetful thus of Chatterton's bright name
> Why is the tribute due of fame
> Still thus denied me in my native seat.
> Aye art thou Genius' deadly foe

2 Thomas Rowbotham, *Wine Street*, 1826 (BMAG M2345). *Bristol's Museums, Galleries & Archive*

3 J.M.W. Turner, *South Porch of St Mary Redcliffe*, c.1791-92 (BMAG K347).
Bristol's Museums, Galleries & Archives

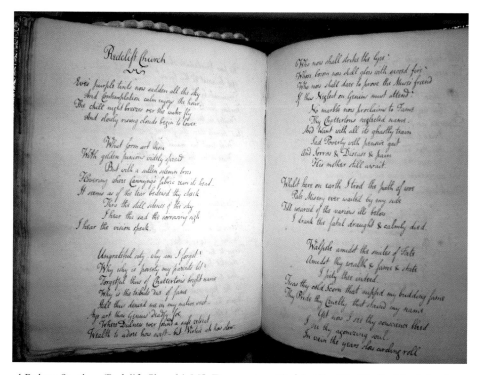

4 Robert Southey, 'Redclift Church'. MS. Eng. poet. e. 10, fols. 78v.-79r. *The Bodleian Libraries, The University of Oxford. Photo: Robin Jarvis*

> Where Dulness ever found a safe retreat.
> Wealth to adore how swift – but Virtue ah how slow.[24]

This, of course, rehearses the same theme explored in my account of Coleridge above, namely that Bristol was preoccupied with trade and material acquisition to the detriment of its cultural life. Chatterton's ghost continues by lamenting the absence of a statue to commemorate his achievements,[25] attacking Horace Walpole for the 'ungenerous crime' of having cast doubt on his medieval forgeries ('Twas thy cold Scorn that nipped my budding fame, / Thy Pride thy Cruelty that staind my name'), and urging Bristol to 'soothe' his mother's 'wintry hours of grief' with some financial support. The poem concludes with Chatterton asking the speaker to publish his complaint, and urging him not to make the same mistake of pursuing the 'meteor fame'. Southey never published 'Redclift Church' (*figure 4*), but eventually paid tribute to Chatterton by producing a three-volume edition of his works. He ignored the advice not to follow a poetic career, and made that same ungrateful city reprimanded by his predecessor's ghost the fulcrum of his early literary life.

Turning to a broader consideration of Southey's West Country poems, these are in various forms and genres, as one would expect from such a prolific poet. There are, for example, a number of sonnets, generally on very personal themes. Corston, three miles west of Bath, where Southey boarded for a year of his highly disrupted education, is remembered fondly as the speaker gazes once more into the stream where he 'wantoned thro' the day' under an apparently ultra-liberal regime. His sentimental recollections are compared to the 'soft sounds' of the same river, heard at greater distance 'on the inconstant breeze'. Another sonnet, written by his own account on the road to Bath, uses his weary ascent of Lansdown, and the beautiful view from the summit back over the 'journeyed plain', as a metaphor for the contradictions of life's journey, feeling regret for past times that were far from ideal as lived experience.[26] And in 1799, on a tour of the north Somerset coast which he described as 'the most beautiful part of England that I have ever seen', Southey found himself confined by bad weather in a pub in the Exmoor village of Porlock (the Ship Inn still exploits the literary association), and wrote a sonnet praising its 'lofty hills', 'woody glens', and 'level bay'; a 'patient prisoner', he found consolation in fabricating 'Dull rhymes to pass the duller hours away'.[27] In these and other sonnets, Southey addresses a place or natural feature to which he brings or creates personal associations, and uses local geography at most for purposes of sentimental reflection or lightly moralising commentary.

In the genre I want to focus on in the remainder of this essay, the inscription, this rudimentary technique is turned on its head, in that it is the place or natural object that addresses an imaginary passer-by – and, by extension, the reader. The basic technique is well illustrated by a poem, 'Inscription for a Cavern that Overlooks the River Avon' (1797), restricted, like the sonnets, to personal themes of domesticity and retirement, the charms of nature, and the sources of inspiration:

> Enter this cavern Stranger! the ascent
> Is long and steep and toilsome; here awhile
> Thou mayest repose thee, from the noontide heat
> O'ercanopied by this arch'd rock that strikes
> A grateful coolness: clasping its rough arms
> Round the rude portal, the old ivy hangs
> Its dark green branches down, and the wild Bees,
> O'er its grey blossoms murmuring ceaseless, make

Most pleasant melody. No common spot
Receives thee, for the Power who prompts the song,
Loves this secluded haunt. The tide below
Scarce sends the sound of waters to thine ear;
And this high-hanging forest to the wind
Varies its many hues. Gaze Stranger here!
And let thy soften'd heart intensely feel
How good, how lovely, Nature! When from hence
Departing to the City's crouded streets
Thy sickening eye at every step revolts
From scenes of vice and wretchedness; reflect
That Man creates the evil he endures.[28]

Here, an imaginary inscription found at the mouth of a cavern tells the visitor, with a redundancy intrinsic to the genre, what they are looking at and how they are feeling. In so doing, it confirms the 'Stranger' as an observant and sensitive individual, who will, moreover, be responsive to the Muse said to haunt the secluded spot ('the Power who prompts the song'). The inscription celebrates the traveller as much as the physical location: by emphasising how hard the cavern is to access, it implies that the Stranger/reader has the where-withal to succeed, that 'no common spot' welcomes someone of uncommon sensibility: the cave, to which the 'sound of waters' rises, functions, that is, as a homely Bristolian version of the classical fount of inspiration. The conclu-sion of the poem, in which the Stranger is urged to remember, on returning from his natural retreat to the 'City's crouded streets', that 'Man creates the evil he endures', seems to highlight the contrast between sensitive poet and unregenerate society – perhaps putting Southey in the Chattertonian role of youthful genius ill-at-ease in an ungrateful city.

For all its semi-mythical qualities, it is worth noting that the cave alluded to in this poem seems to have had real-life significance for Southey. In his commonplace book, under the heading 'St Vincent's Rocks' (the steep cliffs on the east bank of the Avon that Brunel was to choose as the platform for his famous Clifton Suspension Bridge), he outlines a much longer projected poem centred on the topography of the Avon Gorge:

It might begin by saying why I ought to celebrate them. The camp, my cavern, the legend of the building to which there leads no path, Cook's folly and its tale, the suicide at Sea-Mills, Trenchard and Gordon. Chatterton.

5 J.M.W. Turner, *The Mouth of the Avon, near Bristol, seen from Cliffs below Clifton* (c.1791-92) (BMAG K6431). *Bristol's Museums, Galleries & Archives*

Bristol, too, might have its fame. And Ashton might be mentioned. The hot wells, and those who come to die there.[29]

This compendious poem would, it seems, have combined matters of autobiographical importance ('my cavern'; Southey's maternal grandparents lived in Ashton) with material on diverse subjects from the very local and circumstantial (the suicide of a thirty-year-old man, who threw himself off the dock wall at Sea Mills after pencilling anguished diary entries on the wall of a nearby uninhabited building, was reported in the *Monthly Magazine* in October 1797) to matters bearing on the public realm (Trenchard and Gordon being the co-authors of an influential series of essays on civil and religious liberty in the 1720s – a reminder of Southey's republican sympathies). This entry neatly captures how, for Southey, the identity and significance of a place was a complex interweaving of personal associations, literary connections, local legends, and genuine historical traces. In terms of the personal element, it is, of course, tempting to try to identify Southey's cavern, but there are no solid grounds on which to do so. It seems pretty certain that it was not the modern 'Giant's Cave',[30] once a tiny chapel but now a tourist attraction, that is easily viewable from the Suspension Bridge: although this was presumably accessible via the cliff face in the distant past, prior to William West's tunnel being blasted through from the Observatory above in 1837 Southey would have needed mountaineering skills and equipment to get to this particular 'secluded haunt'. Perhaps Southey's cavern was the same one depicted by Turner in a watercolour dating from 1791-2 (*figure 5*). The original of this cave is located just below the top of the cliff in the area known as Sea Walls, and it is possible that a path had been cut along to it in Turner's time; if not, the three figures shown around the mouth of the cave in his painting would certainly have had a 'toilsome' ascent.[31]

'Inscription for a Cavern' is actually quite unusual among Southey's inscriptions in being so exclusively lyrical, focusing, with the exception of the concluding moral, on the close rapport between place and poetic speaker. It is a poem that sits quite comfortably within the genealogy of the nature-inscription as definitively expounded by Geoffrey Hartman in an essay first published over forty years ago. Hartman defines the inscription as verse 'conscious of the place on which it was written' (or might be written) and explores in particular the special form of the nature-inscription, enormously popular in the eighteenth century, in which 'the inscription calls to the passer by in the voice of the *genius loci* or spirit of the place', alerting him or her to the fact that they are on 'significant ground'. He relates this genre to the votive or commemorative epigram, a form with roots in ancient Greek poetry which descended to the Romantics via the intermediate figure of Mark Akenside. For Hartman, the distinctive achievement of the Romantics was to tear the inscription from its literal roots and make of it 'a free-standing poem, able to commemorate any feeling for nature or the spot that had aroused this feeling',[32] a poem in which the voices of nature and of feeling observer merge with one another in verse shorn of unnecessary ornament or rhetorical grandstanding. Southey's 'Inscription for a Cavern' fits this brief perfectly; indeed, Hartman quotes it in his essay.

Many of Southey's inscriptions, however, display a rather different, less uniform texture, and because Hartman sees the inscription as having reached its evolutionary peak in the nature-poetry of Wordsworth, with its unique blend of simplicity and self-consciousness, he is not best equipped to appreciate these other poems (which he ignores). He does, interestingly, contextualise the nature-inscription with respect to the eighteenth-century landscape garden, in which verses were often inscribed on monuments or seats at key locations to provide literary associations to the picturesque scenery and thus deepen aesthetic pleasure. As Hartman suggests, in such circumstances the inscription serves a touristic function, is a kind of 'signpost'.[33] Here comparison might be made with Dean MacCannell's highly influential study of modern tourism. For MacCannell, tourism is a secularised form of pilgrimage, in which tourists search in foreign places for the wholeness and authenticity that it no longer seems possible to attain in advanced urban society. What they actually find and savour, however, is a limited repertoire of sights managed and marketed by the tourist industry. Nothing is a 'sight' in and of itself, according to MacCannell: places, buildings, objects and so on require 'markers' to be constituted or recognised as sights or tourist attractions – a marker being a piece of information about the sight, such as a guidebook description, signpost, or information panel. Markers can be 'on-site', as with information panels that instruct the tourist on what they are looking at, or 'off-site', as with pictures that one might have seen in a magazine or online. If we apply this model to Southey's inscription poems, these might be described as off-site markers masquerading as on-site markers. They are presented, that is, as inscriptions for proposed monuments at the site in question, or as words designed to be otherwise legible at that site, but as written texts they serve as off-site markers which stimulate interest in a place and provide information that will deepen its meaning and significance and foster a suitably appreciative or reverential attitude (in a process MacCannell calls 'sight sacralization').[34]

That information can be very diverse, and is rarely limited to matters of scenic or antiquarian interest, filtered as it is through Southey's distinctive cultural and political concerns. A good example, focused on an 'attraction' in Bristol's hinterland, is his inscription 'For the Apartment in Chepstow-Castle where Henry Marten the Regicide was imprisoned Thirty Years' (1797). Chepstow Castle was a popular stop on the picturesque tour of the Wye Valley, and all visitors were familiar with Marten's story and visited the tower that was named after him. Marten, a hard-line Parliamentarian in the Civil War, who was one of the signatories to Charles I's death warrant, was himself sentenced to death after the Restoration; his punishment having been commuted to life imprisonment, he spent the last twelve years of his incarceration (not thirty, as Southey would have it) at Chepstow. In Southey's inscription, the spirit of the place is evidently on the republican side too, since it represents Marten as a political dreamer whose utopian ideals have been deferred to the millennium:

> Dost thou ask his crime?
> He had rebell'd against the King, and sat
> In judgment on him; for his ardent mind
> Shaped goodliest plans of happiness on earth,
> And peace and liberty. Wild dreams! But such
> As PLATO lov'd; such as with holy zeal
> Our MILTON worshipp'd. Blessed hopes! awhile
> From man withheld, even to the latter days,
> When Christ shall come and all things be fulfill'd.[35]

The austerity of Marten's last years is emphasised by contrasting the monotony of his confinement with the 'fair varieties' (5) of nature that are denied to him. But the most striking aspect of the inscription is that it completely ignores Chepstow's prestige as a magnificent terminus on the downstream picturesque tour of the Wye and foregrounds instead its place in Britain's political history. In so doing, it is entirely plausible that the poem represents, as Nick Roe has suggested, 'a lament for the beleaguered republicans of [Southey's] own generation as well':[36] the 'sad / And broken splendour' (7-8) of the sun that filters through the high bars of Marten's cell window stands for the disappointed dreams of all those English democrats who had mistakenly seen the French Revolution as the catalyst for a universal regeneration.

Another interesting poem in this genre – one of many dedicated to sites within the orbit of Southey's excursions from Bristol – is his 'Inscription for the Ruins of Glastonbury Abbey' (1798), which offers a more eclectic mix of history, myth, and submerged politics. Southey wrote to his wife in May 1799 that Glastonbury was 'the holiest ground in England to the religionist, the patriot, & the lover of romance', and in saying this he was merely embroidering upon his own inscription, published the previous year, which begins by informing the traveller that 'thy steps have reach'd the holiest spot / That Britain boasts'.[37] The poem continues by recalling the intertwined legends of Joseph of Arimethea (said to have built the first church on the site), the Glastonbury Thorn, the Holy Grail (supposedly buried at the base of the Tor), and King Arthur, whose coffin was allegedly discovered in the cemetery at the Abbey in the twelfth century. Then the traveller is questioned rather pointedly on his or her patriotism, and reminded of local connections to a more authentic national hero:

> Dost thou love
> Thy country, and the freedom once her boast?
> Here was it, in these moors, that ALFRED lay,
> Like to the couching lion, and beheld
> Th' invading Danes, and rush'd to victory.
> This fabric, Englishman! may emblem well
> The noble structure of the laws he built,
> Like this majestic once, and ruin'd now! (13-20)

In an appeal to national pride, the traveller is reminded that it was on the Somerset Levels that King Alfred maintained guerrilla warfare against Viking invaders for several years in the ninth century, and is reminded too of his reputation as a legal reformer; indeed, the final two lines, repeating a popular contemporary belief, take the ruined Abbey as a metaphor for the erosion of Anglo-Saxon liberties under the Norman yoke (and perhaps also the current yoke of Pitt's Tory government). Published in October 1798, at a time of crisis in the long war against Revolutionary France and eighteen months after the abortive French landing at Fishguard in southwest Wales, the inscription's invocation of Alfred's military successes against a foreign enemy had clear contemporary resonance. Southey was acquainted with the historian Sharon Turner, whose *History of the Anglo-Saxons* (1799-1805) would invite the same comparisons between past and present, and at great length celebrate Alfred as a wise legislator, patron of the arts, dedicated family man, and benign philosopher-king devoted to the service of his people – precisely the image that George III was currently attempting to construct for himself. It is very much the domestic tourist that this inscription very deliberately addresses, calling up from the local landscape heroic figures from the legendary and historical past to inspire fortitude in defence of the nation, however defective its present social arrangements. As Lynda Pratt very aptly comments, Southey here 'revitalises the inscription for a time of national and international crisis' and 'turns it into a vehicle for political, social, and cultural commentary'.[38]

Returning to Bristol, one can only regret the loss of numerous poems that Southey never got round to writing. These include an eclogue on Bedminster (where his maternal grandmother lived), of which he provides an enthusiastic outline in his commonplace book:

> The bowers, the porch, the yews by the laundry, the yard horse-chesnuts,
> the mortality, as my grandmother called it: the changes now, colloquially

told; and then to catch the sound of Ashton-bells, and speak of the family burying-place. The best kitchen, the black boarded parlour, the great picture-bible. What a treat![39]

This would evidently have been a poem built out of very personal associations. The unwritten topographical poem on the Avon Gorge referred to earlier would have been a totally different venture, mixing the personal with material of general or topical interest in characteristic Southeyan fashion. Although that work never materialised, Southey did return to the subject of the Gorge in his *Letters from England* (1807), an epistolary travel book published under the pseudonym of a Spanish traveller, Don Manuel Alvarez Espriella. His treatment of the Gorge in this work gave classic expression to a popular theme in the topographical literature on Bristol.

Tourists and guidebook-writers had long been troubled by the way in which the natural beauty of the Avon Gorge was being increasingly encroached upon by the signs of human occupation and interference in the landscape. To begin with, there were the new residential developments, the Georgian terraces and crescents which were spreading across the hillside as the *nouveaux riches* abandoned the overcrowded centre of Bristol to colonise the high ground of Clifton. In their symmetry, smoothness, and regularity, these Palladian extravagances were, as Malcolm Andrews has pointed out, the architectural antithesis of the picturesque.[40] To make matters worse, in the early Romantic period much of the new building work was in a state of partial completion: as one development followed another, aesthetic sensibilities were offended by the presence of what seemed like a permanent building site on the edge of one of nature's grandest spectacles.

Further along the Gorge, however, was the prospect that caused most disquiet to residents and visitors alike. This was the limestone quarrying which was constantly and very visibly – and also audibly, owing to the use of explosives – altering the appearance of the cliffs. Quarrying had been going on here for centuries, but the scale of activity in the Romantic period was unprecedented: Samuel Jackson's painting of the view from Sea Walls (*figure 6*) dramatically reveals the changes wrought on both sides of the river. In general, industrial activity was not thought to be necessarily inimical to picturesque beauty, but in the Avon Gorge it seemed that the damage inflicted on the natural scene in the cause of economic gain was too extreme to sustain an alliance between beauty and utility: Ibbetson suggested that the spectacle of quarrying, with the miners 'perpetually changing their grouping and their attitudes',[41] was consistent with

6 Samuel Jackson,
*The Avon Gorge from
Sea Walls, Looking
towards Clifton,*
c.1823 (BMAG
K1501). *Bristol's
Museums, Galleries &
Archives*

picturesque variety, but his was a rare equanimity. As for the other dominant aesthetic category, G. W. Manby begins his account in 1802 by construing the blasting as heightening the appeal of the landscape, distorting the rock into more violent irregularity and, through the thunderous fall of immense blocks of stone with accompanying multiple echoes, creating a 'most awfully sublime' spectacle. But a few pages later he contradicts this stance with an attack on the industrial exploitation of the Gorge:

> These rocks [St Vincent's Rocks] are the property of that opulent and respectable society of Merchant-Venturers of Bristol, who will not allow this beautiful mass to be defaced. It is to be lamented their interference has not restricted the prodigious havoc that is daily making on its neighbouring rock, as the venerable majesty of this truly sublime wonder of nature is receiving daily insult, and robbed of some ancient grace by the rude hand of mercenary labour.[42]

Manby's observations highlight the fact that the benign neglect on which picturesque nature thrives is usually not the most profitable option; equally, it is clear that aesthetically minded observers such as him prefer their sublimity to be a manifestation of the power of nature rather than of chemical explosives. Manby's displeasure at the perceived environmental vandalism became the dominant note in representations of the quarrying in the Gorge and it was memorably articulated by Southey. In his persona of Don Manuel Alvarez Espriella, Southey observes with mock wonderment that 'The people of Bristol seem to sell every thing that can be sold'. He cites the selling of the

Bristol Cross, which ended up in the grounds of Stourhead; he mourns the disposal of a fine brazen eagle lectern from the Cathedral; he is shocked at the selling of false hope to consumptives by the proprietors of the spa ('the people here regard death as a matter of trade'); but what aggravates him more than anything is that here, in the Avon Gorge, the people of Bristol are 'selling the sublime and beautiful by the boat-load'.[43] Southey's judgement on the quarrying was so perfectly epigrammatical that later writers freely quoted or plagiarised it; it was even incorporated into verse, as in *The New Clifton and Bristol Guide* (1826), which references 'Espriella's Letters' for a jovial description concluding with the lines:

> With gunpowder blasted, there fell the SUBLIME,
> And the beautiful too – and they make each knob Lime[44]

Southey's definitive attack on selling the sublime indicates that he took personally the physical and visual degradation of the Avon Gorge – which, after all, contained *his* cavern – 'the cavern where I have written so many verses'.[45] It also shows him – now living in a different part of the country – happily revivifying that familiar negative stereotype of materialistic Bristolians recklessly subordinating culture to commerce.

To conclude, it is clear from the poetry, letters, and notebooks that he produced when living in the Quantocks and the Lake District that Coleridge was a writer capable of responding with great sensitivity to his local environment. In his Bristol period, however, his energies were largely absorbed by radical politics (to which, of course, Bristol was a far from neutral backdrop) and his poetic engagement with Bristol and its hinterland was correspondingly limited. Robert Southey's prolific poetic output, on the other hand, demonstrates a deep and enduring emotional and intellectual involvement with the region. 'Our western country may well claim your attention,' he wrote to one correspondent in July 1792,[46] and it certainly claimed his own attention over the next decade and beyond. Francis Jeffrey, the forthright editor of the *Edinburgh Review* who had little time for modern literature, once said – and it was not intended as a compliment – that Southey turned everything in his notebooks into poetry.[47] Were this true, we would have a still larger legacy of West Country poems, including many more with Bristol themes. As it is, though, we have an impressive range of short poems that engage with the people, landscapes, legends, and history of this part of the world. Southey's inscriptions, in particular, considered as touristic markers, compose a highly

7 E.H. Baily, *Memorial Portrait Bust of Robert Southey* (1844), north choir aisle, Bristol Cathedral. *Photo: Robin Jarvis*

selective and partisan itinerary of places that he believed should be commemorated for their cultural and historical associations or that offered inspiring lessons for his own troubled generation. He is himself commemorated by a portrait bust in Bristol Cathedral (*figure 7*); perhaps Bristol, the 'ungrateful city' that he always regarded as his spiritual home, should do more.

In Her Place: Ann Yearsley or 'The Bristol Milkwoman'

Kerri Andrews

> Engrossing Leeves! in wishes unconfin'd,
> Else would they fix on one extensive Mind:
> Is not thy Soul capacious as the Globe?
> Yet too insatiate, thou must needs disrobe
> Poor Bristol of the only gem She prized,
> And cruel, leave her senseless, dull, despised.
> Tho' too exulting, thou may'st deck the scene,
> Beware! the blaze may scorch thy Cowslip green:[1]

So opens a recently-discovered poem by Ann Yearsley, the 'Bristol Milkwoman', 'Lines Addressed to the Revd Mr Leeves on his Visiting Stella to Cowslip Green'. Written some time in the spring of 1785, it articulates an intriguing anxiety about the fate of Bristol without 'Stella', or Hannah More, the famous dramatist and educator, and Yearsley's patron. The poem's subject is More's move from Bristol, where she had lived in Park Street with her sisters at their well-known school, for Cowslip Green in the rural Mendips some twelve miles to the south-west. Whilst More in reality appears to have craved the peace and quiet of country life after several years in the city,[2] in Yearsley's poem the architect of the move is Reverend William Leeves, the rector of Wrington. Though Bristol was in this period a city of immense material wealth (it was second only to London both in terms of population and the trade coming through its ports), for Yearsley More is the 'only gem' 'prized' by the city: with her loss Bristol is sensibly diminished. Leeves has stripped the city of its only true material and cultural asset, and stolen her away to Wrington. However, once transplanted to the rural idyll of the Mendips, the 'gem' no longer embellishes, but 'scorches', her beauties dazzling, rather than ornamenting; the unfortunate consequence of More's removal from her proper place, of the relocation of Bristol's 'only gem' to a location not used to dealing with such riches.

Yearsley's argument here is that Bristol, a city habituated to trading in

1 A line engraving of Ann Yearsley by Wilson Lowry, published 1787 (BMAG M874).
Bristol's Museums, Galleries & Archives

wealth and jewels, is much better equipped than Cowslip Green to deal with treasures like More. But this is not her primary reason for objecting to More's removal; rather, it is that the Reverend Leeves has no *need* of More or her virtues:

> To lose with calmness, stop the rising sigh,
> Freeze the big tear, ere it disgrace the eye
> Has long been mine: nor would I now bewail
> Should Stella seek some poor uncultur'd vale
> Where sentiment has budded but to die
> And all the souls best powers blasted lie!
> Where spirits like Lactilla's sullen rove
> Whilst more than midnight fills the Grove
> Of branching ignorance – which wide extends
> Whilst its fell dew on the young thought descends
> With deadly weight: a scene like this requires
> A Stella with her soul-pervading fires;
> But thou! what strong necessity is thine?[3]

Leeves, an accomplished composer, poet and scholar, has no 'strong necessity' for More's improving presence. Indeed, Yearsley's speaker goes so far as to accuse him of 'boundless avarice' that he 'must yet sigh for *More*' learning than he already has,[4] the dubious pun emphasising that there is an emotional, as well as intellectual, desire for More. What is perhaps most interesting about this part of the poem, though, is the detailed topography offered by Yearsley of the 'uncultur'd vale' which she inhabits imaginatively. In its naming of the primary location in that vale – 'the Grove/ Of branching ignorance' – the poem evokes the allegorical topography of John Bunyan's *The Pilgrim's Progress* (1678) and makes a similarly strong connection here between the imagined places in the 'vale', and intellectual or mental struggles. The result is a powerful paralleling of real place (Bristol; Wrington; Cowslip Green) and imaginary ('the uncultur'd vale, 'the Grove/ Of branching ignorance'), with More's physical and intellectual presence.

Acknowledging that Yearsley understands place in this poem as a complex interweaving of real and imaginary spaces, social connections, and intellectual exchanges, is important because it challenges the simplistic presentation offered of Yearsley by Hannah More herself when she described her protégée as 'the Bristol Milkwoman'. This description appeared on the title page of

Yearsley's debut volume, *Poems on Several Occasions* (1785) which was published only three months or so after Yearsley wrote 'Lines Addressed to the Revd Mr Leeves on his Visiting Stella to Cowslip Green'. As John Clare, 'the Northamptonshire Peasant'; 'the Ayrshire Ploughman' Robert Burns; or Robert Bloomfield, 'the Farmer's Boy' from rural Suffolk, would find along with Yearsley, being located so specifically by their patrons both 'geographically and in terms of rank'[5] significantly shaped how their works were read. Whilst their local areas were undoubtedly important to these poets (all of whom wrote about the environments in which they lived), the imposition of descriptions such as 'the Bristol Milkwoman' encouraged responses to them which viewed their 'poetic proclivities' as 'emerging from the soil from which they sprang, rather than from their hard won efforts at literacy.'[6] Yet, as Yearsley's poem, 'Lines Addressed to the Revd Mr Leeves' indicates, place for Yearsley meant much more than the immediate local environment to which the identification of her as 'the Bristol Milkwoman' would seek to reduce her. Furthermore, place is a concept with which Yearsley engages in complex and challenging ways. In this essay I want to pay close attention to the ways in which Yearsley explores ideas of place, from her description of her own home in 'Clifton Hill' (published as part of *Poems on Several Occasions*), to her engagement with Bristol's involvement in slavery in 'On the Inhumanity of the Slave Trade' (1788), and her critique of Bristol's governing classes in 'Bristol Elegy' (1796). By doing so I hope to examine the ways in which Yearsley seeks to understand her own place, not just in terms of physical spaces (such as Clifton or Bristol), but also in terms of her role as a Bristol poet, and as a lower-class poet from Bristol eager to secure for herself a place in literary culture.[7]

Yearsley's most explicit engagement with place – in all the senses I mention above – comes in the early poem 'Clifton Hill', written in January 1785 and published in June that year as part of *Poems on Several Occasions*. Bridget Keegan and Donna Landry have both usefully explored the poem's engagement with the traditions of the 'prospect' poem, a genre which, as Keegan notes, 'considers human imprints on a site in history,'[8] and my discussion of this poem also examines Yearsley's work in generic terms. Writing prospect poetry is of particular significance for lower-class poets such as Yearsley, partly because of the genre's historical associations with the 'symbolic' assertion of 'control over the countryside', but also because the poet, writing about 'natural scenery, transform[s] it into poetry that performs geo-historical work', meaning that 'the poet's identity is linked with a particular conception of

2 Francis Danby, *View of Clifton from Leigh Woods* (c. 1818-20). Here the hill top location of Clifton is in evidence from Leigh Woods on the other side of the River Avon (BMAG K851). *Bristol's Museums, Galleries & Archives*

nature'.[9] The prospect poem, then, engages with place in a way that is historically, socially and poetically coded, and in a manner that weaves the poet's identity into the topos in a particular way. Yearsley's poem, however, destabilises these codes, with interesting consequences for the poet's identity, and indeed for the place she is describing.

In considering Yearsley's engagement with the prospect poem, I will be comparing 'Clifton Hill' with three influential examples of the form from the seventeenth and early-eighteenth centuries: Sir John Denham's 'Cooper's Hill' (1642); Alexander Pope's 'Windsor Forest' (1713); and John Dyer's 'Grongar Hill' (1726). In all three of these earlier examples, the poetic speaker is positioned so as to be able to survey the landscape to the horizon, usually describing, if often in general terms, something of the topography before them:

> Through untrac't waies, and ayrie paths I flye,
> More boundlesse in my Fancy than my eye:
> My eye, which swift as thought contracts the space
> That lyes between, and first salutes the place
> Crown'd with that sacred pile, so vast, so high,
> That whether 'tis a part of Earth, or sky,
> Uncertain seemes, and may be thought a proud
> Aspiring mountain, or falling cloud[10]

The speaker of 'Cooper's Hill' has just taken 'wing from thy auspicious height' (directly addressing the hill itself), and seems physically, as well as imaginatively, to soar above the surrounding landscape so high that detail is difficult to come by. John Dyer's speaker, rather than flying from the hilltops, makes a rather more laborious journey to the summit of Grongar Hill, though the effect is similar:

> Now, I gain the mountain's brow,
> What a landskip lies below!
> No clouds, no vapours intervene,
> But the gay, the open scene
> Does the face of nature show,
> In all the hues of heaven's bow!
> And, swelling to embrace the light,
> Spreads around beneath the sight.[11]

Even the speaker of Pope's poem, contained by the less lofty Windsor Forest, manages to find higher ground from which to imagine when '*Jove* himself, subdu'd by beauty still, / Might change *Olympus* for a nobler hill.'[12] Underlying all of these generalised perspectives are eighteenth-century aesthetic values which held that a prospect was not to be 'looked *at*', but 'looked *over*'.[13] In such views:

> [t]he impression made upon the eye was a general one: an impression of the order of its own progress over the objects in the landscape, rather than of those objects themselves. And it is in this respect [… that the eye] is able to move at such speed over the landscape, only because it can organise so efficiently the objects in its path into a preconceived structure, which allows them an identity only as landmarks on the journey the eye makes to the horizon.[14]

According to John Barrell these aesthetic values, and the rules governing their practical application to prospects, were so pervasive throughout the eighteenth century that 'it became impossible for anyone with an aesthetic interest in landscape to look at the countryside without applying them.'[15] As a result of this pervasiveness, Barrell argues, the features which distinguished one landscape from another, which made each landscape distinct, became blurred, because '*A* landscape was fitted into *the* established set of landscape patterns, and so became part of the *universal* landscape'.[16] From this evidence, it appears that both eighteenth-century aesthetics, and literary tradition, strongly favoured the elevated view, the description of a prospect seen from a distance, the generalised sense of place.

The title of Yearsley's poem certainly ties it to these cultural and literary traditions: 'Clifton Hill' cannot but help call to mind 'Cooper's Hill' and 'Grongar Hill', and connects it to the sorts of aesthetic values identified by Barrell. It can be assumed, then, that Yearsley was aware of the precepts governing the prospect poem form, and indeed the aesthetics of landscape, yet her poem appears to conform with them only momentarily, or conditionally. Where Denham and Dyer opened their poems with expansive views – assisted in Denham's case by his fancied flight over the scene before him – which are scanty on detail, Yearsley loads the opening of her poem with specific descriptions. These are not only of the fauna, but also of individual people who might plausibly belong in the landscape, in contrast to the classical deities who populate the poems of Denham and Pope, or the uninhabited view described by Dyer. Yearsley writes:

> How mourns each tenant of the silent grove!
> No soft sensation tunes the heart to love;
> No fluttering pulse awakes to Rapture's call;
> No strain responsive aids the water's fall.
> The Swain neglects his Nymph, yet knows not why;
> The Nymph, indifferent, mourns the freezing sky;
> Alike insensible to soft desire,
> She asks no warmth – but from the kitchen fire;
> Love seeks a milder zone; half sunk in snow,
> LACTILLA, shivering, tends her fav'rite cow;
> The bleating flocks now ask the bounteous hand,
> And chrystal streams in frozen fetters stand.
> The beauteous red-breast, tender in her frame,
> Whose murder marks the fool with treble shame,
> Near the low cottage door, in pensive mood,
> Complains, and mourns her brothers of the wood.[17]

This is very much an individuated topography, and Yearsley's use of landmarks (the 'silent grove', the 'low cottage', the sight of 'LACTILLA' tending her cow) serves not to facilitate 'the journey the eye makes to the horizon',

3 George Holmes, *Bristol from Clifton Wood*. In the foreground of this undated drawing, cows are grazing as they would have done in the days of Ann Yearsley, the so-called Clifton milk woman (BMAG M1747). *Bristol's Museums, Galleries & Archives*

or to follow the speaker in a poetic flight of fancy *over* the landscape, as in Denham's poem, but instead to enable the reader to follow the speaker on her journey *through* the landscape. The experience for the reader is therefore quite different: this is not some generalised or idealised panorama whose description is designed to enable a gentlemanly class to express 'their authority over the national landscape which they owned',[18] but a living, working landscape for which this poem might plausibly serve as guide or word-map; instead of seeking to participate in the assertion of power over an idealised view which was so central to earlier prospect poetry, this poem offers the reader a companionable, egalitarian participation in the life of the landscape; a landscape in which human and non-human agents have an equal share.

It is worth noting here Bridget Keegan's caution against assuming that labouring- or lower-class poets, with 'their more straitened socio-economic expectations' would offer 'readers a greater sense of immediacy' by which their writing might be viewed as 'more "realistic"',[19] an assumption that was made by some contemporary readers of labouring-class poetry, and one that it would be unproductive to make here. Yearsley might be describing a landscape in such a way that the reader could retrace the speaker's steps, but that landscape is by no means unmediated by poetic devices or literary knowingness. Indeed, there is evidence in the poem to suggest that Yearsley is conscious of, and plays with, the kinds of assumptions likely to be made about her as a labouring-class poet (and possibly as a female poet), in a way which serves to further challenge the conventional masculine, land-owning subjectivity of earlier prospect poetry. This can be seen in Yearsley's inclusion in her poem of people who might 'realistically' be found in this landscape, and who do not often feature in earlier examples of the form:

> The ruddy swain now stalks along the vale,
> And snuffs fresh ardour from the flying gale;
> The landscape rushes on his untaught mind,
> Strong raptures rise, but raptures undefin'd;
> He louder whistles, stretches o'er the green,
> By screaming milk-maids, not unheeded, seen;
> The downcast look ne'er fixes on the swain,
> They dread his eye, retire and gaze again.[20]

Though the figure is masculine, his response to the landscape could not be more different to that of the leisured, gentlemanly class from whose point of view prospect poetry was usually written, in which the landscape is seen 'from the commanding position of the noblemen and gentlemen who owned it.'[21] There is no time here for admiration of 'that sacred pile, so vast, so high,'[22] spied by Denham's speaker, nor for the leisured celebration of 'Grongar Hill' which sees Dyer's speaker 'At the fountain of a rill/ Sate upon a flow'ry bed,/With my hand beneath my head',[23] nor even for the relaxed mirth of James Thomson's 'Cottage-Swain', who after a hard winter's day 'Hangs o'er the enlivening Blaze, and, taleful, there,/ Recounts his simple Frolick: Much he talks,/ And much he laughs'.[24] Instead, Yearsley's 'ruddy swain', who clearly is not insensitive to the beauties of the place, strides on, 'stretches o'er the green' and out of the poem, having only briefly registered the rising of the 'Strong raptures'. There is no place here, either in terms of the swain's own business, or in the poem's own structure, for leisured meditation. Instead, the swain, like the speaker and the reader, hurry on: he further 'along the vale', and we to ponder the 'screaming milk-maids' he has left behind, and the means of preserving womanly virtue in rural communities.

Nor does Yearsley's description of the pastoral life on Clifton Hill fit with the conventions of prospect poetry. She writes:

Here nibbling flocks of scanty herbage gain
A meal penurious from the barren plain;
Crop the low niggard bush; and, patient, try
The distant walk, and every hillock nigh:
Some bask, some bound, nor terrors ever know,
Save from the human form, their only foe.
Ye bleating innocents! dispel your fears,
My woe-struck soul in all your troubles shares;
'Tis but LACTILLA – fly not from the green:
Long have I shar'd with you this guiltless scene.[25]

This is a long way from the pastoral lushness imagined by prospect poets whose speakers gaze with complaisance over the farms and smallholdings of the landed gentry beneath their elevated positions:

This scene had some bold Greek, or Brittish Bard
Beheld of old, what stories had we heard,
Of Fairies, Satyrs, and the Nymphs their Dames,
Their feasts, their revells, and their amorous flames!
'Tis still the same, although their ayery shape
All but a quick Poetick sight escape.
There Faunus and Sylvanus keep their Courts,
And thither all the horned hoast resorts,
To graze the ranker mead, that noble heard
On whose sublime and shady fronts is reard
Natures great Masterpeece;[26]

In Denham's poem, the landscape is overseen by the gods who have a care for the well-being of cattle, or of the woods and fields, and there is a long association with magic or supernatural beings, all of whom have contributed to the lushness and fertility of the place. That landscape, Denham makes clear, is carefully managed to yield good harvests, and to provide the monarch with sport; the very image of a gentleman's country estate, embellished by an association with the deities of old. Yearsley's unsupervised flocks, in contrast, have nothing to do with humanity: they roam the common ground, and shun humankind. This unmanaged, unimproved, and most importantly *common* space, allows for a different kind of interaction between human and animal life. Instead of the violence of the hunts of both Denham's and Pope's poems, in Yearsley's poetry there is a place where both humans and animals can co-exist without competition or violence, and indeed genuine companionship between human beings and animals seems possible. In fact, Yearsley seems to be describing something close to empathy: in addition to sharing the physical space in a way not usually seen in this type of poetry, Yearsley's speaker occupies a shared mental space with these sheep. Whilst Yearsley was by no means the first or only writer to imagine herself into the mind of an animal, it is significant that this empathetic relationship occurs on the common land of Clifton Hill, a space where not only animals and humans can co-exist, but where humans share peacefully with other humans the means to make a living.[27]

This, I suggest, is evidence of a conscious effort in 'Clifton Hill' to reverse the power dynamics more typically found in prospect poetry from this period. Bridget Keegan has suggested that 'eighteenth-century topographical poets use the elevated perspective to separate themselves from rural nature, privileging the visual to create distance between observer and observed, symbolically asserting control over the countryside in ways that were both classed and gendered.'[28] Yearsley would seem to do the opposite: instead of 'separating' her speaker 'from rural nature', Yearsley places her speaker within the minds of the creatures that constitute the natural world, and does so in a space where it is not possible to assert control, the land being by law shared ground. This is taken even further when Yearsley's poem shifts from Clifton to the opposite side of the Avon Gorge and the tangled brakes of Leigh Wood:

> The pois'nous reptiles here their mischiefs bring,
> And thro' the helpless sleeper dart the sting;
> The toad envenom'd, hating human eyes,
> Here springs to light, lives long, and aged dies.
> The harmless snail, slow-journeying, creeps away,
> Sucks the young dew, but shuns the bolder day.
> (Alas! if transmigration should prevail,
> I fear LACTILLA's soul must house in snail.)
> The long-nosed mouse, the woodland rat is here,
> The sightless mole, with nicely-pointed ear;
> The timid rabbit hails th' impervious gloom,
> Eludes the dog's keen scent, and shuns her doom.[29]

The distance between speaker and subject is here almost undetectable, as the speaker imagines herself into the lives of several sorts of creature, none of which would ordinarily be considered suitable for inclusion in a prospect poem. The exception of course is the rabbit, though this creature usually appears in poetry only as sport for the gentleman whose land is being described by the polite prospect poet. Nor is this the sort of nature over which any control can be asserted: instead of the well-managed, productive landscapes explored by Pope in particular – whose scene is 'crown'd with tufted trees and springing corn' which, 'Like verdant isles the sable waste adorn'[30] – Leigh Woods (*colour plate 14*) is utterly resistant to improvement, and represents nature at its wildest:

> How thickly cloath'd, yon rock of scanty soil,
> Its lovely verdure scorns the hand of Toil.
> Here the deep green, and here the lively plays,
> The russet birch, and ever-blooming bays;
> The vengeful black-thorn, of wild beauties proud,
> Blooms beauteous in the gloomy-chequer'd crowd:
> The barren elm, the useful feeding oak,
> Whose hamadryade ne'er should feel the stroke
> Of axe relentless, 'till twice fifty years
> Have crown'd her woodland joys, and fruitful cares.[31]

Something approaching a character is given for each tree, indicating again that the speaker is capable of sympathy with all wild and natural things, including trees. There is no attempt to 'assert control' over the landscape; rather there is a celebration of the wildness and variety of the topography, the flora and the fauna to be found here. Whilst the poem is not blind to the brutality of nature, which, as Yearsley notes, 'feast[s] on dreadful food, which hop'd a milder grave',[32] there is no desire expressed here to 'improve' it, or to 'manage' it. Instead, the speaker seems content to co-exist with nature in its present state.

The proximity between speaker and subject contrasts interestingly with the distance between speaker and reader, and indicates that the poet is alert not only to the power dynamics inherent in prospect poetry between author and landscape, but those likely to be present in prospect poetry by a self-educated lower-class writer. This distance between speaker and reader is most apparent in Yearsley's discussion of the Hotwells and its typical clientele:

> Blame not my rustic lay, nor think me rude,
> If I avow Conceit's the grand prelude
> To dire disease and death. Your high-born maid,
> Whom fashion guides, in youth's first bloom shall fade;
> She seeks the cause, th' effect would fain elude,
> By Death's o'erstretching stride too close persu'd,
> She faints within his icy grasp, yet stares,
> And wonders why the Tyrant yet appears –
> Abrupt – so soon – Thine, Fashion is the crime,
> Fell Dissipation does the work of time.[33]

The description of her own poem as a 'rustic lay' is an arch nod to bourgeois assumptions of labouring-class poets as rural poets, or poets of nature: a 'rustic lay' would be the work of someone who has 'the appearance or manners of a country person [...] lacking in elegance, refinement, or education', and the sort of short rural poem 'intended to be sung'. Given the poem's clear alertness to the conventions of prospect poetry, and its deliberate echoing and reinterpretation of earlier examples of the genre, this description is disingenuous, and ironic. It also serves as a deliberate counterpoint to the speaker's condemnation of the vices of the 'high-born', a condemnation in which the reader is implicated by the pert 'Your'. In contrast to the gentlemanly companionship evoked in their poems by both Pope, but especially Dyer, who urges the reader in friendly but imperative tones to 'see the rivers how they run', or to 'See on the mountain's southern side' a particularly lovely view,[34] Yearsley here abruptly distances her speaker from her imagined reader. Instead of speaker and reader being united in admiration and approval of the landscape before them, as in the poetry of Dyer, Denham and Pope, here the speaker and reader are at odds: they come from different classes, different backgrounds, and have very different social values, of which the speaker is openly critical in this, her supposedly 'rustic lay'.

This, then, is very much an alternative prospect poem which refuses to approach landscape or space in the traditional ways associated with the form. Both Bridget Keegan and Donna Landry have suggested that this rejection of the literary conventions of prospect poetry emerges from Yearsley's desire to 'substitute protofeminist for conventionally masculine "subjects"', in order to ensure that 'the dominant consciousness of the poem is always a feminine one'.[35] Whilst it would be impossible to argue that Yearsley's gender is not a factor – any more than her class is a factor – in the decisions made in this poem regarding the engagement with place, to claim that the poem is predicated on a 'protofeminist' challenge to masculine poetic conventions is to miss the wider implications of Yearsley's representation of 'Clifton Hill'. Certainly, the speaker is female, but not necessarily 'feminine', and, as Yearsley makes clear, the consequences of not seeking to assert control over the landscape, of taking time to explore the detail of that landscape instead of generalizing or idealizing, are of benefit to all. This includes non-human occupants of the place, whose day-to-day life is not here evidence of poor (i.e. unimproved) agricultural practices, nor is it inconvenient to the human occupants (no hunter complains about the tangled woods, for instance). Instead, the place that Yearsley represents to us is one that can be, and indeed is, occupied by a variety of entities, including poor and dispossessed human beings (both male and female), and crawling, creeping, bloody animal life. It is perhaps in making these beings fit subjects for a prospect poem – a form, as we have seen, more usually associated with kings and national history – that 'Clifton Hill' most effectively challenges the conventions of that form; if Bridget Keegan's claim that in prospect poetry 'the poet's identity is linked with a particular conception of nature',[36] then 'Clifton Hill' demonstrates that a female manual labourer is fit to be a poet.

Speaking for Bristol

In 'Clifton Hill' Ann Yearsley makes a powerful claim for the value not only of her poetry about place, but her place as a poet, through her shrewd adaptation and reinterpretation of the generic conventions of the prospect poem. Her subsequent work would make even more ambitious claims. When Yearsley's second volume, *Poems on Various Subjects*, was published in 1787 (without the support of Hannah More, with whom Yearsley had parted company in September 1785), it still sought to link the poet with place, though in subtly different ways. Instead of 'the Bristol Milkwoman', Yearsley was presented as the 'MILKWOMAN OF CLIFTON, NEAR BRISTOL',[37] indicating that Yearsley's new publishers, the Robinson brothers, were eager to maintain the public perception of Yearsley as coming from a particular place (both geographically and socially), perhaps as a cultural shorthand for what readers might expect of her work. However, the poetry in the volume itself is suggestive of a writer with loftier goals than being pigeon-holed, like so many other labouring-class authors, as a poet *of* a particular place. Instead, Yearsley's poetry from 1787 suggests an increasing desire to be viewed as a poet who speaks *to* and *for* a place.

Something of this sort can be seen at work in 'Clifton Hill', when Yearsley's

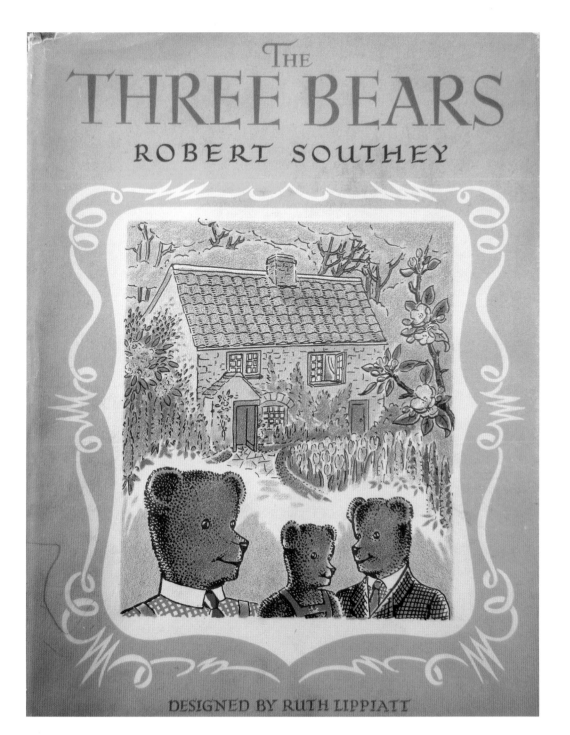

THE THREE BEARS

ROBERT SOUTHEY

DESIGNED BY RUTH LIPPIATT

1 The Bristol-born poet Robert Southey was the first to record the fairy tale of *The Three Bears*.
Bristol's Museums, Galleries & Archives. Photo: Marie Mulvey-Roberts

2 Thomas Chatterton life-size bronze sculpture
(2000) by Lawrence Holofcener, Millennium
Square, Bristol.
Photo: Marie Mulvey-Roberts

3 This gypsy caravan is in the Bristol Museum
and is mentioned in Angela Carter's *Shadow
Dance* (1966) which is set in Bristol.
Bristol's Museums, Galleries & Archives

4 *Chatterton* (1856) by Henry Wallis. © *Tate, London, 2015*

5 John Cabot bronze sculpture by Stephen Joyce at Narrow Quay, Bristol.
Photo: Marie Mulvey-Roberts

6 *Samuel Taylor Coleridge* by Peter Vandyke (1795). This portrait was painted for Joseph Cottle, who published Coleridge's first volume of poems in 1796.
National Portrait Gallery

7 *Bristol Riots: The Burning of the Bishop's Palace* (1831) by William James Müller, (BMAG M4122). *Bristol's Museums, Galleries & Archives*

8 *Mary Robinson as Perdita* (1782) by
John Hoppner.
Chawton House Library

9 Edmund Burke bronze statue by James Havard Thomas
on the Centre in Bristol, first cast in 1894.
Photo: Marie Mulvey-Roberts

10 *Robert Southey* by John James Masquerier (c.1800)

11 *The Abolition of the Slave Trade* (1792) attributed to Isaac Cruikshank. Published by S.W. Fores, 10 April, 1792. *British Cartoon Prints Collection, Library of Congress, Washington*

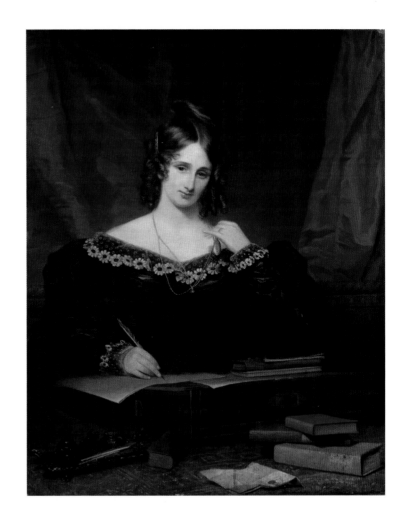

12 *Unknown woman, formerly known as Mary Wollstonecraft Shelley* by Samuel John Stump (1831).
National Portrait Gallery

13 Yew-tree in Brockley Combe. *Photo: Robin Jarvis*

14 *A Sketching Party in Leigh Woods* (c.1830) by Samuel Jackson. *Bristol's Museums, Galleries & Archives*

15 Stage and auditorium of the Cube, King Square, Bristol, formerly the Bristol Arts Centre which staged a key moment in theatrical history with the debut of Charles Wood's *Dingo* in 1967.
Photo: Roxanne Courtney, www.cubecinema.com/ images-of-cube

speaker gives voice to the occupants of particular locations in the surrounding area, in particular Leigh Woods. However, instead of acting as 'the messenger' only for the sorts of 'animals least likely to be perceived by urban reader', to use Mary Waldron's assessment of Yearsley's role in 'Clifton Hill',[38] Yearsley's subsequent poetry has her acting as the 'messenger', voice, or even conscience, of a whole city. Yet even here, Yearsley's claims to speak *for* a place are rooted in her being *of* that place. This is perhaps most evident in Yearsley's decision to publish in 1788 a poem on the evils of the slave trade. Bristol, of course, was heavily implicated in the trade in African slaves: many of the city's merchants had grown rich from their involvement, and parts of the city had been built using money made from the trade. And whilst, for the first time in her career, Yearsley's name appeared on the frontispiece unqualified by a place of origin (either Bristol or Clifton), readers were unlikely to be ignorant that it was the 'Milkwoman of Bristol' who addressed the Earl of Bristol in the opening dedication:

> My Lord,
> Being convinced that your Ideas of Justice and Humanity are not confined
> to one Race of Men, I have endeavoured to lead you to the Indian Coast.
> My Intention is not to cause that Anguish in your Bosom which powerless
> Compassion ever gives; yet, my Vanity is flattered, when I but fancy that
> Your Lordship feels as I do.[39]

The last clause indicates not only the possibility of an important concord between poet and the Earl of Bristol, but also the potential for a reversal of the expected power dynamic. Whilst it might be assumed that the Earl would lead on such matters, this clause represents him as following the poet's example; it is she who speaks for Bristol, both in terms of the city and perhaps also the Earl himself.

As a result Yearsley was able to claim for herself the right to speak directly to the citizens of Bristol, a right she asserts from the beginning of her poem:

> BRISTOL, thine heart hath throbb'd to glory. – Slaves,
> E'en Christian slaves, have shook their chains, and gaz'd
> With wonder and amazement on thee. [...]
>   Yet, Bristol, list! nor deem Lactilla's soul
> Lessen'd by distance; snatch her rustic thought,
> Her crude ideas, from their panting state,

And let them fly in wide expansion; lend
Thine energy, so little understood
By the rude million, and I'll dare the strain
Of Heav'n-born Liberty till Nature moves
Obedient to her voice. Alas! my friend,
Strong rapture dies within the soul, while Pow'r
Drags on his bleeding victims.[40]

There is some ambiguity in the opening sentence whether the poem's speaker is addressing the Earl of Bristol, or a personification of the city itself, an ambiguity heightened by the pre-existing overlap between the two senses of 'Bristol'. The latter, however, emerges as the dominant sense, but the momentary uncertainty lends power to the position Yearsley has established for herself. That position shifts, however, at the start of the second verse paragraph quoted above. Having opened with a typical apostrophe to the city, in keeping with the poet's role as the voice of Bristol, the register shifts to become both more entreating and more insistent, and it quickly becomes clear that rather than speaking directly *for* the city, or *to* the city in this poem, the poet and city are to combine forces in a collaborative effort to counter the evils of slavery. With the city providing 'energy' and the opportunity for 'ideas' to 'fly in wide expansion', the poet brings a voice capable of taming 'Nature' itself. The reference to 'Lactilla' also brings into play the earlier resonances established by the use of that name in poems like 'Clifton Hill', providing a shorthand for the poet's intimate connection with place, and establishing a solid framework for the collaboration between poet and place. The reference to the poet's 'soul' being 'Lessen'd by distance' is obscure – it is possible Yearsley means the distance from the city to her home in Clifton (though this is not particularly plausible given that Clifton was only a couple of miles away), or perhaps it is a reference to her recent absences in London (for which there is some documentary evidence)[41] – but this does not preclude Yearsley bringing together poet and place through imagination. Indeed, this poem represents a compelling argument for the power of the imagination in effecting change, especially when that imagination is bound together, as it is here, with notions of place.

Yearsley's confidence in representing the combination of her own claims to belong to Bristol with her ability to imagine a partnership with the city perhaps has its origins in a slightly earlier poem, from her second volume (published 1787). 'To the Bristol Marine Society' is addressed to a prominent

charitable body dedicated to clearing Bristol's quays of vagrant boys, supplying each with the materials necessary for a life at sea, and securing them
employment in the navy. As such its topic is of a smaller nature, not having
the national, or indeed global, significance of *A Poem on the Inhumanity of the
Slave Trade*, but there is a clear similarity in the positions of the two speakers.
In this earlier poem, Yearsley writes:

> But you! who mourn the majesty of man,
> Too early marr'd in the fair shameless youth;
> You, who have sigh'd, when in the list of sin,
> A blooming champion in her cause he stood,
> Till vengeance met him in her full career,
> And hurl'd him blotted to a timeless grace;
> To you I bend, to you I strike the lyre,
> Rustic and inharmonious[42]

As in *A Poem on the Inhumanity of the Slave Trade*, the poetic speaker here is
entreating a representation of Bristol, though with the description of
'bending' perhaps there is here a hint of supplication, too. However, as with
the later poem, the city provides the opportunity for the poet to exercise her
talents, in a way that is mutually beneficial: the poet is authorised to speak for
the city or its institutions, and the city is celebrated and commemorated.

Indeed, the poem celebrates not only social but also legal structures which
have facilitated the philanthropic efforts in relation to the fate of the vagrant
quayside boys, each of whom has been encouraged to 'fix/ His eye on attrib-
utes which strike his soul/ With deep amazement!'[43]

> Happy ye!
> Who gently shed on poor neglected youth
> The joys of social love; but chiefly thou,
> O Burke, whose sensibility is pain,
> Melting with keenest agony, accept
> The praises of this long-forgotten race.
> BRISTOL shall hail thy name, and sacred hold
> Thy records from oblivion's deep abyss,
> With Glory, nurs'd within her merchants arms,
> Shall blaze refulgent on a wond'ring world.[44]

'Burke' is Richard Burke, who held a judicial position as Recorder of Bristol which had both civic and legal powers, combining in one person two aspects of Bristol's local government. This would have made Burke a key figure in the prosecution of the Marine Society's philanthropic mission, as Yearsley's poem confirms. Interesting here, though, is the way in which the poetic voice is in this closing passage aligned with Bristol; the poem itself becomes a means for 'BRISTOL' to 'hail' Burke's name. The poem's speaker and the desires of the civic powers are as one here, in a way that perhaps echoes the way in which the speaker of 'Clifton Hill' united her voice with the inner lives of the sheep and smaller creatures of the down. The consequences in 'To the Bristol Marine Society' are further-reaching, though, as the poet's voice becomes imbued with civic authority.

The ability to unite the poetic voice with representations or personifications of Bristol's civic power is demonstrated in both 'To the Bristol Marine Society' and *A Poem on the Inhumanity of the Slave Trade*, but later, in Yearsley's 1796 poem 'Bristol Elegy', which was written in response to the 1793 Bristol Bridge Riots and published in *The Rural Lyre*, the relationship between poet and place has changed completely. Instead of unity between poetic voice and place being used to the public benefit of each party, Yearsley ironizes her former role as Bristol's voice, and satirises her former connection with the city. She does this, however, without sacrificing her ability to speak *for* the city, though the poet's relationship with place is very different to that seen in 'Clifton Hill' or indeed in *A Poem on the Inhumanity of the Slave Trade*.

The Bristol Bridge riots, which erupted after the reimposition of tolls on Bristol Bridge, led to the deaths of twenty people and injuries to many more after soldiers were ordered to fire on the rioters. The official version of events, published in *Felix Farley's Bristol Journal* the Saturday after the riots, was full of reports and proclamations issued by members of the Bristol Corporation. The reports claimed that the mob had been 'exhorted and implored to consider the consequences' of their actions by the civic leaders, but that they had refused,[45] and the proclamations urged the public to assist in the identification of the offenders who remained at large. The deaths of Bristol citizens were regretted, and many of those who died were allowed to have probably 'been innocent without any evil intention themselves', but it was represented that they were 'certainly indiscreet and blameable in adding to the multitude by their individual presence, after having been forewarned … that the military would be desired to fire if the Rioters did not disperse.'[46] First-hand accounts emerged shortly after, though, of innocent bystanders, including women and those trying to retrieve the dead, being killed or crippled by the deliberate low firing of the militia.[47] Yearsley's poem rejects the official version of events, and instead represents the riots as a violent clash between a repressive ruling body and a vulnerable and innocent people.

But before the reader gets to the poem, they must first read a curious 'ADVERTISEMENT', supposedly written on the day of the riots, 30 September 1793, though the phrasing indicates that it may, in fact, have been written some time afterwards:

> BRISTOL, 30TH SEPTEMBER 1793.
>
> THE Author disclaims the presumption of judging rich men or wise men: Wealth must be adored in a becoming manner: Wisdom is so beloved – hem – Wisdom ought to be so beloved in Bristol, and every where else, that the man or the woman who possesses it, is as a consecrated vessel suffered to lie by for sacred purposes. Full of these gentle considerations necessary to well-doing, the Author only begs leave to say –
>
> … Time has softened the frowning jealousy of power on one part, and the sense of misfortune on the part of those who lost their children, their friends, and fathers; but as the city of Bristol is the scene for the pathetic poet, and as every poet who has hitherto sung in her shade has been rewarded, the Author expects her civic wreath.[48]

As with the majority of Yearsley's previous productions, the Advertisement to 'Bristol Elegy' makes Yearsley's 'place' explicit: we are supposed to believe that this has been written on the spot, both temporally and physically. This, as in former cases, authorises the poet to speak – she is in the right place, and *from* the right place, at the right time, to be able to comment upon recent events. However, there is no alliance here between Bristol (either personified, or as represented by its institutions) and the poet. Yearsley instead offers a critique of the city which is heavily ironized by the cynical authorial *persona* who seems to choke on the idea that 'Wisdom is so beloved' in Bristol. And, in contrast to the earlier imaginary yoking of civic energy with poetic talent which was supposed to yield so much, Bristol's civic structures here have utterly failed to recognise the opportunities presented to them to secure the city's fame: the only reward Bristol knows to mete out to poets who have 'sung in her shade' is the kind of 'civic wreath' bestowed upon Thomas Chatterton, who 'was abandoned to poverty and death by his fellow citizens.'[49] As Mary Waldron observes, 'This is the "civic wreath" [Yearsley] appears to expect' for herself.[50]

It is therefore of interest that Yearsley's technique in this poem resembles that of 'Clifton Hill'. Instead of aligning herself with civic bodies, as in 'To the Bristol Marine Society' or *A Poem on the Inhumanity of the Slave Trade*, the poetic speaker moves in and out of different individuals caught up in the riots, in a similar way to how the poetic speaker of 'Clifton Hill' moved between animal or plant minds. In that poem the technique functioned to facilitate the representation of an alternative, more democratic sense of place, an aspect of the poem which resonates here:

> HARK! whence those groans of dying men?
>   Am I the slave of visionary, lingering fear?
> How dolefully this night the clock strikes ten!
>   Leaving a mournful silence on the ear.
>
> Behold! there struggles with departing breath
>   The father of a helpless race! – Ah! why
> Did you so rashly point the winged death,
>   And fill with early woe his infant's eye?
>
> See the fair babe bends from its mother's arms
>   To snatch the parting kiss! Turn, beauteous boy;
> Thy fondness through his veins gives new alarms –
>   Yet, ere his lips grow cold, oh taste the sacred joy!
>
> 'Tis done! No more thy little face shall hide
>   In his warm bosom, nor in cheerful mood
> Play with his hair, and smile to hear him chide –
>   He's gone! he leaves thee to a world too rude.[51]

These opening stanzas set up the speaker as an unfixed intelligence which alights in the minds of those who died in the riots in the moments immediately before their deaths. As in 'Clifton Hill', the use of empathy is extremely powerful, and in this poem brings each death into the present, to be relived not only by the speaker, but also the reader, who is forced to accompany the speaker on their migration through the minds of the dead.

There are parallels with the way in which the speaker led the reader around Clifton Hill in the earlier poem, though the type of journey undertaken here is rather different. The effects, however, might be considered to be similar: just as Yearsley's representation of different 'prospects' in 'Clifton Hill' challenged the conventions of the genre, and assumptions of her as a poet, so too in 'Bristol Elegy', with Yearsley's version of events challenging official accounts. Her title, too, perhaps serves to enhance this challenge. Whilst an elegy is 'a song of lamentation, *esp.* a funeral song or lament for the dead'[52] – a meaning which unproblematically applies to Yearsley's poem – it is not at all clear from the title what exactly Yearsley is lamenting. At various times in her earlier poetry, 'Bristol' has stood for the civic structures of the city, for the city personified, and for the inhabitants of that city. No guidance is given to the reader here, though, as to how they should read the 'Bristol' of 'Bristol Elegy'. It is possible, then, that all these earlier meanings are pertinent simultaneously, and that we can read the title as the speaker's lamentation for the loss of the city of her imagination; a city interested in justice and fairness, a city a poet might proudly exclaim has 'to high perfection wrought/ This mighty work', for '*such is Bristol's soul.*'[53]

Conclusion

Ideas of place, in terms of physical space, geography and topography, of the real and imaginary relationships fostered by place, and in terms of social status, are all of concern to Ann Yearsley at various points during her career. By sampling how Yearsley engages with place in four poems produced under varying circumstances and appearing in several publications, it has been possible to see both similarities and discontinuities in her subject positions and literary techniques. Whilst the alignment of poet and place was a common feature of the ways in which labouring-class poets were presented to the public, Yearsley's poetry demonstrates the ways in which place could be reimagined as a liberating space, not only for the labouring-class poet supposedly tied to the one locale, but for other inhabitants of that space, humans and non-humans, flora and fauna. The poems examined here also indicate some of the wider-ranging, and longer-lasting, consequences of a poet aligning themselves with particular notions of place. In *A Poem on the Inhumanity of the Slave Trade* poet and place combine to produce something neither would have been capable of alone: the strength of Yearsley's imagination is coupled with Bristol's bustling, mercantile energy so that both place and poet are empowered to make a statement to the whole nation about the evils of the slave trade. Yet the dangers of forging such connections are also apparent in Yearsley's later poetry, where the bitterness at Bristol's apparent failure to adequately recognise its poetic wealth (from Chatterton onwards), in contrast to its frequently-celebrated material wealth, is uncompromisingly, and ironically, articulated. From her life and poetry, there is clearly much more to Ann Yearsley than the simple adage of 'The Bristol Milkwoman'.

John Gregory, St Mary Redcliffe and the Memorialising of Thomas Chatterton

John Goodridge

The literary memorialising of Thomas Chatterton began modestly enough some two months after his death on 25 August 1770, when his Colston school friend Thomas Cary, described as 'Chatterton's second self', published an 'artless and affecting' poem, 'Elegy to the Memory of Mr. Thomas Chatterton, Late of Bristol', in the *Town and Country Magazine* for October.[1] A month later there followed 'An Elegy, to the Memory of a Young Man lately deceased' by another friend, James Thistlethwaite, printed in the *Gentleman's Museum and Grand Imperial Magazine* for November, and the process has continued more or less ever since.[2] 'Perhaps no other poet', as David Fairer puts it, 'offers such a contrast between a brief and obscure life and a vast and powerful posthumous existence'.[3] The key early stages in this posthumous existence, Chatterton's role in late eighteenth-century culture and the birth of Romanticism, have been richly analysed by Nick Groom, Maria Grazia Lolla, David Fairer and most recently Daniel Cook.[4] The present chapter looks at the response to Chatterton of a slightly later figure from the period after the deaths of the great Romantic poets. John Gregory (1831-1922) was a shoemaker and a poet, a socialist, an activist in many good causes and a leading figure in the foundation and development of an independent working-class movement in Bristol. He twice wrote verses on Chatterton, first through a sequence of four 'Sonnets on Chatterton's Church, Bristol', written in the 1870s, and then in a 42-line poem, 'Concerning Chatterton', printed like many of his poems in a local paper, the *Bristol Observer*, on 25 January 1908. The sonnet sequence richly celebrates the church that had inspired the Rowley poems, before passionately demanding that its doors be thrown open to re-admit their true author, whose belated and inadequate statue stood forlornly on unconsecrated ground to the north. The second poem, three decades further on in Gregory's long life, forms a sequel to the first, and actually brings the statue to life so that 'poor Tom Chatterton' can make his own 'wail' for forgiveness and fair treatment from his erstwhile community.

For in Bristol itself, Chatterton's after-life had been, and would continue to be, characterised by uncertainty, with unpredictably varying moods of pride and rejection. For the vociferous and verbose 'Rowleyan' sect the boy was a mere scribe to the medieval poet Thomas Rowley, a figure who could provide glorious cultural ancestry and perhaps some much-needed 'tone' to their mercantile city. Sadly Rowley didn't exist, and once the 'Rowley Controversy' that had burned so fiercely in 1782 had more or less died down Cary and Thistlethwaite's theme could be taken up again. The harbingers of the Romantic revolution began to canonise Chatterton as the archetype and icon of neglected genius, radicalism and the twin cults of ancient mist and youthful promise, 'hoar antiquity' and 'very heaven'.[5] But he still posed a threefold problem (at least) for Bristol, in his open contempt for the city, his literary 'forgery', and his 'suicide'. (My 'scare-quotes' reflect the contested status of both the latter terms.[6] His dislike of Bristol is less controversial.) There was civic anxiety about Chatterton, uncertainty as to how best to remember the poet, if at all. So whilst the 'Romantic' Bristol of Ann Yearsley, Joseph Cottle, Samuel Coleridge and Robert Southey wrote tributary poems, raised money for the poet's surviving sister, produced new editions of his poetry and campaigned for the raising of a memorial, the Bristol establishment and most especially the church authorities of St Mary Redcliffe were having none of it. This is the primary context for Gregory's poems, which focus on the contrast between the splendour of the church that represents 'Rowley's' world and Chatterton's aspirations, and the rather sorry memorial statue that represents Chatterton's uncertain local afterlife.

Pilgrim in the Valley

The sonnet sequence was first collected in John Gregory's second volume, *Song Streams*, published in 1877. Like Coleridge he was a Devonian incomer to Bristol, originally from Bideford where he had served his apprenticeship as a shoemaker, reading aloud from the Chartist newspaper *Northern Star* to his fellow workers, just as the poet Robert Bloomfield had once read newspapers aloud to his workmates as a junior shoemaker in London. After tramping in South Wales and the West Country for some years, Gregory settled in 1860 in Bristol, where he had lived twice before and had married Ann Arman, a Cardiff girl, four years earlier. During his long Bristol years he would be a key figure in establishing the co-operative movement, a pioneer of the local trade union movement, several times President of the Trades Council; a founder, in 1885, of the Labour League, and a leader of the new Bristol

Socialist Society. Gregory would be at the head of the great wave of strikes and protest marches of 1889, during which indeed some of his own songs and verses were sung. Passionately opposed to war and to capital punishment, he was deeply involved in the social and cultural as well as the political activities of the early working-class movement, admired as a reciter and singer as well as a political organiser and speaker. His work as a shoemaker was not always a reliable source of income, and he was often in severe poverty, but supplying shoes to boys at Clifton College led him to the friendship and patronage of the Headmaster, Revd J. M. Wilson, who made him the college's official boot-repairer, giving some regularity to his day-work. The work of writing poetry was lifelong, and he first published in the *North Devon Journal* in his youth. He was forty, however, before his first full volume, *Idylls of Labour* (1871), was published in Bristol and London, earning him modest success.[7]

A copy of this collection in the Local Studies Collection at Bristol Public Library (B18858) has on an added leaf among its preliminaries a printed commendation by St Agnes Workman's Club of Newfoundland Road, Bristol, dated October 1883. It expresses the club's anxiety to 'bring this Volume of Poems, by one of their Members, more prominently before their Fellow Working Men and the general Public'. It would be a pleasure to their members, they point out, 'to find their own thoughts expressed by one of themselves', whilst the public, 'it is hoped', will find it 'of service' to learn 'what are the thoughts of a genuine Working Man, and of many of his class'. Clearly Gregory's peers see him as their representative and equal, not just in his political work or social activities, but in his poetry too, and this sense of a supportive and actively engaged community is a key element in the poetry, which has a very sociable character. Moreover its publication made it highly accessible to his peers, since he habitually reprinted poems that had been in local newspapers as affordable single sheets that could be hawked or distributed, in the same way that his contemporary the weaver-poet Samuel Laycock so successfully published verses in Manchester during the cotton famine of the early 1860s.[8]

This, of course, is all in the starkest contrast to the predominant biographical image of Thomas Chatterton (1752-1770), as a misunderstood, isolated and socially rejected loner, writing fake medieval materials under an assumed name for a few dubious local antiquarians. An 1806 biography echoes Chatterton's loneliness and obscurity in ghostly sibilants: 'The silence, the solitude of Chatterton, his eccentric habits and singularities of behaviour, were not attributed to the right cause. [...] Silent and unsuspected he was now soliciting the Muse in secret.'[9] One of the principal purposes of Gregory's

1 John Gregory (1831-1922).
Frontispiece to *Murmurs and Melodies*
(Bristol: J.W. Arrowsmith, 1884).

poems, perhaps the most important, would be symbolically and posthumously to 'socialise' this solitary and eccentric boy, within the church and to 'the chime / Of holy bells; and melodies entrancing' (ll. 33-4). That this was one of Chatterton's own favourite and enchanted environments is clear from the testimony of his friend William Smith:

> There was one spot in particular,' says Mr. Smith, "full in view of the church, where he seemed to take particular delight. *He would frequently lay himself down, fix his eyes upon the church, and seem as if he was in a kind of trance. Then on a sudden, and abruptly, he would tell me, that steeple was burnt down by lightning; that was the place where they formerly acted plays.*"[10]

As this reveals, Chatterton himself had 'read' St Mary Redcliffe church as a social space, but only in the distant past and only in his imagination. Gregory wanted to take the poet inside the church, where everyone could celebrate his extraordinary vision.

The first sonnet begins with the flourish of a challenging rhetorical question:

> What hast thou seen, O pilgrim! in the valley?
>   What hast thou found from this great world of ours,
> Rising more glorious or majestically
>   Tha[n] this tall temple, made of sculptor flowers,
> By Art triumphant, and her high born ally,
>   Seraphic Genius? (ll. 1-6)[11]

Imagining a pilgrim for his addressee is a significant way to begin. The sequence is written in praise of the church and its patron saint, St Mary, before turning its attention more explicitly to Thomas Chatterton. Pilgrimages in western Europe usually focused either on the shrine of a major saint like St Mary (for example, the pilgrimage to Our Lady of Walsingham), or a martyred one like Thomas Becket (the Canterbury pilgrimage). If Gregory sees Chatterton as a martyr, as I think he does, then the church would seem to offer both kinds of destination for the seeking pilgrim: Mary the 'great Queen of Hope' (l. 9), and Chatterton the secular martyr who 'sang for bread, /And, starving, died' (ll. 48-9).[12]

But Chatterton is not the only figure to have begged for bread, and 'pilgrim' is a word that has special resonance in Chatterton's poetry, as Gregory would have known. The widely admired final poem in Chatterton's Rowley cycle, 'An Excelente Balade of Charitie', is the story of a 'hapless pilgrim' (l.17) who begs for alms and seeks kindness and shelter in a rainstorm, finding it, Good Samaritan style, where it was least expected.[13] John Gregory seeks a spirit of kindness towards Chatterton's memory in his poem, so addressing a 'pilgrim' in the first line is a double reminder, of the pilgrim in Chatterton's poem, who finds charity not in the grandly apparelled Abbot who spurs his horse past the sodden figure but in the humble 'Limitoure' or mendicant walking friar who comes to his rescue; and of Chatterton himself, the begging pilgrim who wrote the story. The whole of Gregory's sonnet sequence, in fact, is an intertextually alert homage to Chatterton, and follows a pattern of admiration for the church that Chatterton himself had established in his Rowleyan poetry and prose.[14]

Gregory's term 'valley' has a similar richness and range of reference. The church, as the historian of its architecture notes, 'rises from the rocky cliff' after which the parish of Redcliffe is named.[15] To approach it from the Bristol side is to rise, if not quite literally out of a valley, then certainly from the lower-lying ground to the church's north-west, the area of the old Quaker graveyard and the main route to the city and its nearby quayside. Redcliffe and its church 'rise' distinctively, and in implicit rivalry to Bristol and its less impressive cathedral. (And Chatterton, Nick Groom insists, was a 'Redcliffe man' rather than a Bristolian as generally supposed.[16]) This sense of a local pride associated with the height of the area, its 'cliff' and its rising church, is also prominent in the opening lines of Gregory's later poem, 'Concerning Chatterton', as the poet locates himself in its opening lines:

> Where beautiful Saint Mary stands
>   On the Redcliff – a glorious pile,
> And with much majesty commands
>   All who behold (ll. 1-4)[17]

A pilgrim who has emerged from having been 'in the valley' also suggests the struggles of Bunyan's *Pilgrim's Progress*, as well as the common metaphor for the world as a 'vale of tears'. This latter term is in fact explicitly used later in the sonnet sequence, extended to 'this vale of tears and crime' (l. 35), used to describe the flawed sublunary world that Gregory wishes the church's sublime music to 'float above'.[18]

Heaven's Window

The 'temple' that rises so majestically from the 'valley' of the world is charac-terised as a joint endeavour, a product of human art inspired by the supernatural 'Seraphic Genius'. Yet it also transcends the human altogether. It is 'not like a temple made by men' (l. 15):

> A man within its compass barely seems
> More than a miner mole that makes its den
> In a tall mountain's foot (ll. 16-18)

Chatterton had seen it in a similar light: as both a thing of surpassingly beauti-ful art and artifice, 'counynge hendie worke' so fine that it 'well nighe dazeled mine Eyne', and as somehow being beyond the human altogether:

> Full well I wote so fine a Scite,
> Was ne yreer'd of mortall Wight[19]

Thus Gregory's humble pilgrim-addressee, be they an innocent visitor, or an avatar of Chatterton or his imagination, is invited as they rise from the 'valley' to be overwhelmed by the church's interior, every element and sightline of which seems designed to emphasise a dizzying and overawing height. Gregory's effusive description of it over the second and third of the four sonnets emphasises this size and grandeur, and the sublime effect of its overawing power. It is a 'tall temple', a 'palace vast' (l. 6).[20] As a poet colleague of mine recently remarked in conversation, it is the most perpendicular of perpendicular Gothic churches.[21] Its shaping is designed to lift one's eyes ever upwards, but entering it is also like suddenly being in a mighty forest:

> When that the door
> Doth shut you in another world you tread,
> Where arborescent monsters from the floor,
> Shoot to the ribbed roof, whereon they spread
> Their ravelled branches till that roof appears
> The haunt of spirits watching o'er the dead (ll. 21-6)

Gregory's 'arborescent monsters' are well described. Simon Schama has illustrated some of the ways in which the Gothic cathedrals are designed to imitate the sublime effects of trees and forests, and St Mary Redcliffe is notable for the way its 'trees' of finely shaped stone pillars – the effect is partly because of their narrowness – rise so dramatically, the full height of the church, up to the magnificent 'ribbed roof' that completes the sense of being enclosed within a mighty forest by forming a full canopy of vaulting (*figure 2*). As Michael Quinton Smith notes: 'What makes St Mary Redcliffe so exceptional, and indeed beyond compare, is that it is vaulted throughout.'[22] He adds that the 'vault patterns vary greatly'; this is reflected in Gregory's images of 'ravelled branches'. The extraordinary and intricately decorated roof bosses that lock the immense upper structure of the church in place are his 'sculptor flowers'.

The pilgrim who enters the interior of the church walks into 'another world' (l. 22), shut off from the busy and irreverent outside world, as it had once been for Chatterton who liked to sit reading by the tomb of his admired patron-figure, the Bristol merchant William Canynges, putting himself, as it were, doubly in another world.[23] And while Gregory wishes firstly to overwhelm his pilgrim/reader with the sense of a monstrous forest-space unlike anything they can have seen before, he has other agendas. Although this is, as he says, a 'hall of Death' (l. 21), it is also a hall of light, dedicated to St Mary and the principle of love she represents:

> 'Tis a palace vast,
> On which I gaze with beauty-loving eyes,
> Because I know 'twas raised in ages past,
> For the great Queen of Hope's pure Paradise,
> Soul-saving Love. (ll. 6-10)

The speaker feasts on both the 'beauty' of the church and the sense of an ideal from 'ages past' that can still be shared, seeing in these linked ideas the triumph of art and aspiration. The representation in art of an ideal, created and sustained down the centuries by a medium of 'massy might' (l. 14) is what he means by 'Art triumphant' (l. 5). In addition to its overwhelming and sublime sense of height, its key features are light and sound.

The imagery of light begins in the 'swift-winged angel light' that 'leaps from Heaven's window' (ll. 10, 11), illuminating the exterior grandeur of the church. The image prepares the way for the description of the stained-glass windows in the second sonnet, where:

> The grandest dreams
> Of painter-poets flash from shining sheets
> Of saint emblazoned crystal. (ll. 18-20)

Of another Perpendicular Gothic edifice, King's College Chapel, Cambridge, it has been written that the 'slender columns and ribs' allow its correspondingly enlarged windows to offer 'an extraordinary and hitherto unimagined sense of space and light' to its interior.[24] Light enters St Mary Redcliffe through the stained-glass windows, which by the 1870s combined medieval and Victorian craftsmanship. Gregory's 'shining sheets / Of saint emblazoned crystal' may specifically refer to the 'universally admired' new east window, which is indeed 'saint emblazoned'.[25] It is also possible to see a Chatterton connection in Gregory's emphasis on windows in that, as Michael Liversedge has noted, windows 'feature prominently in the iconography of Thomas Chatterton's life and death as it was imagined by Victorian painters.'[26] Most famously, the Henry Wallis painting has the dead Chatterton lying on his attic bed beneath a window in which the London skyline with St Paul's

2 View of the South Transept, St Mary Redcliffe – 'A man within its compass barely seems / More than a miner mole'. From John Britton, *An Historical and Architectural Essay Relating to Redcliffe Church, Bristol* (London: Longman, Hurst, Rees, Orme and Brown, 1813), Plate IX

Cathedral is prominent. Gregory's phrasing emphasises both the inspiration of the 'painter poets' who crafted the saint-filled windows, and the illumination whereby their inspired images 'flash' from the 'shining sheets'. Gregory was a Christian as well as a socialist, and this idea of illumination from heaven coming quite literally through religious imagery would be strongly associated with the ideal of working-class political and cultural enlightenment.

In Gregory's third collection, *Murmurs and Melodies* (1884) there is a poem that more fully deploys the image I have quoted above, of the 'miner mole' to which a human figure is reduced within the church. Gregory berates his fellows for brawling over religion and literalising the word made flesh, and offers them a fable in which three moles in their 'quaint cavern built under the sod' (l. 13) agree that God must be a 'marvellous mole' (l. 24). Like the isolated infant of Plato's imagined cave, they can only conceptualise what they see, but Gregory urges them to look up:

> Now, why did these three miner moles of my song
> In one coincidence agree,
> That God was like them? If we know they were wrong,
> It is only because we can see.
>
> See what, and how far? Are you clear, brother worm,
> Any more than a mole, in your sight?
> When you dream of God in humanity's form,
> You ought to be crying for light. (ll. 25-32)[27]

To cry for light, to look up from one's mole-run, is Gregory's suggestion for the way the workers, the 'miner moles' can transcend and aspire to something beyond the poverty and exclusion of their earthly prison. So it is appropriate that what he calls 'Chatterton's Church' should offer the illumination of art and light, to which the earlier poet also aspired.

The topic of illumination, casting light, may often have a special significance for autodidactic poets like Gregory. At a practical level, light to read was a precious commodity. One thinks of the coal miner-poet Joseph Skipsey as a young trapper-boy, reading his Milton by the light of begged candle-stubs while he waited for the next coal wagon to come rumbling out of the Stygian darkness.[28] Gregory apparently 'used to think of miners underground, and factory girls', regretting that they lacked light,[29] and he begins his Preface to *Song Streams* with an unforgettable image:

Courteous Reader, by the dim glow of a few bottled glowworms I once saw a countryman reading the Bible. This anecdote I pen that you may comprehend the extreme difficulty a toil drudge has to overcome ere he accomplishes the feat of launching into the flood of literature such a volume as this. (p.[v])

Beyond the simple need for light to read, John Gregory was fascinated and inspired by light, which he habitually associated with looking up to the 'scenery above', the sky and the stars, the sun and the moon. As George Hare Leonard records in his memoir of Gregory:

It was his prayer that everyone should have eyes to see, and a chance to behold the 'perfection' he saw. 'Isn't it beautiful?' he would ask, and he was sorry that men were 'so busy with something else' that they had no time to look up at the sky. Even the common lamp in the room at night was for him a revelation of 'the glory' with its pillar of fire and its dazzling rays.[30]

Holy Bells

The third sonnet turns from light to sound as a source of inspiration:

As a full moon, in the blue heavens dancing
Among the stars with harmony sublime,
Soars from her silver couch with smiles enchancing,
Shall this fair fabric from the grasp of time
Rise with replenished splendour to the chime
Of holy bells; and melodies entrancing,
Shall float above this vale of tears and crime (ll. 29-35)

Bristol has a notably strong bell-ringing tradition and gives its name to ringing methods such as 'Bristol Surprise'. St Mary Redcliffe had a ring of four bells in 1636, eight by 1689, but as Smith observes: 'One of the most significant, and still most famous, achievements of the Victorians [i.e. Victorian restorers of the church] was the installation of the noble full ring of twelve bells'.[31] Their pealing, for Gregory, is not so much a call to prayer or to mark a special occasion, as the appropriate accompaniment to the church's ability to escape the very 'grasp of time' and 'float above' the earthly mire, like some kind of Gothic spaceship. Not only the music of its bells, but the church itself can rise like the moon above the earth.

Music more generally was vital to Gregory and to the social and political institutions he was involved in. He made songs as well as poems; he sang and played the zither, and one of his poems is entitled simply 'Sing!'[32] As for bell-ringing, Gregory's attitude is clear in one of his newspaper pieces, evidently an essay on bells, which opens with great gusto, puns (which Gregory loved to make) and exclamation:

> Who does not love the bells? and what sweet-tempered minstrels they are! The harder we beat them the louder they laugh, and a bell will not sing until it is hung. Strike it, then, and what is the result? Ten thousand drops of silver fall from its exhaustless store. Who does not love the bells?[33]

In a poem of punning transformations of the tools of his day-work, he re-imagines the ringing of the cobbling hammer, as 'Saint Crispin's Bell':

> A merry man, of Crispin's clan,
>   Sat in his attic high,
> His sole lay in his old shop pan,
> And his last end hung nigh;
> Then as he sat on iron flat,
>   His thumping hammer fell,
> And while it rang he gaily sang—
>   I ring Saint Crispin's bell, ah! ah!
>   I ring Saint Crispin's bell.[34]

Even the dissonant noise of a working environment can aspire to the music of 'holy bells'. Nor was the desire for the beauty of music, ringing bells and 'melodies entrancing' just a personal pleasure: it played a vital role in the early Bristol socialist movement, as Sally Mullen records, drawing on earlier accounts: 'For the Bristol Socialists, "socialism was a movement inspired by art as well as economics". Records of the Society illustrate that recitations, music and poetry – particularly that of John Gregory – made the meetings "whole".' Furthermore the movement 'had its own workman composer, J. Percival Jones, who composed and adapted old melodies and tunes to fit socialist songs', whilst other members 'wrote their own songs and Rose Sharland, E.J. Watson and John Gregory each had songs printed'.[35] Gregory is self-evidently central in this activity, contributing music that was felt to be a vital affirmation of communitarian 'wholeness', and that would have been part of a regular round of indoor and outdoor meetings and social activities, and events ranging from socialist Sunday schools for children in the Haymarket to political meetings out on Durdham Downs.[36]

Again one is returned to the poignant contrast between the highly socialised creation and circulation of music, poetry and ideas in Gregory's world, and Thomas Chatterton's lone creativity and longing for the imagined sociability of his *alter ego*, Thomas Rowley and his monkish community, with its plays and rituals and shared love of art and poetry. But there is also an important positive comparison to be made here, in that Chatterton's activities have in common with Gregory's a faith in the transformative power of art. Indeed where Gregory most specifically harks back to Chatterton is in his belief that a medieval ideal can continue to give sustenance. For both poets this ideal is embodied in St Mary Redcliffe. In Gregory's sonnet sequence, the ideal is evident in the fabric and decorative arts in the building, inspired as they were by Mariolatry, as a specific, artistically inspiring manifestation of the universal principle of love.[37] Like his contemporary William Morris, and like other writers and thinkers of the time, most especially John Ruskin but perhaps also the strongly Chatterton-influenced Dante Gabriel Rossetti, Gregory's love of medieval craftsmanship was not simply antiquarian or nostalgic. What was of interest was as much a radical political ideal linked to a political goal of the recovery of craft traditions and practices which the modern capitalist economy, with its alienating factories and its division of labour, had erased. This, as much as Gregory's pacifist and Christian ideals, is the underlying message of his 'Soul-saving Love' (l.10). William Morris visited Bristol and was engaged in the same political activities as Gregory – including radical songwriting. The two men probably knew each other.[38]

For Chatterton the church is a repository of stored medieval culture. It is where the manuscripts were stored that his father found, which have been aptly described as his 'only patrimony'[39] and formed a material base for the Rowley *oeuvre*. It is also a repository and memorial for the dead. As Gregory writes, 'Beauty greets / You in this hall of Death' (ll. 20-21); while the patterns of vaulting spread out 'till that roof appears':

> The haunt of spirits watching o'er the dead
> That slumber in a sepulchre of years,
> Wherein we muse by its famed founder's bed. (ll. 25-8)

The 'famed founder' is not of course the only person memorialised in the church, but as Smith points out, William Canynges' monument (a double memorial, for there are two effigies of Canynges) is 'in the prime position in the south transept at the foot of the great south window, partly blocking it' (p. 95). As we have seen, Chatterton liked to haunt this space with his book, and an idealised image of Canynges accordingly provided his Rowley world with a patron/father figure.

Gregory notes the memorial function in the church, and the peaceful 'slumber' of the 'famed founder's bed', watched over by the church's (presumably benevolent) spirits, quite early in the sequence. In doing so he is preparing the way for the final sonnet, which dramatically shows the contrastingly impoverished Chatterton memorial: it is outside not in, unquietly standing rather than peacefully slumbering, unguarded rather than watched over, open to the sky and the elements (which would in fact slowly crumble the statue). His final peroration follows on from the prophetic sequence that began with the 'holy bells' raising the church above the 'vale of tears and crime' and towards heaven:

> Up unto God like the glad gushing rhyme
> Of bards who see the golden age advancing,
> When Sharon's Rose shall bloom in every clime
> Beneath the blessing sun (ll. 36-9)

Gregory widens the image of the desert blooming with flowers (from Isaiah, 35:1) to 'every clime' in order to offer, if only in simile, a utopian vision. The final sonnet, though, slides from prediction to instruction:

> In these dear days this earth shall not be damned
> By a dire dearth of love. Love shall with joy
> Open her palace doors that now be slammed,
> Defying entrance to the 'marv'lous boy'.
> He in the cold outside stands carved in stone
> Like some unshriven soul. He sang for bread,
> And, starving, died. We to his ghost instead
> Bequeath the granite that shall not atone
> For our forefathers' shame. What deed were worse
> Than this exclusion from his dearest fane[.]
> These are the days when juries round a corse

3 'Socialist Sunday School, Haymarket' Undated postcard. John Wall Papers (BRO 37886/1/5). *Bristol Record Office*

> Of him that dares seek Death say 'twas insane.
> What then of Chatterton? Forgive his sin,
> Open the temple doors, and let him in. (ll. 43-56)

The prediction that 'Love shall [...] Open her palace doors' is echoed in the instruction to 'Open the temple doors'. A number of familiar topics in the posthumous life of Chatterton are touched on here. The phrase 'marv'lous boy', most famously used by Wordsworth in 'Resolution and Independence' (1807), throws emphasis on the youthful and prodigious qualities of Chatterton's achievement. The idea of Chatterton dying in want (specifically want of a loaf of bread, with its symbolic overtones) comes from early testimony, but has been seriously questioned by recent scholarship.[40] But rather than merely dismissing this as a cliché of Chatterton mythology, it might be more productive to note that Gregory begins to write with greater acuteness at just this point, using the simile of an unshriven soul, and throwing emphasis on shame and guilt, and the need to atone. It may be significant that he and his family had themselves experienced serious poverty and hunger for bread in the past. He wrote about this tenderly in another, explicitly autobiographical poem, which also gives some idea of how hard-won is his optimistic talk, in the sonnet sequence, of the victory of love:

> Brave in those days,
> My wedded mate, the mother of my flock,
> Her sharp privations bore. A famished babe
> Clung to her milkless bosom, and about
> Her feeble form the elder children cried,
> 'Oh mother, give us bread!'[41]

To sing for bread, as Chatterton is said to have done, is both to beg and to busk one's poems, and there is a strong sense of humiliation in failing on both counts – or perhaps one should say, of being failed, since Gregory's clear message is that Chatterton's death remains 'our forefathers' shame', and that the posthumous gift of a statue will 'not atone' for this.

Mercy

The question of suicide and sanity is also a familiar one. Gregory appears to be making the general and comparative point that inquest juries for suicides '[t]hese [...] days' tend to bring in a verdict of insanity, rather than applying this specifically to Chatterton; but actually it is precisely relevant to Chatterton. It is important in terms of both his general reputation, and the placing of his memorial.

The story of why and how Chatterton's statue was 'excluded' from the church is pieced together by Louise J. Kaplan in her psychoanalytic reading of Chatterton the 'imposter poet', and given rich detail by Nick Groom in his study, *The Forger's Shadow* (2002).[42] A rising tradition of commemorative ceremonies for Chatterton led to the 1838 proposal for a monument to be raised in the churchyard, though notwithstanding preposterous stories to the contrary the site did not contain his bones, which were probably laid to rest in the burial ground of the Shoe Lane Workhouse in Holborn but have never since been found, nor the site identified with any precision or certainty.[43]

Objections were made, as Kaplan puts it, 'on the grounds that Thomas Rowley was the real poet and therefore to honor Thomas Chatterton would be to honor a mere transcriber' (p. 30). If he wasn't a transcriber then he was a forger; and in either case he was a suicide. These sorts of objections would not go away; indeed I heard them aired myself as late as 1980, when I first made my own pilgrimage to the church in search of the poet. In 1838 the vicar was the principal problem since, as Kaplan puts it, he 'could not tolerate the idea of a monument to an unbeliever, a liar, a forger, a depraved person who had taken his own life in defiance of church law.' (p. 31) The statue must be sited on unconsecrated ground and be inscribed with some pious lines from Young's *Night Thoughts* (1742-5) about infidels needing to respect the hereafter. Although Chatterton's body, as Groom points out, was never treated like that of a suicide (whatever the inquest might have said), anxiety about suicide haunted even his greatest admirers, and Robert Southey's claim that there was hereditary insanity in the Chatterton family appears to have been an attempt to put away the charge of suicide through a method which, as we have seen, was commonly used by inquest juries to avoid both the shame and the undignified posthumous treatment then meted out to suicides.[44]

The Chatterton monument was erected in 1840, quite close to the north-west corner of the church, but dismantled again by the vicar, the Revd Mr Whish (Groom names and shames him) six years later, to allow the restoration of the North Porch. Re-erected under a new vicar in 1857 (*figure 4*) it stood rather further away from the church in unconsecrated ground until 1967 when it was removed for the second and final time. Several reasons for this may be claimed – the changes to the topography of the area and the route of Redcliffe Way; aesthetic dislike of the crumbling statue; yet another unsympathetic vicar. This one, Canon Cartwright, was happy to quote from Chatterton's praise for his church as 'The pride of Bristowe and the western land' in a church guidebook, apparently briskly unaware of the irony in the word 'pride', usually associated with Chatterton in more negative ways.[45] The fine Gothic pediment was broken up and destroyed, the little statue itself wrapped up and left in an outhouse adjoining Chatterton's house on Redcliffe Way, where it remained, and where Nick Groom found it thirty years later, 'in a state of utter neglect', the face 'badly eroded, the eyes sunk back like sockets in an ancient skull'.[46]

The house itself, a Grade II listed building, was and remains a lonely survivor among offices and busy traffic, sticking up, as Beryl Bainbridge put it in 1984, 'like a tooth in the gum of the motorway'.[47] It was 'creatively squatted' in 2011 by a group of young people who wanted to draw attention to its neglect, and as of June 2015 appears to have been sympathetically restored by Bristol City Council, who are tendering to let it as a café: perhaps not the most apt memorial to the young poet who once lived there and was notably abstinent in taking food and drink, but better than letting it continue to crumble. The decayed statue has been spirited away, presumably by the city authorities who own the property.[48]

This sorry history has continued far beyond the lifetime of John Gregory, who died in the spring of 1922, aged 91. What had he wanted for the marvellous boy? What did Chatterton mean to him? In a lifetime rather longer than that of five Chattertons he certainly had plenty of time to think about this. The obvious answer is a memorial inside the church, like that of Canynges. But there are indications of a deeper and more metaphysical agenda, and in fact he appears to question in the sonnet sequence the value of imprisoning the poet in 'granite' at all. He presses this argument further in the later poem; indeed it dominates all but the last four lines of the 'wail from poor Tom Chatterton' (l. 10) which itself forms the bulk of 'Concerning Chatterton':

> Here in this holy temple yard,
>> Like a lost soul, forlorn and lone,
> I, Chatterton, the proud Boy Bard,
>> Stand in this monument of stone.
> A world too mean to give me bread
> Gave unto me this gift instead.
> Since a black hour when I was bit
> By hunger, and constrained to quit
> My starving body, I should say
> Four generations have, to pray,
> Passed through this temple yard; for me
> If they had prayed, I need not be
> Here as I am, out in the cold,
> An outcast from St. Mary's fold,
> An exile vile, a mere scare crow
> Set up by mother church to show
> Much lack of pity, love, and grace,
> That thrusteth me from her embrace.
> Am I within this statue pent
> For everlasting punishment?
> Must I for sin be made a guy
> To caution all that pass me by,
> Lest they should leave their bodies dead
> To men who would not give them bread? (ll. 11-34)

Poor Tom's a-cold, and imprisoned too, 'within this statue pent', like Ariel in his cloven pine. The stone that Chatterton's ghost has been forced to inhabit

4 The Thomas Chatterton Memorial
Undated postcard. John Wall Papers
(BRO 37886/7/1). *Bristol Record Office*

has made him into a 'scare crow', a 'guy', a warning for passers by – almost a hanged criminal. (In the sonnet sequence he is 'carved in stone / Like some unshriven soul', ll. 47-8.) This may perhaps reflect a familiar Protestant and Nonconformist Christian suspicion of statuary. But Chatterton's imagined 'wail' at the statue's unattractive appearance also emphasises the idea that he has merely been fobbed off with a rotten statue by those 'too mean to give him bread', or their descendants. Gregory was highly aware of the importance of symbolic gestures, such as the positioning of a statue, and would not hesitate to decry what he regarded as unchristian behaviour. One of his obituarists recalls a telling incident in this respect, one that also gives a glimpse of the toughness underlying this gentle and optimistic man, and his ready resort to Christian imagery. Gregory 'was never afraid of his convictions or of giving forcible expression to them':

> What a rumpus there was at one of the Socialist Society's public meetings
> on Durdham Downs during the Boer War, when he retorted to some

'Christian' critics that they had wrapped the body of Jesus Christ in the fold of a bloody Union Jack! As an opponent of Imperialism, too –

'Knaves on Empire-building bent
Must have blood to make cement.'[49]

In 'poor Tom Chatterton's' speech Gregory particularly emphasises the statue-spirit's sense of exclusion. Chatterton has been ostracised by the church; and trapped in the statue he is 'forlorn and lone', 'out in the cold', an 'outcast from St Mary's fold'. This last is perhaps the key term: he has been cast out from the safety of the church's 'fold', deprived of the socialised and inclusive grouping that would allow him to share Gregory's vision of love in the inspiring art and craft of the church's interior, where the church's flock abides, light flows in through 'shining sheets', and the mighty bells ring out.

When one considers the numerous ways in which Chatterton was enlisted in the second half of the nineteenth century: sentimentalised in the famous Wallis painting, historicised by David Masson, modernised by W. W. Skeat, romanticised in Rossetti's sonnet, and finally appropriated by Oscar Wilde, Gregory's approach seems a distinctive one.[50] He could be described as resisting the universalising tendency of these various sorts of responses, by restoring Chatterton to a specific locality and, importantly, reclaiming him for the principle of universal love and the radical socialist and Christian communities that, for Gregory, espoused this ideal.

The impassioned plea in both poems is not simply to move the statue to a more appropriate spot ('some proper site', as Tom Chatterton says at the end of his 'wail', l. 39); nor yet to replace it with something more dignified or attractive (as many thought it should be, for it was never widely regarded as a thing of beauty, though the pediment had its admirers). But as the last lines of the sonnet sequence dramatically insist, Gregory wants the world to 'forgive his sin, / Open the temple doors, and let him in' (ll. 55-6). Chatterton must be pardoned forthwith for any and all sins, crimes and errors of judgment he is held to have committed, and admitted to the church, perhaps literally, but certainly also in the wider sense of being properly accepted into the community from which he came.

As for Gregory's own feelings about Chatterton, no explicitly personal agenda is stated. He does not make the obvious connection, for example, with his own struggles to make his way in the world, as a poet of humble origins facing hunger and rejection and struggling to get a foothold, though we have detected a certain sharpness around the subject of Chatterton's unheeded call for bread. It may be that the simple act of memorialising the earlier poet in these verses, and arguing for his full acceptance, says enough. And interestingly enough Gregory himself was the recipient of some post-Chattertonian guilt, the tone of which suggests that the Chatterton agenda was unavoidable in the Bristol of his time. On 27 October 1908 the *Bristol Times and Mirror* reported on the well-attended opening meeting of the season of the University College Literary Society, to hear a paper by Professor G.H. Leonard, MA, on 'The Poems of John Gregory', as follows:

> The lecturer claimed that the real lover of English literature should not be so wholly occupied with the study of the English Classics that he should forget contemporary writers who claim a hearing, and who, for the full fruition of their powers, need sympathy and their meed of praise. Too often 'their ghosts are crowned to make amends.' He thought it specially right that the Literary Society of the College should remember the writers, past and present, specially connected with the city, pointing out the loss to the world of letters which resulted from the fact that Chatterton, missing the help, intelligent sympathy, and discipline which might have been given him in Bristol, was left to perish miserably in his pride. Such help, it may be hoped, the University of Bristol, when it comes, will ever be ready to extend to genius in whatever rank of life it may be found.

There is that Chattertonian 'pride' again, ascribed to him most prominently by Wordsworth and here set against the wholly theoretical 'intelligent sympathy' he 'might have' received – in a better world, perhaps; though Leonard's hope for the University's future good behaviour towards 'genius in whatever rank of life it may be found' was certainly realised to the extent of an honorary Master of Arts degree, awarded to Gregory four years later in 1912. It is nonetheless worth noting that Gregory's 'Concerning Chatterton', published in the same year Professor Leonard gave this talk, in contrast to almost every other commentator there had ever been, allowed Chatterton to feel pride in himself without authorial condemnation or an automatic link to his premature destruction. He is simply 'I, Chatterton, the proud Boy Bard' (l. 13).

Further post-Chatterton remorse, albeit mingled confusingly with local pride, would surface in a memorial article on the 'Death of Mr J. Gregory, The Shoemaker Poet, A Personal Recollection', by William C. Pocock of the 'Poets' Fellowship, Bristol' (an organisation reminiscent of the 'Juvenile Club'

5 'Open the temple doors, and let him in' – View of the North Porch, St Mary Redcliffe. From John Britton, *An Historical and Architectural Essay Relating to Redcliffe Church, Bristol,* Plate VII

Your faithful Comrade John Gregory to J W H Wall

6 John Gregory in later life. Undated postcard photograph, autographed to his friend and fellow shoemaker, poet and socialist John Wall (1855-1915) (BRO 37886/7/1). *Bristol Record Office*

made up of Bristol apprentice poets to which Cary, Thistlethwaite and Chatterton belonged in the 1760s). This was published in *The Bristol Adventurer* (described as 'a new weekly paper'), for 26 May 1922, a few weeks after Gregory's death:

> The treasure-house of English poetry has been enriched by [Gregory] to a greater extent than many of us realise, and Bristol has again bequeathed a splendid legacy unto this treasure-house. The poetry of John Gregory is by no means so widely known as it deserves to be or eventually will be. It takes Bristolians an unconscionably long time to realise they have among them a real, if minor, genius, and the lesson of Chatterton passes unrecognised and unrepented.

And Pocock concludes his tribute with a dramatic imperative exclamation, one that might serve to summarise the energetic and impassioned efforts on behalf of the spirit of Chatterton I have discussed in this chapter: 'O Bristol, be worthy of your worthiest sons!'

For Ray Gosling, 1939-2013

E.H. Young, Popular Novelist
and the Literary Geography of Bristol

Chiara Briganti and Kathy Mezei

> The geography of classical modernism is determined primarily by metro-
> politan cities and the cultural experiments and upheavals they generated:
> Baudelaire's Paris [...] Kafka's Prague, Joyce's Dublin [...] Woolf's London.[1]

> In the sloping, one-sided street called Beulah Mount, no two houses are
> alike [...] the houses, standing shoulder to shoulder [...] are united in an air
> of personal dignity, unmoved by changes of fortune, and in the proud
> possession of the finest view in Upper Radstowe. On the other side of
> the road the ground drops for a steep two hundred feet to the river. [...]
> On the right the suspension bridge spans the gulf: away on the left, masked
> by the houses built on the more gradual slope, are the docks, the low swing
> bridges, the factories close to the water's edge, the ships loading or unload-
> ing, and at night [...] mysterious sounds rise from that quarter of the city
> and are pierced, at high tide, by the mournful challenging cry of steamers
> making for the sea.[2]

Passages such as this panoramic opening to E.H. Young's novel, *Jenny Wren*,
evoking the urban geography of Bristol and Clifton, permeate the novels of
this popular interwar author in a recurring refrain. Like other writers at the
beginning of the twentieth century, as Andreas Huyssen notes in the opening
quotation above, Young draws upon the city, its streets, houses, railway
stations, cafés, monuments and shops to explore both bourgeois society and
ideology in a provincial town and the bodies and psyches of her characters.
For her readers everywhere – and she was a best-selling author in Britain and
America in the interwar years – Young created a literary geography of Bristol
and its surrounds.[3] For Young, the quaint streets and houses of her fictional
Upper Radstowe represented 'a miniature of all societies, with the same
intrigues within and the same threatenings of danger from outside'.[4]

    Through reflections gathered while wandering the streets of Paris, the
French symbolist poet, Charles Baudelaire (*Les Fleurs du mal* (1857); *Le Spleen de*

Paris (1869), and the cultural critic, Walter Benjamin (*Arcades Project* (1927-40)), famously portrayed the alienation, class distinctions, consumerism, boredom and anxieties of an industrialised metropole that would characterise much early twentieth-century writing. Reading Baudelaire's poetry, Benjamin observes how he projects the gaze of the alienated man, 'the gaze of the flâneur, whose way of life still conceals behind a mitigating nimbus the coming desolation of the big-city dweller. The flâneur still stands on the threshold – of the metropolis as of the middle class'.[5] As Rachele Dini explains: 'the flâneur, or urban wanderer, is free to wander because his time is his own. He thus embodies, concurrently, the freedom of the man of independent means, and the freedom of the criminal: the man who has inherited time, and the man who steals it'.[6] In Young's novels set in Bristol, with the exception only of *William* and *Chatterton Square*, the role of flânerie is female. Not an individual of independent means, she either steals time literally, as in Hannah Mole's case, or in the case of the middle-aged housewives Celia and Rosamund, she steals it figuratively from the humdrum routine of her days.

In their experimental novels, modernists like Virginia Woolf and James Joyce, fascinated (and, in Joyce's instance, also repelled) by their native cities, mapped their characters' inner journeys throughout a day of 'street haunting' in London (*Mrs Dalloway* (1925) and Dublin (*Ulysses* (1922)). Young, too, sent her protagonists touring the squares and lanes and parks of Clifton in quest of self-knowledge, solace, privacy, and to satisfy an 'insatiable interest in men and women and an eye for the ludicrous, the pathetic and the incongruous'.[7] When Celia or Miss Mole or Rosamund or Jenny or William or Mr Blackett stroll through the streets of Bristol, their observations and experiences reflect a modern, if provincial, flâneur or flâneuse who steps out of his or her familiar and private domestic space to observe the ever-changing spectacle of the city. Importantly, Celia and Miss Mole and her other young and middle-aged female protagonists-flâneuses relish a recent freedom to walk through the streets on their own, even at night, unhampered by chaperones, though they may be chastised for their behaviour by husbands, brothers, sons, or employers.

Yet, while Young's literary imagination is located in and inspired by Bristol and the nearby pastoral beauties of the Somerset countryside, her art is a domestic modernism, ostensibly remote from the radical experiments of Joyce or Woolf's literary geographies.[8] Written in conventional and chronological narrative form, with a decidedly present omniscient narrator who nevertheless defers revealing crucial secrets, her novels explore the daily,

1 Emily Hilda Young
by Howard Costar
(1932)
© *National Portrait
Gallery, London*

minute lives of families inhabiting the streets and squares of Clifton. Rather, her unconventionality lies in her irony, wit, tart dialogue as well as in her understated acceptance and sympathetic portrayal of alternative domestic arrangements and sexual transgressions – single mothers, illegitimate children, love affairs, adultery. Nor does she hesitate to expose, subtly, the dangers and risks lurking in rumour and scandals and moral pretention.

Throughout the seven Bristol novels (*The Misses Mallet* (1922), *William* (1925), *Miss Mole* (1930), *Jenny Wren* (1932), *The Curate's Wife* (1934), *Celia* (1937) and *Chatterton Square* (1947)), landmarks such as the Easterly steeple, the Downs, the Green, the harbour, the Avon gorge, the cliffs, the Brunel bridge, the tidescape of the Avon and Frome rivers,[9] Leigh Woods and

Monk's Pool signal significant moments of introspection or revelation. With its Georgian houses and squares, tree-lined streets, village green, and quaint shops, Clifton became the vividly portrayed Upper Radstowe and Bristol became Radstowe (echoing its earlier name, Bristowe) of the novels. The city of Bristol offered an ideal site to explore the 'art of living', which became a vital theme of her novels. As Young explained in *Celia*: 'the art of living, the only one Celia tried to practise, was as exacting as any other: it might be that it was the most exacting, for no concessions could be made to the artist whose skill was in doing without them'.[10]

The spectacular Brunel bridge, alluring, magical pools like Monk's Pool, and the verdant downs of Clifton provide an incongruous stage for the chance encounters of ordinary people and the unfolding of minor dramas. This bridge, straddling city and countryside, and the scenic Avon gorge, connecting land and sea, metropolis and empire were fitting symbols of the on-going dialectic in Young's work between urban modernity and untamed nature in all their contradictions. Like Jane Austen, to whom she was often compared, Young turned her wit and her observant eye to play upon the bits of ivory that were inlaid in everyday family life; and like Austen, her bits of ivory did not accommodate the seamier and unsavoury side of this once thriving shipping port, its role in the slave trade in the eighteenth century, and the problems of drink, prostitution, press gangs, unemployment, and poverty endemic in port cities. But Young, a ship-broker's daughter, was not deaf to the music of trade and commerce, the noisy, busy docks, the ships, moored to the wharves, and to 'the ordered confusion of river, docks, factories.'[11]

From Surrey to Bristol to Dulwich

The third child of six daughters and one son, of William Young, and Frances Venning, Emily Hilda Young was born in 1880 in Northumberland. The family later settled in Sutton, Surrey into a house called Beaconsfield. Educated first at Gateshead Grammar School, Young was then sent at age ten as a boarder to Penrhos College, Colwyn Bay, Wales. She developed an abiding interest in Greek and modern philosophy and logic, and throughout her novels pursued concepts of the good, the shadow and the real, and the ideal. Hers was a creative family: one of the daughters was the renowned actress, Gladys Young (West), who first made a name for herself on stage and then in film and radio. Another daughter, Norah Sanderson, became an artist and sculptor, who fashioned a bust of Young's profile. There is a photograph of the bust in the 1950 *The Bentleian* (13), the school magazine for the

Bentley Grammar School in Bristol.

Her marriage in 1902 to John Arthur Daniell, a lawyer, took her to Bristol – first in the suburbs, then, in 1907 to Clifton. Their flat in Saville Place is commemorated by a plaque erected in 1992 by the Clifton and Hotwells Improvement Society (*figure 2*).[12] An avid and expert rock-climber, Young received many accolades for her grace, skill, and adventurousness. It was likely at this time that she met R. B. Henderson, with whom she was going to spend the last thirty years of her life. Young (as E.H. Daniell), recollecting her rock-climbing days in Wales for the Pinnacle Club, wrote that she had gained her first sight of Tryfaen in 1906 'when R.B. Henderson and I left the family party [...], took the train to Port Madoc and bicycled up to Pen-Y-Gwryd.[...]' ('Reminiscences' 1938, p. 27).[13]

Although it was in Bristol that Young embarked on her writing career, it was not until her fourth novel that her characters deserted their wildly romantic Brontëian landscapes to move to the streets and squares of this bustling city. After her husband was killed at Ypres in 1917, Young relocated to London, to live with R.B. Henderson and his wife Beatrice. Ralph Henderson had attained a post as headmaster at Alleyn's School, a boys' grammar school in Dulwich. Their highly unconventional arrangement, a proper ménage à trois, continued as a well-kept secret for 22 years. How ironic that Henderson, while living this secret and 'immoral life', served as moral advisor to the Archbishop!

During the years in Dulwich, a leafy and hilly south London suburb rather like Clifton,[14] Young published eight novels, all with the exception of *The Vicar's Daughter* set in Bristol. Although Young joined the Society of Authors and participated in P.E.N., she did not mingle with London literary society. One biographical entry, probably written by Young herself, firmly states: '[s]he goes to no public dinners, knows no celebrities, and does not care for the society of "lions"'.[15] We do not know if she ever returned to or even visited Bristol while she lived in London and it is intriguing that she set her best known and most successful novels in a city where she had lived for 16 years, but that she did not draw upon Dulwich (or London), where she resided for over 20 years, as a source of literary geography. Perhaps, as Joyce did with Dublin, she needed the physical distance from the city to be able to inhabit it with her imagination. Young also published two children's novels, *Caravan Island* (1937) and *River Holiday* (1942), neither of which is set in Bristol.

Following Henderson's retirement from Alleyn's, Beatrice left for Weston-super-Mare, while Henderson and Young set up house alone in Bradford-on-Avon, Wiltshire (*figure 3*). Here Young wrote her last novel, *Chatterton Square*,

2 Commemorative plaque,
Saville Place.
Photo: Kathy Mezei

and during the war, served in the Civil Defence. She died in 1949 at home from lung cancer. In her memory, Henderson established an annual 'E.H. Young' Lecture at Bristol University in his will. Begun in 1961, this series presented speakers who would address the subject 'Truth is worthy of pursuit for its own sake' from different disciplines. Henderson also created the E.H. Young Prize Fund at the Bristol Grammar School where he had been a student along with Young's husband, Arthur Daniell. This prize was awarded for an essay on Greek thought, a subject which had engrossed Young.[16]

A Popular Author in the Interwar Years

In keeping with her focus on domestic and everyday life, a focus frequently touched by philosophical reflection, Young published in and was reviewed by publications directed at middle-class women and/or the middlebrow reader, such as *Good Housekeeping* and *Punch* as well as in journals and newspapers that drew upon a more selective readership – *Time and Tide*, *The Times Literary Supplement*, *The English Review*. Her novels were issued by established British and American presses (Heinemann, John Murray, Jonathan Cape, Harcourt, Brace and Company). She was marketed, packaged, and promoted by republication in cheaper series like the Travellers' Library and the Reprint

3 Prior's Close, Bradford-on-Avon. Young and Henderson lived here from 1940-49.
Photo: Kathy Mezei

Society. *Chatterton Square* was selected by the Book Society and *William* was one of the first ten Penguins mass-produced as cheap reprints by Allen Lane in 1935.[17]

In 1930 *Miss Mole* won the coveted James Tait Black Fiction Prize, one of the two oldest book prizes awarded annually for best fiction and best biography; the book subsequently underwent six re-printings in 1930 alone. In 1931, Cape began issuing a collected edition, consisting of *Moor Fires, The Misses Mallett, The Vicar's Daughter, Miss Mole, Yonder*, and then, following Young's death in 1947, Cape again reprinted her novels as the 'Collected Works of E.H. Young'.

With the exception of her first novel, *A Corn of Wheat* (1910), all of Young's novels were published in America, mostly by Harcourt, Brace and Company who held shares in Cape. All, again with the exception of *A Corn of Wheat*, were extensively reviewed both in Britain and America. During the 1980s and early 1990s, Virago reissued eight of the eleven novels in their Virago Modern Classic series, with The Dial Press of New York publishing the Virago edition of *The Misses Mallett*. The several productions of Young's work on BBC radio and television attest to her popularity and/or to her sister Gladys's perseverance in promoting her work. *William, Miss Mole*, and *Chatterton Square* were dramatised during the 1940s and 50s on the BBC. In 1985

Miss Mole was read in ten parts on BBC's 'Story Time', probably as a result of the Virago reprint in 1984.

Until recently, Young received little scholarly attention, even in the 1930s when she was at the height of her popularity. In June 2000, Stella Deen and Maggie Lane held the first International E. H. Young Conference, 'The Life and Work of Emily Hilda Young', at the Bristol Grammar School, where Henderson and Daniell had been pupils. This reclusive, once beloved writer is now being recognised by scholars (Deen, Fritz, Lane, Wallace, Briganti and Mezei), particularly with the current interest in popular and middlebrow literature, non-canonical women writers, and diverse forms of twentieth-century modernism.[18]

Touring the literary geography of the novels

Reflecting on the pleasure and flair of Young's fiction, Henderson remarks that the 'setting – all of Hotwells and of Clifton and much of Bristol, has already become part of the story [of William]'. Yet it is *Miss Mole*, he suggests, that 'affords the proper opportunity for a description of Clifton'. In the first chapter, 'we have Clifton in all its charm made so plain to us that those who have never seen the place can yet feel quite at home in it'.[19] Bristol's cityscape serves not only as a setting for Young's novels, but also as a map of and accompaniment to her characters' inner journeys. Nor does Young hesitate to resort to a lavish use of pathetic fallacy: the seasons, weather, river, forests, meadows, trees and flowers, frequently sentient and anthropomorphised, reflect and/or inspire the characters' moods. Thus, 'autumn, laying on all things a gentle, reluctant hand, stifles the very cries of the streets'.[20]

Both *William* and *Miss Mole* present us with unusual protagonists; William, empathetic, nurturing and wise, probably based on Young's own father, is a prosperous ship-builder, with four daughters, a son, and a wife from whom he 'kept nothing but the meaning of his words'.[21] Miss Mole, witty and optimistic, is a plain, impoverished spinster, with a secret past love affair, who hires herself out as a companion or housekeeper. Both strive towards a Platonic idea of the Good, a concept which had preoccupied Young in her studies in Greek philosophy; both, in seeking this elusive Good, manipulate the lives of families and household through conversation and covert actions whose consequences comprise the plots of the novels.

With *William*, her fifth and most successful work, published in 1925, Young began to perfect the art of depicting ordinary domestic life and families in middle-class Upper Radstowe. Thus, the novel begins with

William's daily walk from his office in the harbour to his comfortable home. Through William's observant eyes, Young evokes the sights, sounds and smells of this port city, the 'flowering trees, for which Upper Radstowe was famous', the 'sound of footsteps, of voices, the hoofs of horses, the horns of motor-cars',[22] of hooting from the river boats, and the distinct smells of the muddy river and of burning wood.

We learn that for William, 'romance, streaked with irony' abides in 'his own low, white house, sheltered by a sweep of garden',[23] and in the 'happy, haphazard intertwining of countryside and city'.[24] Like Miss Mole and Celia in the later novels, he finds charm in 'fine old houses' that 'keep company with poor ones' and in little alleys that lead unexpectedly to wide gateways; and sounds of labour mingling 'with those of pleasure' delight him.[25] The muddy tidal river, flowing outwards to the open seas and adventure and backwards through the heart of the city to home, is emblematic of William and his desires. Life to William 'was interesting, a great adventure enlivened by countless minor episodes'.[26] And certainly no one interests him more than his favourite daughter, Lydia. Living in dangerous, sophisticated, bohemian London, Lydia rebels against the constraints of provincial Radstowe, 'constantly doing things which were not possible in Radstowe, meeting the kind of people who did not live in Radstowe, wearing clothes at which Radstowe would have been astonished'.[27] Indeed, to the consternation of her family, except William, she embarks on a scandalous affair.

While William cunningly seeks to sort out the 'matrimonial muddles'[28] of his offspring, Miss Mole, novelist manqué, invents a past for herself and plots to bring some contentment to the troubled household of Reverend Corder, a Nonconformist minister and a widower with three unhappy children. Published in 1930, *Miss Mole* offers a subtler and more cutting portrait of middle-class pretensions, poverty, religious hypocrisy, and provincial *mores* than *William*. As Henderson noted above, in the opening chapter, Hannah Mole, a thin shabby figure, who has lost all illusions except those she created for herself,[29] takes the reader on a picturesque night tour of Upper Radstowe, an ode to a beloved cityscape, its tram-cars, steep hills, glowing lamp-posts, the masts and funnels of ships. In the guise of a flâneuse fascinated by all she encounters, Miss Mole nostalgically compares the remembered city of her childhood to the present busy commercial centre. More so than in *William*, houses and streets are personified, exemplifying the class distinctions and the often oppressive presence of religion; for instance, the houses on Beresford Road, where the Corders live, give the 'impression that nothing unusual or indecorous can happen within their walls'.[30] A 'specialist in roofs', Miss Mole surveys, criticises, and comprehends the people in her small world. Gazing over the roofs in 'every shape and colour'[31] from her attic room, she attempts to impose her wide-reaching vision upon them, while seeking to deflect the looming outfall of her 'sinful' past. This sinful past is associated with her 'pink cottage' in the countryside, a now tainted pastoral idyll, where she experienced her only and unsatisfactory love affair. And it is during another night journey, once again homeless, comforted by the 'cliffs and the dark river and the sparkling docks she loved so well',[32] that she encounters romance, which concludes the novel on a surprising and happy note.

Of bridges, doors and art

According to George Simmel:

> [...] the bridge reveals its difference from the work of art, in the fact that despite its synthesis of transcending nature, in the end it fits into the image of nature. For the eye it stands in a much closer and much less fortuitous relationship to the banks that it connects than does, say, a house to its earth foundation, which disappears from sight beneath it. [...] Yet by means of its immediate spatial visibility it does indeed possess precisely that aesthetic value, whose purity art represents when it puts the spiritually gained unity of the merely natural into its island-like ideal encloseness.[33]

Jenny Wren (1932) is not the most mature or successful of Young's novels, but arguably the one in which she draws most richly on the metaphorical complexity of the bridge. (We note that the earlier novel, *The Misses Mallet's* original title was 'The Bridge Divided', whose plot centres on the complicated relationship between two families on either side of the bridge.) In *Jenny Wren*, the bridge is, of course, engaged to dramatise the division between the dignified town from the country, 'with lanes and woods and secret places for lovers', protected by 'sheltering trees, roofed with a great stretch of sky presently to be pricked by stars'.[34] Less predictably, however, Young builds on the 'will of connection', which in terms of the bridge, becomes what Georg Simmel sees as 'a shaping of things'.[35] That 'will of connection' implies that which, exerted by the three main characters, will result in the final shaping of the novel.

The ill-assorted marriage of Sydney Rendall, a 'man of good breeding' and a scholar, with Louisa, 'an ignorant country woman'[36] with embarrassing speech and manners, has left their daughters, Jenny and her sister Dahlia, untethered to any particular class. Louisa, now a widow with a compromised reputation, has placed a burden on them that is not made any lighter by her decision to borrow money from her former lover, to leave the countryside and cross the bridge and to open a lodging house in Upper Radstowe.

As quoted at the start of this chapter, the novel opens with a long and lovingly detailed description of Beulah Mount. Before the narrator has time to close in on the Rendalls' house, 15 Beulah Mount, the 'gaiety [of] a terrace built in an age of leisure and of privilege' is interrupted by the vision of Brunel's glorious suspension bridge. As in all Young's novels, this is a bridge that does not recoil from spanning the gulf between the pastoral and the urban, the mournful challenging cry of steamers making for the sea and houses that stand 'shoulder to shoulder, like a row of eager but well-behaved spectators, united in an air of personal dignity, unmoved by changes of fortune'.[37] The tone changes brusquely as the narrative moves indoor into the Rendalls' new life in the boarding-house. The sisters' situation is tellingly presented as not the 'living in' but 'the removal to Upper Radstowe' and Jenny turns from the contemplation of tree trunks 'turned lustrous by some accident of lightning' to her 'distasteful' duty of dusting the room of Mr Cummings, the only lodger. The precariousness of the Rendalls' situation is reinforced obliquely when only half a page later we are told that Miss Jewel's lodging-house, on the higher side of the terrace, is the proud possessor of two permanent, respectable lodgers. Jenny, who especially smarts from the contrast between the leisured life which her father had led her to expect and the social stigma of keeping lodgings', is 'perpetually conscious of division in herself': 'there was the Jenny Rendall who had been educated as befitted her father's daughter, and there was the other who dusted Mr. Cummings' sitting-room and suffered because the Dakin girls narrowed their normally broad smiles when they met her in the street'.[38]

The filaments that attach 15 Beulah Mount to the households on either side may be slender, but the barriers that Louisa perceives between herself and her daughters are impassable, their separateness emphasised by the three flights of stairs that run between their attic and her bedroom. And they are just one example of the thick web of contrasts and divisions of which the novel is made – the division between the Rendall parents, and among the various inhabitants of Beulah Mount; the division between the wealthy Merrimans' solid presence figured in their country estate and the Rendalls' precarious hold on middle-class Upper Radstowe. Although Jenny repeatedly crosses the suspension bridge into the bucolic countryside for clandestine meetings with Cyril Merriman, the bridge between classes cannot be overcome and her dream of romance is shattered. It is during the first of these meetings that Cyril mishears Jenny's surname and she, failing to correct him, reinvents herself as Jenny Wren and disowns her family. The narrative delights in detailing further divisions. A visit to the Green on a Sunday affords Dahlia with a vivid spectacle of social differences: mothers from the poorer streets, a few husbands charged with babies in perambulators, shabby motor cars filled with family parties, and 'some small, shining ones containing only a man and a girl'.[39] And when the characters from Beulah Mount converge into the Gardens to watch a performance of Shakespeare's *Twelfth Night* it would be tempting to expect that the narrative will come to its close by mirroring the trajectory of the comedy, the genre in which reconciliation and social integration crystallise in the marriage plot. But in fact the expected marriage plot fails to come together: Louisa marries the boorish Thomas Grimshaw, a marriage to which she agrees in a useless effort to salvage her reputation so that Jenny can marry her 'centaur emblazoned on a field of green and white and gold'.[40] But the 'centaur' cannot overcome imagined class difference, and Jenny runs off with the lodger, Edwin Cummings, while Dahlia will marry the ungainly curate, Cecil Sproat.

These uneasy relationships and their negotiated resolutions comprise the plot of the sequel, *The Curate's Wife* (1934), which focuses on the other sister, Dahlia, 'whose marriage [to Cecil Sproat] had not taken her many yards from her late home'.[41] Her house which, despite its morose face, ungainly figure, inconvenient arrangement, 'had its place in the medley of houses round 'The Green' and which Dahlia preferred to 'a bright little labour-saving villa without a single cupboard',[42] serves as centre stage for the enactment of 'minor episodes' and domestic dramas in a small circle clustered around Cecil's parish. Thus, Dahlia who loves but is not in love with her husband, eventually does fall in love with him, while Jenny, after an unpleasant interlude with Edwin Cummings in his second-hand shop, takes refuge with Dahlia and finds romance next door, with the Vicar's son. As Dahlia points out to her husband:

> If we [she and Jenny] had chosen to be doctors or nurses or schoolmistresses we should have been very serious about it because we'd chosen, not just happened on it... It's so easy to forget that marriage can be a career, too.[43]

In *Celia* (1937) Young continues to probe the intimacies and intrigues of married life in lower middle-class Upper Radstowe. Thus, the literary geography of *Celia* ranges over the same terrain as do the previous four novels: 'There were the Downs, there was Upper Radstowe with Nunnery Road flanking it on one side as the river did on the other [...]'.[44] Celia too roams, seeking privacy and solace, observing how the Downs 'might have been a scene set on a stage', with the 'permanent significance of a fine picture depicting a scene of no apparent significance',[45] and finding 'simple pleasure [...] in the sight of familiar places and people'.[46] An indifferent housewife, distant wife, but attentive mother, Celia moves in 'a narrow world, but what more was the greater world than a container of personalities and the pain and the happiness they could bestow on their fellows?'.[47] Fittingly, much of the novel is set in the 'narrow world' of Celia's small flat in a Georgian terrace (*figure 4*). Here are enacted and discussed complications of middle-age, marriage, children, and livelihoods; here the rooms and their furniture – the 'barbaric marriage bed', the heavy carved furniture chosen by her husband – symbolise her entrapment. Celia's father, a draper, was 'in trade' and her husband, Gerald, an architect who builds shoddy little villas Celia despises, has trouble making ends meet, thus drawing our attention to enduring class distinctions and to the hardships of the Depression years. Describing the panoramic view of Radstowe, the narrator notes how 'from the docks a dense growth of buildings, factories and shops and shabby rows of houses spreads westward and almost unnoticed from a distance'.[48]

Like William and Hannah Mole, Celia derives pleasure from word play and ironic retort, but in contrast to them, she must learn that her own romance is an illusion, that people such as her rather bovine sister, May, have unexpected strengths and grace, and that her own husband is more worthy than she imagined. As the novel opens, Celia is admiring the view out of her attic window; she muses that the Easterly spire must point heavenward, but 'there were times when she thought it was more like a little black exclamation mark on a big, blank page, making some sly, malicious comment on itself and on all it had observed from its place on the hill'.[49] The Easterly steeple foreshadows Celia's journey through the social geography of Upper Radstowe, her family and friends, and her own inner being.

Chatterton Square, Young's last novel, published in 1947, but written during the war, is her darkest novel. And tellingly, it is also the novel in which the bridge, which had gradually faded after *Jenny Wren*, has almost disappeared from view. A sense of constriction and claustrophobia permeates the square

4 Celia's House in a Georgian terrace. *Photo: Kathy Mezei*

and its two adjacent houses, replacing the expansion of gorge and bridge; the Green has locked gates and spiked railings 'high enough to thwart stray urchins.'[50] Doors abound, but there is no respite from surveillance.

While Beulah Mount is prosperous, with houses 'unmoved by changes of fortune',[51] Chatterton Square (the real Canynge Square) 'has seen better days'; its houses may not have printed cards in the windows advertising lodgings, but their inhabitants are 'certainly not householders'(*figures 5 and 6*).[52] Ominously, the looming war and Neville Chamberlain's futile politics of appeasement hover over the neighbouring Fraser and Blackett households.

Bertha Blackett, who despises her 'conceited ass' of a husband, practises a domestic appeasement, which, while offering her some perverse satisfaction and amusement, merely postpones the unmasking of his self-delusions and pomposity. In contrast to the generous and thoughtful William's promenade to and from work, Herbert Blackett struts through the streets of Radstowe, satisfied that 'he looked like an elegant poet with his pointed, little black beard', and wrongly assumes that everyone, including his wife and three daughters, knows 'he is different'.[53] When he returns home, 'walking with the quick, hard step of his indignation with events',[54] Rosamund Fraser, lovely,

5 Model for the Fraser's house, Canynge Square. *Photo: Kathy Mezei*

6 Model for the Blackett's house, Canynge Square. *Photo: Kathy Mezei*

fortyish, an abandoned wife, mother of five children, including two sons of conscription age, sweeps the shreds of flowers scattered on the pavement during her daughter's wedding because she cannot bear to let Mr Blackett tread on Chloe's flowers. Despite her good-humour, courage, and intelligence, she too acquiesces in domestic appeasement, staying with her errant husband, and thus denying her love for the wounded war hero, Piers, who has bought a farm across the bridge.

In contrast to Mr Blackett, Rosamund (and her household) fears that Chamberlain's 'peace for our time' and 'peace with honour speech' and stance after the Munich Agreement only postpone the inevitable and necessary conflagration. Like so many of Young's characters, she hurries out 'in search of comfort on the hill.' And once again, nature reverberates with the character's mood; Rosamund sees in the trees on the other side of the river 'not the golds and yellows of autumn showing here and there, but a dishonourable tarnish creeping over them'.[55] The novel ends with Mr Blackett, shaken by the truths finally spoken by his wife, stumbling through the nightscape of Radstowe, and returning to the square and his home 'like some sad old dog'.[56]

But it is Rosamund who has the last word, envisioning her excursion into the country and to Piers' farm, where she feels sure the next crop in the bare field will be a good one.

Each of these novels has evoked a memorable and at times nostalgic literary geography of Bristol. Throughout Young's work, we encounter a cumulative mapping of streets, bridge, squares, village greens, idiosyncratic houses, rivers, and lush fields that frame the novels, correspond to the characters' moods and journeys, and offer homes, solace, amusement, trials, companionship, and a sense of belonging perhaps too rare in today's globalised and highly mobile world.

The Bristol New Wave: Radical Drama 1957-1968

Dawn Fowler

In October 1963, Mrs Nora E. Cowood remembering 'pleasant evenings spent in the Little Theatre' decided to attend a play in Bristol and she found herself an audience member at Charles Wood's *Cockade* trilogy. After watching the first two one-act plays, appalled at the 'filthy language and disgusting "humour"', she sought out the theatre manager. Under assurance that the third play followed a similar pattern she left the theatre feeling 'disgusted and degraded' and wrote a subsequent letter of complaint to her local newspaper:

> I now cease to wonder at the violence, unchastity and indiscipline of masses of our young people if this is today's 'adult entertainment'. If this is 'kitchen sink drama' it is wrongly named, for my sink is a place where I keep things clean. Those in authority frequently ask what can be done to raise the standards of morals in this country. I suggest they make a start by banning such plays from public theatres.[1]

The letter accused the author of 'delving into the grimy recesses of his mind' leading Wood to suspect that his contemporary playwright, Joe Orton, had written it as a prank although Orton promised he was not responsible (and the name suggests that perhaps Wood himself had played a role in the letter).[2] Either way, Mrs Cowood was, in fact, watching a vastly diluted version of the play. Wood had planned originally to have an expletive title as his fellow Bristolian, film director John Boorman, describes:

> I travelled up on the train from Bristol to London one morning in his company. 'What do you call the plays?' I asked. 'I'm thinking of calling them Piss,' he said. 'Why?' 'Because it is one of the finest words in the language. Simple, onomatopoeic, insulting, essential.' The Lord Chamberlain refused it, as Charles expected. He was ready with the perfect euphemism: Cockade. He loved sticking it to the censors.[3]

This first rejection by the Lord Chamberlain was only the beginning in a long run of conflict between Wood and the theatrical censoring body. Established in 1737 and abolished in the Theatre Act of 1968 the office of the Lord Chamberlain was tasked with approving every public theatrical performance in the UK, and had prohibitive power over anything deemed too provocative, violent or blasphemous for unrestricted viewing. Richard Findlater argues that in the beginning of his writing career in Bristol Wood had 'more trouble with the Lord Chamberlain than any other dramatist.'[4]

This story is emblematic of a new wave of Bristol writing that emerged in the 1950s and became a creative benchmark of the city until the late 1960s when some of the key writers began to drift towards London and elsewhere. The whole country went through huge social, political and cultural change through that period yet, as this chapter argues, it was Bristol that led the way in irreverent and subversive new writing. While never identifying as a unified group or collective it is significant that a generation of the most important and influential British dramatists of the twentieth-century – Tom Stoppard, Peter Nichols, and Charles Wood – began their writing careers in Bristol or, as in the case of Harold Pinter, saw their work premiered in the city.

Of this list only Nichols (b. 1927 and educated at Bristol Grammar School and Bristol Old Vic Theatre School) was a Bristol native and has written tellingly in his autobiography that, 'in the early and middle 1960s, several unknown writers and directors happened to be living in Bristol [...] as with the Chelsea set, if there was a group, we never knew where it went for drink.'[5] Wood has also been wary of affiliation with a particular movement stating that 'I was not aware of being part of a New Wave'[6], but does recognise that there was an idiosyncratic or colloquial quality to the writing of the period that differentiates it: 'There was a time when I could tell almost who had written it just by listening. Even if I didn't know what the play was or anything. I could say that's so and so, that's Peter Nichols, that's Pinter.'[7] Wood also recalls afternoons with Nichols 'propping up the bar in the pub at the bottom of Blackboy Hill in Bristol and proposing outrageous things to each other', then 'each going our own way after grabbing and storing as many ideas from each other as we could'[8] – suggesting that even though there was no official creative collaboration going on it was certainly ingrained into the social fabric including pubs of the city. Bristolian playwright and novelist A.C.H. Smith, furthermore, describes 1960s Bristol in his recent memoir as an imaginative and artistic hub:

> The city was full of talented arts people, living there, not just passing
> through [...] as well as Stoppard, Wood and Nichols, John Arden was

1 *Evening Post* article celebrating local writer Charles Wood's nascent success at the BBC

holding a fellowship at the university drama department (the first such department in the country), George Brandt was teaching there, and its students included Alan Dosser, now a leading director, and Tim Corrie, the film agent. [...] Until he became a full-time writer, John Hale ran the Bristol Old Vic, where the general manager was Nat Brenner. Nat later ran the theatre school, where he and Rudi Shelley are revered names among the thousands of actors they've taught, including Jane Lapotaire, Greta Scacchi, Jeremy Irons and Daniel Day-Lewis. At the BBC, John Boorman and Michael Croucher were developing a distinctive school of documentary films. Artists, many of them taught or teaching at the college of art, included Paul Feiler, George Tute, Derek Balmer and David Inshaw. Angela Carter and my predecessor editor at *delta*, Christopher Levenson, were involved in an attempt to set up a writers' group. Bristol had its own dance company, its own orchestra. Even Richard Hawkins's chauffeur at the BUP, Keith Floyd, went on to a different sort of celebrity.[9]

Smith here pinpoints a range of factors that have been instrumental to the thriving theatre tradition Bristol currently enjoys, not least the opening of the country's first drama department at Bristol University in 1947 (helmed by playwright John Arden) and the accompanying Wickham Theatre on Cantock's Close off Park Row (opened in 1964), the strong regional identity embodied in the Bristol Old Vic at the Theatre Royal on King Street (opened in 1766), and the population of actors, directors and designers trained at the Bristol Old Vic theatre school on Downside Road in Clifton (opened in 1946, and where Wood's wife Valerie [née Newman] trained as an actress).

Clearly there was a creative reason to reside and write in Bristol beyond the cheaper-than-London accommodation and living expenses. Tom Stoppard found himself in the city after a peripatetic childhood, leaving his native Czechoslovakia on the outbreak of war and settling in Britain in 1946. Uninspired by school and, like Pinter, eschewing the idea of a university education, Stoppard became a junior reporter at the *Western Daily Press*, a Bristol-based newspaper, at the age of 17. In these formative years he began attending regularly performances at the Bristol Old Vic and elsewhere. In 1958 he watched the then 24-year-old Peter O'Toole as Hamlet which 'Had a tremendous effect on me. [...] It was everything it was supposed to be. It was exciting and mysterious and elegant. I used to dash back from evening jobs, or rather get the reporter on the rival newspaper to cover for me, to catch the end of it.'[10] This revelation is not surprising from the later author of *Rosencrantz and Guildernstern are Dead* (1966-7) and the screenplay for *Shakespeare in Love* (1999). Other key works include: *The Real Inspector Hound* (a sly look at the art of theatre criticism, 1968), *Jumpers* (1972), *Travesties* (1974), *Arcadia* (1993), *The Invention of Love* (1997) and *Rock 'n' Roll* (2006), as well as a wealth of further plays, screenplays and radio plays.

Stoppard and Charles Wood worked in the city on the *Evening Post* at the same time as for the *Western Daily Press*. There were opportunities for new writing from the BBC which opened on Whiteladies Road in 1934 where increasingly inventive television and radio plays were being produced. At the *Post* Wood laid out classified adverts and Stoppard was a reporter and eventual theatre critic. A.C.H. Smith writes of the dawning realisation in Bristol that arts pages were an integral component of 'posh London papers'[11] and that he and a 24-year-old Stoppard worked as writers for the *Evening Post*'s newly commissioned arts pages from 1960 to 1962. Copy included reviews of Bristol theatre, and new film releases but the pages also ran long essays by Stoppard on major playwrights and interviews with actors such as Peter

O'Toole and Albert Finney.[12] Smith and Stoppard recognised the importance of Martin Esslin's now seminal book *The Theatre of the Absurd* and ran a leading article on it with an extract on its publication in 1961. The book is now an integral theatre text having grouped and identified the stylistic and political importance of plays by Eugene Ionesco, Edward Albee and Samuel Beckett amongst others.[13] Their reign over the arts pages for *Western Daily Press* not only allowed Stoppard an extensive education in theatre and new writing but also acknowledged and campaigned for the importance of regional financial support for the arts which forms such an important part of the civic and cultural life of a city.

Critic, journalist and former literary producer for the National Theatre, Kenneth Tynan, supports the view that Bristol provided a uniquely creative platform for writing:

> During this period, Bristol was a seedbed of theatrical talent. Geoffrey Reeves, who directed the first performance of *After Magritte* and collaborated with Peter Brook on several of the latter's productions, was then a research student in Bristol University's Drama Department. He recalls Stoppard as 'a cynical wit in a mackintosh, one of the very few sophisticated journalists in town – though I would never have thought of him as a potential playwright'. [...] During the nineteen-sixties, Stoppard's *Rosencrantz and Guildenstern*, Wood's *H* (a chronicle of the Indian Mutiny of 1857), and Nichol's *The National Health* were all to be presented at the National Theatre, thereby provoking rumours of a Bristolian conspiracy to dominate British drama.'[14]

As well as Bristol's mainstream theatres, the Old Vic and the Hippodrome on St Augustine's Parade (opened 1912), another significant factor in the nurturing and promotion of more subversive writing was the chance to have work produced in smaller venues such as the Little Theatre on Colston Street (opened in 1923 and turned into a bar for the Colston Hall in 1980), a 300-seat space where Wood and Nichols both had early work produced. The Bristol Arts Club in King Square (later the Bristol Arts Centre and now known as the Cube) was a theatrical space built by amateur dramatists in a building previously used as a workshop space for the Bristol Institute of the Deaf (*colour plate 15*).

This space saw the acting debut of Jamaican-born St Pauls resident Alfred Fagon (*figure 2*) as the Nigerian Officer Orara in Henry Livings' *The Little Mrs Foster Show* in 1966. Fagon later became a noted writer whose plays include *11*

Josephine House (1972), *In Shakespeare Country* (1973), *No Soldiers in St Pauls* (1975), *Death of a Black Man* (1975), *Four Hundred Pounds* (1983) and *Lonely Cowboy* (1985). Fagon is now viewed as an essential and influential figure in the development of black British theatre. In March 2013 the Bristol Old Vic used its studio to revive and explore Fagon's plays and poetry for a week, and a statue of him by David G. Mutasa stands in Grosvenor Road Triangle, St Pauls.

Despite forming a range of uniquely different voices there are frequent themes that can be found in the work of these dramatists that reflect a rejection of traditional theatrical *tropes*. None had received a formal university education. Wood and Nichols were friends who had both been soldiers whereas Pinter was a conscientious objector during the war. Stoppard was younger, had fled the Nazis as a child, and began his success at the end of the 1960s. Their early work is experimental in terms of form and language, preoccupied with issues of class, race and gender, and provocative in terms of Britain's post-war position in the world. Colloquialisms, slang and uncompromising humour characterise an unnaturalistic approach to dialogue. New audiences could be found for the ramshackle, low-budget productions in the city's new theatre spaces, which were open to thinking differently about innovative drama. Using specific examples this chapter considers how Bristol writing in this period, from the premiere of Pinter's *The Room* in 1957 to the end of censorship in 1968 has led to original forms of writing and to excitingly radical dramatic landscapes.

The premiere of Pinter's first play *The Room* at Bristol University Drama Department is often overlooked, partly because the far more famous classic *The Birthday Party* had its London premiere in 1958 (with an infamously lacklustre response from critics). Published versions of the play erroneously cite the first performance as having taken place at the Hampstead Theatre Club in January 1960, followed by a production at the Royal Court in March the same year. However, it is significant that the future Nobel Prize-winning playwright, poet, actor, screenwriter and political activist found his first audience in Bristol in a production described by Michael Billington as the 'event that would propel him towards his unavoidable destiny: the impossibly difficult business of writing plays.'[15] Pinter's description of his own work was typically understated:

> I went into a room one day and saw a couple of people in it. This stuck
> with me for some time afterwards, and I felt the only way I could give it
> expression and get it off my mind was dramatically. I started off with this
> picture of two people and let them carry on from there. It wasn't a delib-

2 Bust of Alfred Fagon by David G. Mutasa on Grosvenor Road, St
Pauls, Bristol. The inscription reads 'Alfred Fagon 1937-1986 Poet
Playwright Actor "Through Grief to Happiness" erected on the first
anniversary of his death, 29 August 1987 by the friends of Fagon'.
Photo: Marie Mulvey-Roberts

erate switch from one kind of writing to another. It was quite a natural
movement.[16]

The play written from this initial stimulus was performed in a converted
squash-court at the University of Bristol in May 1957. British actor, director
and founder of the Orange Tree Theatre in Richmond, Auriol Smith, was a

student in the drama department at the university and President of the Green Room Society. She asked a fellow student, the actor Henry Woolf, who was completing a post-graduate course in directing for advice on producing a new play. Woolf was a friend of Pinter's and wrote to him, in a tale which has now achieved apocryphal status, promising a production at the university if he could have a manuscript within a week. Pinter wrote the play in four days:

> 'The first Pinter production,' claims Woolf, 'cost four and sixpence. It shouldn't have even been that much. I'd told the stage manager not to give the character of Bert real bacon and eggs except for one performance because we had no money. I'd budgeted the production, literally, at one and ninepence, and she went and spend four and sixpence. But it went down very well. It was menacing and very funny.'[17]

The Room, like Osborne's *Look Back in Anger* (1956), often cited as the revolutionary 'kitchen-sink' drama of 1956, takes place in a bedsit but the similarities end there. An elderly couple Rose and Bert co-exist in their room as Rose talks ceaselessly while fussing around her silent husband. As so often in Pinter plays, and in what would become a signature trademark of his work, there is a pervasive feeling of menace overriding the action. As Rose is visited by her neighbours Mr Kidd and Mr and Mrs Sands her fear about life outside the room and her subsequent isolation raise more questions than they answer. Who holds power in the space? Who dominates the conversation and why? What secrets are people hiding? It is eventually revealed that Rose has a fear of a mysterious man who creepily 'lies there…waiting'[18] in the damp basement. At the end of the play this character, a blind, black man named Riley arrives with a message for Rose: 'Come home, Sal,'[19] before Bert beats him unconscious.

A review of *The Room* in the *Bristol Evening Post* stated with modest foresight: 'Throughout there runs a rare vitality, and, with experience and greater conciseness, one feels Mr Pinter may well make some impact as a dramatist.'[20] In December 1957 *The Room* had a revival at the National Student Drama festival which was held that year at Bristol University. The festival was sponsored by *The Sunday Times* and attended by that paper's influential theatre critic Harold Hobson. Later Tom Stoppard went to hear Pinter give a paper at a conference at the university and was so impressed by what he heard that he prepared a column of quotations for the *Western Daily Press*. The beginning of Pinter's career as a playwright in Bristol is important not least because it is a significant event in theatre history but because it offers a usefully symbolic starting point to the dramatic experimentation that was forthcoming in the decade to follow. Certain characteristics of *The Room* are clearly influential in the development of Bristolian theatre. As an unassuming one-act play it marks a departure from the grand, proscenium-arch stage of the Bristol Old Vic and heralds a more studio-based, cheaply produced theatre with simple set designs and actors who could be recruited from the student body or the theatre school. It also marks a more experimental theatre in terms of form and content. Pinter challenges the audience's attitudes on race, age and gender and the play can be read as a cautionary tale against isolating oneself against the outside world.

If the University of Bristol was pivotal in the beginning of Pinter's career, then it was the Bristol Arts Centre that did the same for the work of Charles Wood, whose experiences as a Bristol resident arguably informed his work more than any other Bristolian writer of the period. Born in 1932 in Guernsey, Wood grew up travelling itinerantly with his theatre-manager father and actress mother, attending art college in Birmingham, before pre-empting National Service and joining the army in the 17th/21st Lancers from 1950 to 1955. After 18 months in Canada and a stint with Joan Littlewood's radical Theatre Workshop in London, Wood moved to Bristol and a job in the art department of the *Evening Post* until 1963. Wood's uncompromising treatment of his dramatic material, particularly his depiction of the Armed Forces, has seen him gain a reputation as a subversive or iconoclastic literary figure who divides public opinion. In defence of his position, however, he has stated: 'What's the point of writing anything at all unless you are trying to change attitudes which is what subversion is – trying to change attitudes to all kinds of things. To theatre itself amongst other things.'[21]

The *Cockade* trilogy which so upset Mrs Nora E. Cowood at the beginning of this chapter, contained the militaristic themes that would become emblematic of Wood's long career. As a former soldier it is not surprising that drama reviewing and reflecting on Britain's role in past wars would be Wood's primary concern in his own writing. After watching a full-length play for the first time 'from curtain to curtain', as a twenty-two year-old on leave from the army, it had struck Wood 'all the way, line after line how odd it was the play had nothing to do with anything important like me being near Korea', and there is no doubt that when he came to write his first plays he wanted to tackle what he considered the important social and political issues of his time. As he explains, writing about soldiers and army life was a popular choice because 'at that time it was known to a great many people because almost everybody had been in the army, everyone had done National Service or had been through the war.'[22] The commonality of the National Service experience saw a significant number of writers inspired by their own time in the military, and Wood's early work is consonant with the concerns expressed by other authors throughout this period.

Wood wrote prolifically for film, television, radio and theatre between 1957 and 1968. There were three iconic films for Richard Lester: *The Knack* (1965), *Help!* (with the Beatles, 1966), and *How I Won the War* (starring Michael Crawford and John Lennon, 1968). For stage were the plays: *Dingo* (1961, performed 1967), *Cockade: Prisoner and Escort, John Thomas* and *Spare* (all 1963), *Meals on Wheels* (1965), *Don't Make Me Laugh* (1966), *Tie up the Ballcock* (1967) and *Fill the Stage With Happy Hours* (1968); for television: *Traitor in a Steel Helmet* (1961), *Not at All* (1962) and *The Drill Pig* (1964), and for radio *Cowheel Jelly* (1962). This early stage of his career was inextricably linked to his life in Bristol. *Meals on Wheels*, for example, is described by Wood as 'a play set in Bristol, about Bristol, and for the Bristol Old Vic.'[23] The play is a knockabout farce centred around an old-before-his-time man in his thirties who brings his elderly father meals on wheels on a small trolley while saving for his family members to be cryogenically frozen until a cure is found for old-age. The play was supposedly based on a real scandal in Bristol and the city council refused the play a licence. The Lord Chamberlain also had multiple issues with the play, in the end requesting a new copy of the script as the original had been annotated so much. In the end, it was produced at the Royal Court in London as one of the few plays directed by playwright John Osborne. However, outside of its original context the play was misunderstood by the London audience as Alfred Hinchliffe observes:

> Wood was living in Bristol when he wrote *Meals on Wheels* and decided that he ought to write something about Bristol for Bristol. He came up with this farce which the Council renamed 'Muck on a Truck' and banned. The Royal Court produced it but Wood felt, defensively perhaps, that it was out of place there, having been written for Bristol to get angry about rather than in general terms of anger.[24]

If the Lord Chamberlain's censors and local council were not always support-ive of Wood's work in this era the Bristol theatre community provided a more welcoming reception. Wood's first play, *Cockade* was produced in Bristol before Wood won the *Evening Standard Award* for Most Promising New Playwright in 1963 after the *Cockade* trilogy was performed at the Arts Theatre in London. The trilogy consisted of three one-act plays *Prisoner and Escort* (Wood's first play originally written for television in 1959), *John Thomas* and *Spare*. By the time the trilogy made it to the Little Theatre Wood had already had two television plays produced by BBC West Region, both directed by Patrick Dromgoole, who at that time was a young director and producer based in the Hotwells area of Bristol.[25]

Prisoner and Escort was a play based loosely around a responsibility Wood was sometimes given during his time in the army, which was to escort prisoners from Catterick Military Camp to the army prison at Shepton Mallet. In his fictional version, however, it becomes a play concerned with the endemic abuse of the vulnerable by the military. Harry Jupp (a name that sounds like 'Hurry Up' if spoken quickly) is a hapless prisoner in a war of words with his two brutish escorts, Blake and Hoskinson. Jupp's crime, ostensibly, is publicly urinating on the boots of a visiting German Officer during a military inspection parade, and the play takes place in the confined spaces of a railway carriage as he is carted to prison. The real criminals of the carriage, though, emerge as the escorts, as they bully, cajole and eventually hang Jupp by his wrists with handcuffs from the luggage rack. A young woman, on her way to Birmingham, enters the carriage and after being subjected to a tirade of sexist abuse by Blake and Hoskinson she reveals that her soldier brother Fred was murdered by his own comrades. In comparison, Jupp's inarticulate protest against the military parade turns out to be based in real psychological suffering or even post-traumatic stress over lost family members across the two World Wars:

> My grandfather was gassed. His two brothers sucked down mud and were drowned walking into a threshing machine at Passchendaele. My elder brother was used by the Japs and died vomiting. My father – he was lucky – his brothers weren't, they copped it between the legs – both of them – but dad was lucky he lived to see them all die. Then a D.P. climbing out of a camp on V.E. night slit his throat because he was a sentry.[26]

Recognising the despair and loneliness of the central characters Edward Mason wrote that 'The solitude of life is the theme that emerges. It is the kind of life in which what counts is to endure [...] more people than we like to think live such a life in England today.'[27] Indeed the scenarios Wood creates in his early plays appear to be deceptively simple, yet the questions they pose about wider societal issues are not.

The *Cockade* trilogy was completed by the play, *John Thomas*, which depicts a lonely man who secretly dresses in Nazi uniform, and the surrealistic *Spare* (a word used to describe soldiers going mad in battle), where soldiers from different eras take part in an endless drill, always having 'spares' to replace them when they die. Throughout the trilogy, Wood's soldiers use local words rendered from their own dialects written out on the page phonetically and audiences were typically divided in response. After *Prisoner and Escort* was televised one letter to Wood admonished him: 'I felt ashamed that a Bristol author could write such tosh [...] the world has a far better assessment of the army than the incorrect implication placed on it by the author.'[28] Another stated with breathless excitement: 'I watched your play "Prisoner and Escort" with deep interest. I am in a position to give you the most thrilling true story with absolute authenticity, based upon my own experiences, in a military prison during the war.'[29]

Cockade put Wood on the map as a theatrical voice, and most significantly introduced him to the producer Oscar Lewenstein, who, after watching the play in London writes: 'In 1963 I saw at the Arts Theatre Club an evening of short plays by Charles Wood under the title *Cockade*. Here was a very interesting new writer.'[30] Lewenstein immediately asked Wood to do a treatment of Ann Jellicoe's absurdist play *The Knack* (1965) for the director Lindsay Anderson. When Anderson abandoned the project Richard Lester was brought in to replace him, marking the beginning of a long and fruitful partnership between director and writer. Wood and Lester went on to work together on a number of films throughout the sixties and Wood's position as a major new voice in theatre and now on film was established.

The one play that could not be forgotten by all who saw it in Bristol, however, was Wood's *Dingo*, an extraordinary piece of theatre, whose road to production took six years. A.C.H. Smith has written:

> I don't have a President Kennedy moment about where I was when I heard they had shot him, but I know just where I was sitting in Bristol Arts Centre on April 28th, 1967 to watch Charles Wood's *Dingo*, banned from public theatres by the Lord Chamberlain, that ludicrous relic, and so performed under a club licence, in a boxing ring set, directed by Geoffrey Reeves.[31]

The integral role of the former Bristol Arts Centre (now the Cube) in the first performance of this radical drama is a key moment in theatre history and testament to the boldness of its cast and crew. *Dingo* takes place on the battlefields of Alamein in the Western Desert during World War II. The eponymous central character, cynical and battle-weary Dingo, negotiates his way through an increasingly surreal, grotesque and harrowing landscape first on active duty in the desert, then as a prisoner of war. Where the play proved particularly controversial, however, was in its thinly veiled depiction of General Viscount Montgomery and Winston Churchill and the propagandistic techniques of theatre and film during war. The politically charged subject and radical style of *Dingo* left Wood's agent, Margaret Ramsey, at a loss over how to market the play to theatres:

> I read [*Dingo*] and I don't honestly know what to think about it from a 'show-biz' point of view. You see I use the word 'show-biz' advisedly. I think it's the kind of play we might get on if you were already a success but would be very difficult to set up as a first play.[32]

To Wood's utter astonishment it was the National Theatre who bought the rights to the play in 1964, and there was interest in the role of Dingo from the actor Albert Finney. The thought of such a high-profile performance must have been incredibly exciting for an emergent writer still trying to make a name in the theatre, but *Dingo*'s road to production was fraught with difficulty. The Lord Chamberlain demanded vigorous cutting including the 'deletion or substitution of all the obvious four letter words'; 'more explicit stage directions to clarify the action in passages he considers needlessly horrific'; and 'the blasphemy'. Most detrimental to the play was the instruction to remove the 'impersonations of living persons' with a warning that 'the general should not be identified as Viscount Montgomery.'[33] The problems with censorship and with senior members of the theatre's board meant that *Dingo* never received a National Theatre production. Following revisionary histories of the Western Desert Campaign that were emerging in the 1960s,[34] Wood articulated a growing feeling of unease surrounding official or received accounts. Ronald Bryden wrote:

> [*Dingo*] expresses something felt very strongly by the generation grown up during and after the war which had not been said and needed saying. They constitute over a third of the British population now. It's a pity the National Theatre couldn't speak for them too.[35]

3 Brechtian Masterclass: Henry
  Woolf appears as the Comic in
  the Royal Court production of
  Charles Wood's *Dingo*

With nowhere for *Dingo* to go and to the utter fury of his London agent *Dingo* was first performed at the Bristol Arts Centre on 28 April 1967, with Royal Shakespeare Company actors Tom Kempinski as Dingo, Leon Lissek as Mogg, and Henry Woolf as the Comic (*figure 3*). The director, Geoffrey Reeves, was an acolyte of Peter Brook, and he had directed a student production of *Cockade* at the University of Birmingham. He consequently approached *Dingo* with enthusiasm, consulting a military adviser, Gary Sayer, who in the initial weeks of rehearsal made the cast endure an hour of army drill every morning. All involved were paid 'practically nothing' but 'just wanted to do the play because they liked the idea of it'[36] testifying to its demanding but stimulating challenges.

A highly significant aspect of *Dingo*'s production in Bristol is that Wood himself designed the set. 'It was wonderful to build a set while the play was being rehearsed', he tells us, 'to hear the play coming together whilst you were trying desperately to get some sort of structure around it. I enjoyed that.'[37] As a former graphic designer, newspaper illustrator, and satirical cartoonist, Wood was undoubtedly aware of the power of striking, representative images. In *Dingo* a German prisoner of war camp became a boxing ring lit by a single light bulb, surrounded by barbed wire and searchlights; the 'Bloody Beaches

4 General Montgomery's notes for his speech to the troops before the battle of Alamein appeared in the programme for the Royal Court production of Charles Wood's *Dingo*

of Normandy' are highlighted on a front cloth depicting a 'badly drawn map of the European theatre of war.'[38]

Between Acts I and II footage was shown from World War II newsreels depicting images of 'Princess Elizabeth, Glenn Miller, and the White Cliffs of Dover.'[39] The use of documentary footage alongside the dramatic action blurred the boundaries between reality and fiction within the play. It is therefore not surprising that Wood cites the government-sanctioned wartime propaganda film *Desert Victory* (1943) as an influence on *Dingo*. This public information picture mixes action filmed on the Alamein battlefield with staged combat performed by actors, and Wood's citation of it shows he was clearly aware of the manipulative power of cleverly edited propaganda. While this served to inform the audience of the archetypal propaganda produced during the war, it was also representative of the kind of jingoistic material that Wood was reacting against.

Although Wood's account of Alamein remained contentious he was able to find both the collaborators who could finally realise his vision, and an audience who were willing to engage with his historical revisionism. The Bristol Arts Centre provided an intimate performance space where the audience was close to the action and huge bags of real sand were brought in to recreate the Western Desert. Indeed, Wood stipulates that the play works best 'in warehouses, drill/church halls, small ramshackle theatres',[40] testifying to his desire for *Dingo* to appeal to working-class audiences, well-versed in popular forms of entertainment.

The full extent of Wood's black comedy is revealed in act I scene v, when Tanky carries the corpse of Chalky onto the stage and sits it on his knee. Chalky has been burned to death in a sitting position and is described as a: 'charred, thin as a black, dried-in-the-sun, long dead bean. His arms are bent over his pinhead to open his hatch. Bits of still intact khaki drill flap from the crook of his elbows, crutch, and around his ankles.'[41] This is a bold subversion of the standard ventriloquist act and the repulsiveness of the image was emphasised by Derek Weekes, a member of the audience at Bristol, who wrote that he was:

> quite unable to convey the full nightmarish impact of the torso on stage. At Bristol, in a small auditorium, it was uncomfortably close, inescapable, and, long after other parts of the play had vanished from the memory, it remained seared into the mind.[42]

Dingo persuades Tanky to throw away the body in disgust by pretending that Chalky is a dead German soldier: 'That Chalky? Never. They wouldn't have it. They'd be up in arms if they thought that was a [sic] killed on the field of honour green. Cross their legs and shout no more.'[43] Wood has suggested that the British public would have been more likely to question the death toll at Alamein if they had been fully informed about the horrendous way soldiers were dying. Instead, Wood argues through his mouthpiece Dingo that people are protected from the painful images of war. The charred corpse is acceptable as a German soldier, Dingo states, because 'Evil enemy die like that.'[44] Tanky is able to acknowledge the gruesome torso as that of the enemy because the punishment seems deserved, whereas he believes that Chalky's death was unfathomably unjust. The corpse is indicative, however, that large numbers of both British and German soldiers suffered the same terrible fate.

Dingo remains a marginalised play in mainstream terms, although in his introduction to the play Wood states that 'students perform it well',[45] and tellingly, it is a text that remains popular in university seminars. Perhaps the best hope for *Dingo*'s future lies in the 'small, ramshackle' theatres that thrive on improvisation and experimentation, and which Wood describes as the ideal performance space for his play. What is clear is that the reappraisal of events during World War II is still underway, and while that continues to be the case, *Dingo*, as the sole British play of the 1960s to challenge dominant narratives of the Second World War battlefield, is perhaps still too subversive for mainstream British theatre.

Peter Nichols has written with modesty that 'Charles's early television plays had dazzled and depressed me. Wherever I went, there seemed to be talents finer than my own.' Later he adds, 'no one has goaded and hurt me more than Wood and Stoppard' testifying to the ironic circumstance that a flourishing writing scene can produce bitter rivalry as well as encouragement and inspiration.[46] Nichols, in fact, by any stretch of the imagination, has written hugely significant works and played a singularly important role in the development of British drama. For the theatre Nichols' plays include: *The National Health* (National Theatre at the Old Vic, 1969), *Privates on Parade* (Aldwych, 1977), *Passion Play* (Aldwych, 1981), *Poppy* (Royal Shakespeare Company at the Barbican, 1982), and several plays with Show of Strength theatre company in Bristol from 1995-2000. His first work for the stage was a play called *The Hooded Terror* (1964) at the Little Theatre in Bristol, as part of the same season of new writing that had included *Cockade*. It was the Citizens Theatre in Glasgow, however, that would stage the ground-breaking *A Day in the Death of Joe Egg* in 1967 before it moved to the West End where it has had several high-profile revivals. Nichols set the play in Bristol and based the story partly on his own autobiographical experience with a disabled child. The play is radical in its honest and unflinching look at disability and its effects on a family as well as its theatricality and use of black humour.

In terms of landscape, possibly the most 'Bristolian' of Nichols' work was the BBC Wednesday Play comedy *The Gorge* (broadcast 4 September 1968, dir. Christopher Morahan). *The Gorge* depicted the fortunes of a teenage boy Mike (Billy Hamon) on a tortuous day out with his family to nearby Cheddar Gorge. The family pile into their Ford Zephyr and drive over the Cumberland Basin for a Bank Holiday trip. Nichols perfectly depicts the dynamics of family life and how agonisingly irritating they can be for a teenager as the day disintegrates into chaos. *The Gorge* was played at the Watershed cinema as part of a Bristol Festival of Ideas event 'Bristol Films of the 1960s and 1970s' in May 2012, alongside Charles Wood's *Drums Along the Avon* (1967), directed by James MacTaggert and starring Leonard Rossiter. In typically surreal fashion it interrogated racial integration in Bristol along with *The Bristol Entertainment* written by John Hale (1972). Watching these films alongside one another with shots of the harbour, Bristol streets and the Clifton Suspension Bridge it was evident that each was rooted in a strong sense of place and regional identity, and that the city itself had impacted on the social issues and attitudes that were explored. 'Together,' stated the programme, 'they show a Bristol, that in many cases, no longer exists'.[47]

The story of Bristol theatre in this decade is one which stresses the importance of local funding in the arts, the integral role university arts departments play in the cultural life of a city, and the fundamental necessity of theatre subsidy in the development of exciting artists. It is unthinkable that the writers mentioned in this chapter may not have been discovered had the artistic scene in Bristol not supported and provided a platform for early endeavours. It seems stranger still that despite having long and illustrious careers Nichols and Wood are not better known in the city that nurtured them. Bristol has thrived on its reputation as a cultural and artistic centre, not least because of the theatre scene that has swelled to encompass The Tobacco Factory, the Bristol Old Vic studio, Circomedia, Mayfest, and many other small pub and café theatre venues such as the Alma Tavern. A revival of late 1950s and 1960s Bristolian drama would be a truly radical step for any theatre brave enough to do it.

Angela Carter's 'Bristol Trilogy': A Gothic Perspective on Bristol's 1960s Counterculture

Zoe Brennan

Urban terror, sex and violence characterise three early novels by Angela Carter: her debut *Shadow Dance* (1966), *Several Perceptions* (1968) and *Love* (1971). Popular and well-reviewed at the time of their publication, they were subsequently labelled the Bristol Trilogy in the 1990s.[1] They not only share a Bristol setting, but also a focus on the dark underside of the lives led by the city's bohemian youth.[2] This is a more realistic locale than readers of Carter's later work might expect underwritten as it is by extraordinary environments such as the futuristic America of *The Passion of New Eve* (1977) or the harsh Siberian landscape of *Nights at the Circus* (1984). Although insisting that the trilogy's locations were 'absolutely as real as the milieu I was familiar with',[3] Carter still manages to transform Bristol into a Gothic cityscape in which her characters play out their intense and destructive relationships. In this chapter I explore her use of the city, as well as suggesting that she is subversive both in her refusal to laud countercultural norms and in challenging the London-centric bias of urban Gothic.

Carter is widely regarded as one of the most influential women writers of the late twentieth-century and produced critical essays, radio plays, poetry and short stories in addition to the nine novels for which she is best known. Recently there has been a renewed media interest in her life and work. The twentieth anniversary of her death in 2012 saw the publication of *A Card from Angela Carter*.[4] Produced by her friend and literary executor Susannah Clapp, the book is built around the postcards that Carter used to send on her travels. Academics have been discussing her fiction since the 1980s although the trilogy has been relatively neglected. This may be because it has been dismissed as merely formative work which has resulted in its being out of print at various times. Perhaps because of this critical oversight, Carter is often characterised as a writer of magical realism where supernatural events are treated in a realistic way. Although the trilogy is ostensibly realist, it too challenges the boundaries between fact and fiction in the lives of its protagonists and borrows heavily from the Gothic genre. Underpinning, and uniting, Carter's oeuvre is her enthusiasm for questioning perceived wisdoms, as illustrated by her oft-quoted pronouncement: 'I'm in the demythologising business.'[5] In the trilogy the 'myth' on which she turns her incisive gaze is that of the joyfulness of youthful rebellion and the consequences for those who 'turn on, tune in and drop out'.[6]

What was Carter's relationship to Bristol? Born in 1940 and brought up in South London, she attended the local grammar school and then, following in her father's footsteps, worked briefly as a journalist with the *Croydon Advertiser*. In 1960 she moved to Bristol with her first husband, Paul Carter, and was to spend the majority of the decade here. At the age of 22, she was given a place to read English literature by the rapidly expanding Bristol University. Carter turned to writing fiction after graduation and later said that she had wanted to depict a restless and amoral youth culture and exploit Bristol's atmosphere of 'provincial Bohemia'.[7] Winning the Somerset Maugham award for *Several Perceptions*, she used the prize money, as stipulated, partly to travel, leaving her husband in the process and moving to Japan for a couple of years. On her return to England in 1972, and after a brief stint in London, she settled in Bath before finally leaving the West Country for good in 1976.[8]

It is worth returning to this idea of 'Bohemia' as it was a particular subculture in which she was interested: that of largely middle-class bohemian youth, ex-university students, folk-singers and the beatniks who, influenced by the 'summer of love' of 1967, transform into the hippies. Marc O' Day in his essay, 'Mutability is Having a Field Day', suggests that each novel in the trilogy is set at a particular moment 'within the wider history of the counterculture'.[9] *Shadow Dance* belongs to a 'post-beatnik, pre-hippie phase', while *Several Perceptions* captures the 1960s as they peaked and *Love* charts its waning.[10] The mods and rockers who were certainly part of Bristol's alternative scene during this period are barely mentioned and neither is their 'turf'. Favoured haunts included the rockers' Starsreach Café in Staple Hill and one of the mods' hangouts, the 'Never on Sunday' café in Fairfax Street (the setting, in 1969, for one of Bristol's largest mods and rockers clashes).[11] One possible reason for these omissions is that Carter, who described herself as a 'wide-eyed provincial beatnik',[12] moved in middle-class circles and both mods and rockers were proudly working-class and keen to set themselves apart from the beats / hippies as well as each other. So not surprisingly in the trilogy, she keeps to the territories that she knew such as Montpelier, and Clifton with its students and lively folk scene in which Carter and her husband took part and that revolved, in the late 1960s, around the Bristol Troubadour Club.

The novels: themes and characters

Before a more in-depth discussion of the trilogy's use of Bristol, I would like to offer a brief synopsis of the novels each of which focuses on a central male character in his mid-twenties. The main protagonist moves to the city (usually to study) and becomes part of its counterculture. At *Shadow Dance*'s centre is Morris, a failing husband and artist, who runs a squalid junk shop with his theatrical and sociopathic friend Honeybuzzard. The story focuses on the aftermath of Honeybuzzard's scarring of the hippie Ghislaine, with whom Morris tried having an affair, culminating in her ritualistic murder in an abandoned Georgian mansion. *Several Perceptions* begins with the failed suicide attempt of the protagonist Joseph, 'sad, hopeless and full of baffled murderous thoughts',[13] who is haunted by the war in Vietnam and nightmarish dreams. The novel is about his gradual recovery amongst a carnivalesque cast of outsiders from tramps through to American 'flower children'. It is the most optimistic of the trilogy ending with an extravagant Christmas party in which the hopeful aspect of the 1960s translates into various characters seemingly healed of their woes. Such an atmosphere is conspicuously absent in *Love* which traces an incestuous love triangle between Lee, a promiscuous narcissist, his aggressive and voyeuristic brother Buzz and the unbalanced art-student Annabel. The novel portrays their increasingly fraught relationships riven with alcohol, casual sex and mental breakdown concluding with Annabel's suicide.

In many respects, the novels contain what you might expect from a portrait of the 'alternative' scene in this era. They are filled with alcohol and marijuana, casual sex and a disdain for mainstream values. The characters do not pursue a consumerist 'square' routine. Even when they have jobs: Morris at the junk-shop, Joseph in a morgue and Lee as a teacher, these are not framed as 'careers' and narrative attention is directed to their existence outside of working hours. Yet Carter's stance on this lifestyle is insurrectionary insofar as instead of celebrating its revolutionary aspects she emphasises the rootlessness and disorientation of its players. The trilogy's Gothic interest in psychic dislocation and collapse amplifies the protagonists' sense of alienation. The genre has always allowed for an interrogation of the socio-political anxieties of whichever period it portrays. Here Carter gives room to the uneasiness

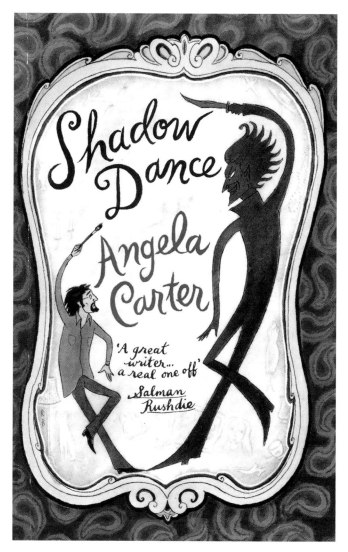

1 The cover of Angela Carter's novel *Shadow Dance* (1966) published by Virago, which is the first in the 'Bristol Trilogy'

generated by the notion that those 'swinging' individuals were not having the 'time of their lives'. Characters claim personal freedoms but then do not know what to do with the liberty they gain. They have dismissed the *mores* of their parents' generation, but failed to establish a more life-affirming philosophy in which to believe.[14] Reflecting on the decade, Carter wrote 'towards the end of the sixties it started to feel like living on a demolition site – one felt one was living on the edge of the unimaginable: there was a constant sense of fear and excitement'.[15] Her account of the era is clearly neither sentimental nor nostalgic, perhaps because she was part of the scene upon which she turned a cynical and politicised eye.

It is noteworthy that Carter largely ignores the political activism for which Bristol is known. The 1960s were an era of public demonstration as perhaps most famously symbolised by the Bus Boycott of 1963 where successful public protest led the Bristol Omnibus company to drop its employee race bar.[16] Students joined people across the city to picket bus depots and in 1968 they marched again in support of higher student grants, staging an eleven-day sit-in at the administrative centre of the university. Carter would have been aware of these activities and had been on CND marches herself, introduced to them by her husband. Yet this face of the epoch does not fit with the particular portrait that Carter wants to capture. Instead of public dissent there is suicide, murder and uncertainty. One concession to youthful protest is found in *Several Perceptions* where Joseph breaks into Bristol Zoo to free a badger who 'had apparently gone out of his mind' running 'ceaselessly round and round its tiny wire enclosure making small desperate whimpering noises'.[17] Joseph's hardly subtle identification with the badger reflects his personal sense of entrapment. Carter chooses to highlight the futility of such rebellion when the joy he feels at freeing the beast onto the Downs is undercut by the notion that it might 'die the same night under the wheels of a car.'[18] Nevertheless, even this potentially unsuccessful action is beyond most of the trilogy's characters who are largely too narcissistic and self-absorbed to act for any sort of greater good.

The trilogy's female protagonists are even less likely to engage in political activism than their male counterparts. They have no identity outside of their heterosexual relationships and are often psychologically and physically abused. Apart from Annabel in *Love*, their perspectives are absent from the narrative and, to use *Shadow Dance* as an example, they tend to fit one of two stereotypes: either grey, passive 'Victorian' women, such as Morris' wife Edna or promiscuous flower children, such as Ghislaine.[19] Sarah Gamble in *Angela Carter: Writing From the Front Line* (1997) suggests that this representation of women 'could come as a nasty shock to any reader accustomed to thinking of Carter as a feminist writer.'[20] Gamble argues that the ability to create different sorts of lives 'unfettered by the traditions or moral assumptions of an outmoded past' is 'a freedom that the text [*Shadow Dance*] often seems only to extend to men.'[21] Whilst I agree, I do not think that it is some sort of oversight by Carter but rather a reflection of the power inequalities she saw around her: the world might have been changing but the power balance between the sexes remained suspiciously static. Later she wrote that it was in the 1960s that her awareness 'of the nature of [her] reality as a *woman*' developed.[22] In these novels the female characters' circumstances are different to those of men and their reality is that they are economically and mentally at the mercy of their male partners.[23] Carter claims she was not radicalised regarding gender politics until after her visit to Japan (in the early 1970s), but I would suggest that the novels contain a scathing critique of a counterculture that defined itself in opposition to the dominant culture whilst actually replicating its sexism and misogyny.

However, both male and female characters are textually 'reprimanded' for not challenging the gender status quo because as Alison Lee points out, women in the trilogy are 'complicit in their own victimisation' and allow themselves to be used 'for sex, but not for friendship.'[24] Later in Carter's career, her fictional women seize the opportunity for sexual autonomy and become active desiring subjects rather than passive sexualised objects.[25] Yet despite the contraceptive pill's availability since 1961, the trilogy is littered with young women who pay the price for 'sexual liberation', most obviously, with unplanned pregnancies. In *Several Perceptions*, Joseph's downstairs neighbour, Anne, mourns the son she was forced to give up for adoption whilst in *Shadow Dance* Honeybuzzard's girlfriend Emily will be left alone to face her pregnancy after 'betraying' him to the police for Ghislaine's murder.

Urban Gothic

Imperilled heroines at the mercy of male villains are very much the stock-in-trade of the Gothic of which, as I have suggested, Carter's trilogy makes ample use. Kelly Hurley points to the genre as containing texts:

> that practice narrative innovation despite the frequent use of certain repetitive plot elements; that depict supernatural or seemingly supernatural phenomena or otherwise demonstrate a more or less antagonistic relation to realist literary practice; that actively seek to arouse a strong affective response (nervousness, fear, revulsion, shock) in their readers; that are concerned with insanity, hysteria, delusion, and alternate mental states in general; and that offer highly charged and often graphically extreme representations of human identities, sexual, bodily and psychic.[26]

The three novels contain many of the traits recognised by Hurley. They may not include the supernatural but still demonstrate an antipathy for a wholly realistic approach to life. Constantly blurring the division between fantasy and reality, Carter constructs them around characters' disturbed dreams and dysfunctional personalities, suitably taken to the extremes demanded by the genre.

The trilogy embraces another crucial aspect of the Gothic and that is its particular use of space and setting. From the genre's genesis in the middle of the eighteenth century, location has played a central role in intensifying Gothic anxieties. Authors have situated their stories in haunted castles, dungeons and remote mountainous regions allowing them to build suspense, create a sense of entrapment or exploit the exotic 'otherness' of distant topographies. The late nineteenth-century revival of Gothic literature saw the publication of novels such as Robert Louis Stevenson's *Dr Jekyll and Mr Hyde* (1886) and Bram Stoker's *Dracula* (1897). In addition to showing Dracula at home in his eerie Carpathian castle, Stoker allows his monster to haunt the streets of London, as does Stevenson with the vicious Hyde. Texts like these inaugurated what critics have dubbed the 'urban Gothic' which features the city as 'a dark, claustrophobic, and labyrinthine space, haunted by doubles, secrets, and traces of the past, refracting personal, social, or political concerns onto the urban terrain.'[27]

This dynamic of the psychological colliding with the topographical underpins an extract from the first chapter of *Shadow Dance*. Carter describes Morris leaving a pub when some youths drive by and chuck a bottle out of the window which smashes at his feet. She juxtaposes this casual violence with an ethereal vision of Bristol:

> [...] it was a remarkable and romantic night. There was a deep blue, secret and mysterious sky with a low, white satin moon appliqued on its bosom and the voluptuous shadows of the city trees moved with black shadows. Morris walked quietly and his footfalls made small, private noises, as if he was the last man left alive in the whole world. Pit, pat, his footsteps, one, two.
>
> He began to pretend there was nobody alive but himself and everyone else was dead. [...] The empty houses appeared to him like rocks or cliffs, the parked cars at the roadside abandoned shells of deep-sea creatures [...].[28]

The landscape is transformed by Morris' imagination and turned into a muffled underwater world. But the city also exerts its own sense of enchant-ment. He thinks about being the sole inheritor of Bristol and beyond, reflecting his desire for solitude. There is a subtle crumbling of divisions between interior and exterior spaces as the city simultaneously reflects and shapes a character's subconscious. Carter has spoken about this connection between space and psychology in relation to traditional American and European Gothic stories. Explaining her attraction to 'cruel tales, tales of wonder, tales of terror, fabulous narratives', she says that they 'deal directly with the imagery of the unconscious' and represent 'the externalised self' through their depiction of 'forsaken castles' and 'haunted forests'.[29] Readers can see the same technique deployed throughout the trilogy although Carter modernises the locations onto which the unconscious is projected, the gloomy dungeon and wild mountains are replaced by smoke-filled pubs and deserted streets.

In this episode from *Shadow Dance*, Carter also emphasises the uncanniness that results from those unexpected moments of calm that occur in usually busy thoroughfares. This type of defamiliarisation is an effect that runs throughout the trilogy. A further illustration appears in *Several Perceptions* where Joseph, out for a drink, walked 'past terraces studded in lights' and once again Clifton's buildings are transformed into 'cliffs' but this time, 'with fires of barbarians burning' as if in 'the mouths of caves'.[30] Characters roaming around at night make it easy for Carter to alter prosaic spaces into something otherworldly and queer. In Freud's seminal essay 'The Uncanny' (1919), he explains that this sensation occurs when the boundary between the familiar and unfamiliar is troubled or, as David Punter phrases it, when 'the barriers between the known and the unknown are teetering on the brink of collapse.'[31] Freud bases his discussion, about the tension between these oppositions, on the German words meaning 'homely' and 'unhomely' (*heimlich* and *unheimlich*) and this choice proves helpful when thinking about Carter's 'Gothicising' of the city.[32] She transforms, for example, Joseph's neighbourhood from a 'homely' place into somewhere unnerving where he is certainly not 'at home' and imagines being cast out amongst the 'barbarians'.

Bristol Gothic

I am now going to discuss the trilogy chronologically and explore further examples of an *unheimlich* Bristol. Although Carter occasionally delineates the city in terms of its beauty, as with her previous description of 'a remarkable and romantic' evening, it is mainly framed as a decaying environment that reflects the crumbling of cultural and social certainties experienced by her characters. They do not populate a prettified or electrifying urban space but instead are propelled towards tired cafes trying to rebrand themselves as trendy coffee bars; dingy pubs with over-flowing ashtrays and rundown corner shops.

Partly this sense of deterioration reflects Bristol's inheritance from the Second World War. The city suffered heavy bombing in the Blitz with one of the worst raids beginning in the early evening of 24 November 1940. It lasted six hours, and in just one night a quarter of the medieval Castle District, the commercial and entertainment heart of the city, was destroyed, as well as much of Park, Castle and Union Streets. Bristol's Mayor at the time, Thomas Underwood, noted that the 'City of Churches had in one night become the city of ruins.'[33] The bombardment continued intensively well into 1941, although it was not until 1944 that the last enemy aircraft left Bristol's skies.[34] At the start of the 1960s, when Carter arrived there, much of the centre was still in ruins and peppered with derelict sites, abandoned or used as car parks. As the decade progressed, town planners began to refashion the city constructing new locations such as the Broadmead shopping centre. These developments were not without controversy. Protests increased throughout the 1960s with various groups complaining that important buildings and streets of historic value were being demolished for faceless tower blocks, car-parks or road widening schemes (as was the fate of the seventeenth-century Redcliffe Hill). As Bryan Little comments in *The Story of Bristol* (1991), 'waves of new office building in the 1960s and 1970s changed the character and scale of the ancient city. Bristol suffered as badly as any British city from insensitive and badly situated new developments.'[35]

Like her Gothic predecessors, Carter is distinctly interested in how individuals are haunted by the past and as a result the modern sites of redeveloped Bristol, cut off from their history, are of little import in the trilogy.[36] However, Bristol's changing geography features in *Shadow Dance* insofar as Morris and Honeybuzzard make their living selling things that they have taken from abandoned buildings awaiting demolition. One night they make a foray to 'William Square' where they learn that the tenants have just been turned-out either to make way for a new road or for the 'slum' clearance that was taking place at the time (residents were rehoused in local authority estates built on Bristol's outskirts).[37] Carter deftly sketches a scene of abandonment:

> They drew up in a black, deserted street where the lamps made lonely

puddles of light on cracked paving stones and walked some distance to a crazy square that stank of rubbish thrown into abandoned areas. Cats, lean and predatory, lurked in overturned dustbins and the blind windows on each side were all boarded. White notices flapped on peeling doors announcing that the city council was about to pull all the houses down.[38]

Breaking into one of these houses, Morris and Honeybuzzard's eventual haul include a 'collarless, Steptoe shirt', 'a cake-tin produced as a souvenir of the coronation of Edward VII' and their prize a 'genuine old oil lamp'.[39] Their goal is to find 'American-bait' those 'small, whimsical Victorian and Edwardian articles that could be polished or painted and sold as conversation pieces.'[40] O' Day proposes that we are now so used to 'endless revivals' and 'instituted nostalgia and pastiche' that 'we forget how surprising it was when it happened on a grand scale for the first time' in the 1960s.[41] One result of this wholesale interest in the past was a sudden growth of antique and second-hand shops, famously in London's Portobello Road and Camden Town, but not exclusively confined to the capital. Bristol certainly possessed its share of junk shops with several in the Triangle, Clifton and on Christmas Steps (sharing the lane with several pubs and a well-loved fish and chip shop).

The exact situation of Morris' junk shop in *Shadow Dance* is not clear, although a friend describes it as 'in the slums' to which Morris bristles 'Americans think it is all very quaint and Dickensian'.[42] Carter is more precise in her description of its interior where 'dirty windows strained sunlight into a thick, rich puree, so that one had the sensation of swimming in soup' contributing to the 'sub-aqueous, deep-sea atmosphere in which piles of furniture and rags and tea-chests seemed the encrusted, drowned cargoes of long-dead ships.'[43] Once again, Morris feels that he is underwater, an apt metaphor for the lack of clarity he senses in his life. The shop is transformed into a shipwreck in which he is trapped and cut-off from the mainstream world.

Morris retreats into Bristol's history to escape his own present. He plays the tortured artist to Honeybuzzard's Gothic seductive villain and spends much of the novel feeling guilty about his part in the attack on Ghislaine. Asking Honeybuzzard to 'teach her a lesson' for mocking his inability to consummate their adulterous affair, Morris had not thought his friend would maim her. Consequently, he tries to avoid seeing Ghislaine's now-grotesque face, taking refuge in Bristol's old buildings such as the Central Library, opened to the public in 1906. Morris lurks around its reading room amongst the 'old age pensioners' who vampire-like 'hung in bat-like clusters around and over the cool radiators as if to force some pale ghost of warmth from them to nourish their old bones.'[44] He also returns time and again to the Bristol Museum with its 'echoing coolness' and 'Best of all [. . .] the reassembled skeleton of an Irish elk on a landing. It was a huge and primeval beast and he looked at it endlessly.'[45] His interest in older spaces is driven by nostalgia for a past he did not experience and his love of artefacts is fuelled by pleasure: when 'he was confronted with a pile of discarded uselessness, he would worry it and tease it like a happy dog with an enormous bone'.[46] Morris is 'at home' with the 'atmosphere of hope decayed' redolent of 'the odd, disjointed fragments of other people's lives.'[47] It resonates with his sense of failure and perversely reminds him that he is not alone in experiencing feelings of 'domestic catastrophe'.[48]

The next novel in the trilogy, *Several Perceptions*, captures 'the disorientation and discontinuity of the mid-1960s countercultural mind and lifestyle.'[49] It is based in and around Clifton village which at the time was the student quarter, as well as home to other groups pushed to the outskirts of the mainstream, 'official' city. The story begins with Joseph finishing his shift at the hospital morgue and walking home. He goes via the Downs and Carter provides a detailed description of his route which takes him past the Obelisk dedicated to William Pitt and pronounced, with a flash of humour typical to the trilogy, as 'modest in size as Obelisks go'.[50] In this opening section it is very clear that Carter's Gothicising tactics are based on a recognisable landscape and readers today could probably still retrace his route. Joseph continues on to Clifton:

> It was a once-handsome, now decayed district with a few relics of former affluence (such as the coffee shop, a suave place) but now mostly given over to old people who had come down in the world, who lived in basements and ground floor backs, and students and beatniks who nested in attics. [...]

> Many of the shops were boarded up, to let, or sold second-hand clothes, or had become betting shops but, nevertheless, this street had once been a shopping promenade of a famous spa and still swooped in a sinuous neo-classic arc from the Down.[51]

The resort to which Carter refers is the Hotwell Spa which flourished relatively briefly during the eighteenth century, offering the waters to the *beau*

2 Rear of Hope Square, Clifton, before refurbishment, 1956
(BRO 40826/HSG/126/4). *Bristol Record Office*

monde, such as the poet Samuel Taylor Coleridge and novelist Fanny Burney.
Due to a number of factors, the spa declined in popularity and was eventually
discontinued.[52]

By the mid-twentieth century, the area had declined even further. The
Bristol of the eighteenth-century cultural elite had been transformed into a
space for those ostracised by contemporary society: both young and old alike.
Carter describes how fat 'pigeons' strutted around the streets 'among the
maimed and old as smugly as if the district had not seen the last of its good
times long ago.'[53] Although fifty years later Clifton's 'good times' have

returned, little has changed in terms of attitudes toward the old. The most aged are still positioned on the margins of society both in terms of cultural representation as well as spatially with the growth of nursing 'homes' designed for 'warehousing' the senescent. Carter does not banish them from the texts and, although peripheral, Gamble has suggested that it is old women who are the true survivors of the novels.[54]

As with the rest of the locality, Joseph's home in *Several Perceptions* juxtaposes past refinement with present disarray: a 'huge, elegant terrace' its 'iron embroidery of balconies bled rust in wet weather', and 'plaster-work crumbled away continuously so this twilight region of one-room flats had a leprous and mice-nibbled look.'[55] Carter deploys the language of illness, wounds and disease to describe this liminal 'twilight' space. It is a spatial reflection of Joseph's state of mind which is slowly crumbling, haunted as he is by vivid and unsettling nightmares. Soon after he arrives home he decides to kill himself and there is no-one to stop him. The one-room flats are not conducive to flourishing partnerships (the like of which are absent from the trilogy). There is no dramatic event that sparks his decision to gas himself, but in a 'cool and casual fashion' he decides it is a 'simple way' to say 'no' since 'nothing was worthwhile'.[56]

What sets this middle novel in the trilogy apart from the other two, is that towards its end readers are offered a glimpse of the more playful and performative aspects of the decade . The same location that accommodates Joseph's failed suicide attempt also restores him. The tension between the degenerative and generative is represented by the house in which Joseph's friend holds a Christmas party. It might possess 'floorboards friable with rot' and 'cracked ceilings' that 'bowed and sagged'[57] but it still amounts to a 'baroque ballroom':

> The marble fireplace, carved with a chastely sumptuous design of urns and garlands, roared with flames; swags and garlands of plasterwork topped the walls and all around the fireplace and the frieze were Woolworth's paper chains, pinned up as from the simple enjoyment of a riot of colours and shapes. [...]

> The heavy almond-green velvet curtains had been roughly streaked with gold and silver paints; the walls [...] daubed with targets, fishes and tropical birds.[58]

The room, decorated like a stage set, allows Carter to illustrate the creative and exuberant face of the decade. The novel's various marginalised figures gather together to experience a magical happening: a nod to the artistic events of the early 1960s. Amongst the chaos of music, dancing and casual sex, characters feel free to adopt the roles that have eluded them in the everyday world. For Joseph, he makes peace with the present: 'I'm friends with time again'[59] and experiences a serenity which lasts to the end of the text.

Several Perceptions may finish on an affirmative note but that atmosphere does not carry over into *Love*, the last of the trilogy, which 'pinpoints the moment when the sixties counterculture self-destructs'.[60] Youthful experimentation with alternative ways of living allow for the damaging fantasies of Lee, his brother Buzz and Annabel to become reality with devastating effect. Carter makes good use of both domestic and public locations to establish a sense of impending doom that intensifies as the novel progresses. The transformation of Lee's room provides a succinct instance of Carter's larger strategy. As a student, his curtain-less room is 'Furnished entirely by light and shade, the characteristics of the room were anonymity and impermanence' and 'In this way, Lee expressed a desire for freedom'.[61] Move forward a couple of years and not only is he still there but not 'free' in conventional terms as he has acquired a wife Annabel. She completely takes him over as symbolised by her transformation of his room. Its walls are now 'painted a very dark green and from this background emerged all the dreary paraphernalia of romanticism, landscapes of forests' that surreally include 'trees with breasts' and 'women whose heads were skulls.' Where once the windows were undressed, now 'Heavy velvet curtains' frame them and 'puffed blue dust at a touch'.[62] As well as highlighting Lee and Annabel's basic incompatibility, the pictures she has drawn offer a clear reflection of her eccentric imagination which slowly, and disastrously, comes to dominate her psyche. The curtained windows make Lee feel claustrophobic, as does the marriage which he temporarily escapes with a variety of affairs, causing Annabel to turn masochistically to his feral brother Buzz for solace.

A novel's opening pages often contain resonances that are felt throughout the narrative, which is certainly the case in *Love* as Carter begins and ends it at Brandon Hill Park, Bristol's oldest park (*figure 3*). It is home to Cabot Tower, built in 1897 in a Gothic revival style by local architect William Venn Gough to commemorate John Cabot's voyage to America, 400 years earlier (*figure 4*). Annabel is described walking through the 'harmonious artificial wilderness, randomly dishevelled by time' which has 'spread its green tangles across the high shoulder of a hill only a stone's throw from a busy road that ran through

3 Cabot Tower on Brandon Hill Park, Bristol. The park is described in the opening and closing of Angela Carter's novel *Love* (1971), which is set in Bristol.
Photo: Dominic Newton

the city dockland.'[63] The boundary between the natural and unnatural is eroded by the phrase 'artificial wilderness'[64] indicating how the park is a liminal space, neither belonging entirely to the city nor the country. Carter is not the only writer to send her youthful characters to Brandon Hill. The television series *Skins*, first aired on E4 in 2007 and shot largely in Bristol, uses the park as a meeting-point where characters can gather without interference from parents and away from daily pressures. Carter similarly exploits its potential as a location 'apart' from the mainstream imbuing it with an aura of uncanniness:

> [...] the magic strangeness of the park was enhanced by its curious silence. Footfalls fell softly on the long grass and few birds sang there, but the presence all around of the sprawling, turbulent city, however muffled its noises, lent such haunted, breathless quiet an unnatural quality.[65]

4 Close up of the
  Gothic features of
  Cabot Tower.
  Photo: Dominic Newton

Once again, Carter zeroes in on the incongruity of silence in the midst of
the metropolis and transforms the quotidian sounds of birds singing and
footsteps into something unearthly. Annabel favoured the 'Gothic north,
where an ivy-covered tower with leaded ogive windows skulked among the
trees' over 'the Mediterranean aspect of the park' that 'held no excitements
for her.'[66] Her preference hints to the reader of what is to come, as she
becomes increasingly drawn to her own chaotic interpretations of the world.
Yet even this early on in her story, the sight of the winter sun and moon
together in the sky at twilight 'filled her with a terror which entirely consumed
her' as it does not fit her personal mythology.[67]

　　After a short stint in a psychiatric ward, Annabel inhabits one of the more
unlikely venues in the trilogy, the enormous Mecca Centre on Frogmore Street

which opened in May of 1966 with a party held for 800 local dignitaries. Even Carter, with her interest in a dingy and menacing Bristol, could not ignore the 'Mecca' which dominated the surrounding Georgian streets and offered itself as the epitome of mid-1960s glamour. Containing an ice rink, bowling lanes, a casino, several bars and a cinema, it hosted such luminaries as The Who (July 1966) and Jimi Hendrix (February 1967). It was a space which offered itself to a mix of Bristolians; the old, the young and those from both the dominant and alternative cultures. The jewel in its crown was the sumptuous ballroom, 'The Grand Locarno' with its famed illuminated ceiling. One of its bars was described by the *Bristol Post* as possessing 'the south seas climate of the Bali Hai' and it is here that Annabel, surprisingly, takes up a job as a hostess in an effort to appear normal.[68] Carter says it was 'decorated to represent a grove of palm trees spreading green fronds over small, rustic, wooden tables', its 'walls were lavishly garnished with fishing nets' and 'luminous, tropic fish, flowers and fruit'.[69] Although something about Annabel makes the other staff uneasy, 'since everything around her was artificial' the 'contrived, if tentative, reconstruction of herself as a public object passed for a genuine personality'.[70] Carter explores the countercultural belief that individuals could create themselves anew by, for instance, not following in their parents' footsteps and exposes the subsequent dangers of such an attitude. Annabel is, in many ways, the trilogy's most psychologically disturbed character and when undergoing this process of refashioning loses track of any 'real' identity. This sensation intensifies to the point where she cannot 'extricate herself from her fantasies'[71] and is so terrified that she kills herself.

Carter's refusal to support dominant discourses means that in her hands the club becomes a discomfiting location. Its lights undergo the Carter treatment: 'above the dancing floor hung a rotating, many faceted witchball upon which a spotlight was permanently directed so roving tracks of light scurried about the floor all the time like shining, fleshless mice'.[72] Assuredly this revolting image of flayed rodents does not comply with the ambience intended by its designers. Carter makes the familiar unfamiliar and builds up unease by adding that 'concealed lighting effects' caught 'the dancers in sudden, cold, blue blizzards or washed them' in a bloody 'crimson'.[73] Soon after this description, Lee starts a fight after noticing one of his lovers at the centre of 'an unpleasant scene of petty sexual bullying'.[74] Carter here further counteracts official narratives of the Mecca as 'the' glamorous place to be by reminding readers of the seedier side of nightlife involving violence and assault.

London and the provinces

Perhaps the ease with which Carter can portray a strange Gothic Bristol stems from her having an outsider's view of the city. Coming from London, she can be characterised as moving from the cosmopolitan centre to the marginal provinces (a term she applied to Bristol). The trilogy's main characters also follow this route and so perhaps it is to be expected that the capital provides a benchmark against which everywhere else is measured. That we live in a London-centric culture, at least politically and media-wise, is a phenomenon to which we have become accustomed and one which Carter's contemporaries also faced. For instance, although the term the 'swinging sixties' is now applied to certain aspects of the decade, it was originally a label applied solely to London by *Time* reporter Piri Halasz in a 1966 article about the capital.

To suggest that readers might discern a London-centric attitude behind some of the protagonists' attitudes towards Bristol, or even those of Carter herself, is not necessarily to suggest a geographical hierarchy with London residing at the top. Yet a handful of characters do possess a sense of superiority over native Bristolians. Honeybuzzard, for example, in *Shadow Dance* warns Morris not to concern himself with the trials of the 'shadows', his term for anyone outside their clique, but particularly the locals. Compared to his larger-than-life and colourful presence, it is a derogatory term and he repeats: 'How can you be sorry for shadows?'[75] He returns from a trip to London with a new girlfriend, Emily. Even before they are formally introduced, Morris instantly recognises that she is not local: 'her appearance was not quite that of the girls of the city and he thought: 'London. Or, maybe, Liverpool.' Her hair is 'curled in dark commas into her cheeks below the ears' and an 'easy skirt of blue denim' with a 'red and white striped sweater' is finished off with 'bright white knee socks' and 'a pair of two-tone, lace-up, low-heeled shoes'.[76] Emily's clothes mark out her 'tribe' but in this instance it also informs the watcher about her geographical background as she is slightly at odds with, and presumably ahead of, provincial fashions.

It is not just Bristol's inhabitants that 'trail' behind London's lead in terms of trends. Carter describes how Morris' local café, 'coloured a nutritious brown' and where the tables and chairs were 'solid and immovable oak', is 'forced, against its will, to become a coffee bar.'[77] The result is that style rules over substance; the heavy tables

> were replaced by steel and plastic structures so light they had to be screwed
> into the ground to prevent them overbalancing at a touch. New chairs

were introduced, covered with yellow lemon simulation leather that adhered to arse and thighs in warm weather.[78]

The furniture is flimsy and uncomfortable and readers can sense Carter's critique of the mind-set that pursues fashion and celebrates the transient over the enduring and consoling. Morris is pleased to find that at least the familiar waitresses remain, although he unflatteringly says that once they were 'women, as one could see by their dresses' and now are 'withered away, their sex ground down by the stubbed-out cigarettes of the years'.[79] He nicknames them 'Struldbrugs' after immortal characters from Jonathan Swift's *Gulliver's Travels* (1726). Naively, the protagonist Gulliver thinks that immortality is an exciting prospect only to discover that the Struldbrugs are despised by the rest of the land. In addition, they continue to age and their appearance is described as 'ghastly' (and unsurprisingly, considering Gulliver's misogyny, the women are more horrible than the men).[80] Whilst it is easy to read Morris' sense of the waitresses' difference as relating to age, it is also relevant to his role as a 'visitor' to the city. Gulliver, after all, travels to many strange lands and reports the peculiarities he encounters and tellingly Morris aligns himself with this character.

Carter's mention of the waitresses is one of the few examples in the trilogy where we glimpse the 'normal' Bristolians who make up the majority of the city's population. A notable departure is found in *Several Perceptions* where Joseph's friend Viv is the one local character who plays more than a bit part. He speaks in 'the drawling accent of the city' and uses 'all the local endearments, my queen, my lover and my star.'[81] Although not a 'square', as he lives on 'benefits' and earnings from playing gigs with his band The Electric Opera, he is also not one of the bohemians. Perhaps it is no coincidence that he prospers: characterised as 'well-adjusted' and 'sweet tempered'[82] he is rewarded with plentiful female attention.

Unsurprisingly Viv's appearance also sets him apart. He has black hair 'glossy as a well-polished boot' and he wears a 'pin-striped suit of navy blue, a Mafia-style shirt of rough black silk and a fatly knotted lilac silk tie'.[83] Not for him are the eclectic borrowings of the hippies such as Kay, the party-giver, who 'wore Levi jeans and jacket' with a 'flannel shirt, lacking a collar, probably bought at or stolen from a jumble sale then dyed a cheerful orange in the communal spaghetti saucepan; green round wire-rimmed sunglasses' and 'dirty white plimsolls'.[84] Kay's outfit is another example, but more benign, of the spirit of self-creation taken to such extremes in *Love*. Items are abstracted from their original context and placed in a different one to make an individual statement: the shirt with its collar belongs to a smarter category of clothing than the denim with which it is now worn and so on. In the trilogy, Carter often details the costumes donned by the characters. She wrote on the subject that 'Fashion is part of social practice' and stresses its importance by adding 'it is an industry whose demands have helped to shape modern history, and choosing our clothes is the nearest most of us will ever get to practical aesthetics.'[85] It is worth taking note of the protagonists' outfits, as it tells the reader something more about their psychology and life-story.

Returning to London, the capital is a presence lurking at the margins of Carter's novels. What is unusual is not that it is there, but that it is pushed to the boundaries of the trilogy. Contemporary English literature and its attendant criticism tend to duplicate the wider culture's bias towards London.[86] The Gothic genre has a particularly close and enduring association with the metropolis. Emily Alder, discussing the urban Gothic, talks about 'the iconicity of London' and Robert Mighal goes even further to suggest that London and New Orleans are *the* 'quintessential' Gothic cities.[87] Carter, by setting her tales in the West Country, as well as writing what she knew, exploits the 'Otherness' of an environment that is 'not-London' to create an atmosphere that many readers found unsettling and alien. She explained in a subsequent interview that 'very few reviewers believed it [Bristol] was real' pointing to their unfamiliarity with the region.[88] However, the British reviewers did not see the locale in as dissipated terms as suggested by one American who, commenting on *Shadow Dance*, said it was set in 'a British slum where streets smell of urine, vomit, and stale beer' much to Carter's amusement.[89] In her refusal to centralise the capital there is an element of her self-confessed literary unconventionality. Gamble explains that she had a 'tendency towards wilful perversity' which 'delighted in toppling belief systems of any kind; an iconoclastic process from which nothing was exempt.'[90] In the trilogy, one of the dogmas that Carter challenges is the pre-eminence of London in the urban Gothic genre.

Conclusion

Carter's portrait of 1960s Bristol is not an 'official' stance on either the era or the city. For instance, she does not focus on its restructuring into the supposedly 'cosmopolitan' location beloved of the town planners. Mainstream society hardly makes an appearance in the trilogy and so this is, necessarily, only a partial tale of the city in that decade. I have spoken about her omissions and pointed out that even in terms of the younger generation it is a partisan account. The mods and rockers are missing, as is an acknowl-edgement that not all baby boomers were 'swingers' or, even if they were, that they were not unquestionably part of the ex-university set. From a differ-ent angle, her perspective is not what we might expect of a confessedly countercultural writer. She does not eulogise the scene or tell tales of a groovy and 'happening' community that thrives alongside the mainstream culture.[91]

Instead Carter's 'unofficial' representation of the city imaginatively trans-figures it into a Gothic space. Her characters move through streets resonant with Bristol's history and root through the basements of once-grand Georgian terraces searching for junk. Although locations are recognisable, or would have been to her peers, she draws from them a strange and uncanny atmosphere. The identities of the protagonists play out on the landscapes reflecting and revealing a sense of dislocation, which intensifies as the trilogy progresses.

Gothic texts are known to engage with cultural anxieties and their authors often project specific concerns onto monsters to be battled. Carter follows this strategy, at least in the first and last books of the trilogy. Her monsters may be human, and seductive to other characters, but Honeybuzzard and the selfish brothers Lee and Buzz personify fears about where ultimately the rebellions of the 1960s would lead. This is an 'insider's' anxiety, not the recur-ring complaint about the youth of today but a questioning about whether or not behind the hippy's mantra of 'peace and love' lies anything apart from emptiness, or worse, chaos. Despite Carter's seeming disenchantment with her peers, as Gamble pertinently points out, a lasting inheritance from the period was 'the notion of acting against the dominant culture'.[92] By setting the trilogy in Bristol, Carter is challenging the 'dominant' urban Gothic convention of centralising London and it seems fitting that she invokes a marginalised city in literary terms to represent her socially marginalised protagonists.

Enchanting the City:
Diana Wynne Jones and Bristol

Catherine Butler

Reading as Enchantment

Readers have always been fascinated by the relationship between writers and the places that are important to them. Whether we consider place as a point of origin, as a source of inspiration, or as subject matter; whether we think of it as inanimate or invest it with sentience; whether we wax lyrical, mystical, or geological, many of us will acknowledge that places play a significant role in shaping our imaginative experience of books, as well as influencing the writers who produce them. The potency of place has been central to my own critical writings, and to none more so than *Four British Fantasists* (2006),[1] a study of four children's fantasy writers, including the Bristol writer Diana Wynne Jones. This book (as indicated in its subtitle) put a specific emphasis on the roles of 'place and culture' in its subjects' work, exploring place in terms of landscape history, archaeology, folklore, and human community.

When I wrote *Four British Fantasists* one of my great pleasures – indulgences, perhaps – was the excuse to seek out the locations where some of the events described in these authors' books took place (or did not take place, these being fictions). Clearly some of the writers being discussed – such as Alan Garner, who put maps in the front of his books – anticipated and tacitly encouraged such expeditions. My primary purpose in making them was to establish the ways in which significant places might be said to have had an effect – a publicly discussable, academically respectable effect – on my subjects' novels. But I was also interested in what drew *me*, and in the ways the experience of such visits fed back into my reading.

The longing to go on pilgrimage that Chaucer wrote of more than six hundred years ago remains an important element of literary experience for many readers. Thousands yearly travel to Dorset and West Yorkshire in search of the landscapes that inspired Hardy and the Brontës. At King's Cross Station thousands more pay their respects at a shrine to Harry Potter in the form of a luggage trolley sunk into the wall, its handle burnished by the touch of many hands. Admirers of Lucy M. Boston's *Green Knowe* books who visit her home in Hemmingford Grey may be allowed to venerate the originals of the toys that feature in her fiction, just as previous generations did the relics of saints. The language of religious pilgrimage may seem overblown, but I would argue that the impulses behind modern literary tourism are in fact quite similar to those that took folk on pilgrimage in Chaucer's time. For the religious, a shrine like that of Thomas à Becket is a place where two worlds meet: the world of the everyday, the bustling city of Canterbury filled with reeves and pardoners and goodwives; and the world of the divine, where a saint was sanctified in martyrdom. God might be everywhere, but such places could give you a better view of God's interactions with the world. Beckett's shrine, being a site where those two worlds touched, was a kind of incarnation – a mystery made flesh. However, one need not be religious to find fascination in the ways that books too may contrive to be incarnations, yoking together being and meaning, investing mere phenomena with significance. In doing this work they are engaged in what the philosopher Jane Bennett refers to as the 'enchantment' of modern life, the fight against and emergence from a reductive sense that all human experience is rationally calculable, which she sees as having achieved cultural dominance since the days when it was given classic expression by nineteenth-century social theorists such as Max Weber. According to Bennett's polemic:

> the contemporary world retains the power to enchant humans and [...] humans can cultivate themselves so as to experience more of that effect. Enchantment is something that we encounter, that hits us, but it is also a comportment that can be fostered through deliberate strategies. One of those strategies might be to give greater expression to the sense of play, another to hone sensory receptivity to the marvelous specificity of things.[2]

Enchantment is a question not just of intellectual assent but of bodily practice and awareness, of re-mooring the mind in the world of physical experience. It is easy to see how poetry, in its attention to specificity, and novels, in their attempts to capture and integrate as broad a range of human experience as possible, might be recruited to this project; but perhaps it is in fantasy literature that it comes closest to being a defining principle. It is conveniently exemplified in a passage from Diana Wynne Jones's novel *Deep Secret* (1997). Here, one of the book's narrators, Maree Mallory, describes the distorting glass in the windows of her uncle and aunt's Bristol house:

> When you look out at the front – particularly in the evenings – you get a
> sort of cliff of trees and buildings out there, with warm lighted squares
> of windows, which all sort of slide about and ripple as if they are just
> going to transform into something else. From some angles, the houses
> bend and stretch into weird shapes, and you really might believe they were
> sliding into a set of different dimensions. [...] With everything rippling and
> stretching, you almost think you're seeing your way through to a potent
> strange place behind the city.[3]

Maree's uncle explains the effect prosaically: the glass dates from the Second
World War, when the house was caught in the blast from the Luftwaffe's
bombing of Bristol docks and the windows had to be hastily replaced. He
adds that the rarity of the glass now adds to the house's value – just the kind
of conversion of mystery into calculability against which Bennett writes and
that is liable (in Maree's words) to 'destroy all the strangeness'.[4] However,
Maree's cousin Nick maintains that the windows 'give you glimpses of a great
alternate universe called Bristolia'.[5] Later, Nick has Maree drive him around
the city, now seen through the double lens of mundanity and enchantment
as both Bristol and Bristolia:

> Nick unfolded a large, carefully coloured map. 'I think we'll start with
> Cliffores of the Monsters and the Castle of the Warden of the Green
> Wastes,' he said seriously.
>
> So I drove him to the Zoo and then past the big Gothic school there.
> Then we went round Durdham Down and on to Westbury-on-Trym and
> back to Redland. After that, I don't remember where we went. Nick had
> different names for everywhere and colourful histories to go with every
> place. He told me exactly how many miles of Bristolia we'd covered for
> each mile of town.[6]

Their travels eventually take them from 'Biflumenia – I mean Bedminster' to
'Yonder Bristolia where most of the magic users live',[7] on the far side of the
Clifton Suspension Bridge. Although Nick's version of Bristolia is a game
that he has invented (just as *Deep Secret* is a novel Diana Wynne Jones has
invented), it becomes a way of re-enchanting the physical city, one that readers
may experience on subsequent journeys through its streets. In this respect it
bears comparison with the immersive fiction, *These Pages Fall Like Ash*, created

1 *These Pages Fall Like Ash.* The audience participates in a locative experience set in Bristol. The narrative is told across both a physical artefact and a digital text. Not only are there two texts which come together but also two cities, one real and another accessible through a mobile device. The story is about a moment when the two cities converge. *Photo: Circumstance*

in 2013 as a collaboration between University of the West of England academic Tom Abba and Duncan Speakman, with input from the fantasy novelists Neil Gaiman and Nick Harkaway.[8] *These Pages Fall Like Ash* is both a physical book (*figure 1*) and an extended 'event' spread over several weeks in the spring of that year, in which readers were invited to explore locations in the city, where they would be able to unlock sections of a counterpoint narrative using a mobile device. By piecing together the book with the electronic texts and imagery, the story emerges of a parallel Bristol, Portus Abonae,[9] which occupies the same physical space but a different reality. The experience of 'reading' *These Pages Fall Like Ash* was described by Sarah Ditum in *The New Statesman*:

> You see the river and the ghost signs, the ancient pubs and the not-so-ancient university buildings more sharply as you make the effort to see something else entirely in their place. Early on, it becomes clear that the fiction involves two cities sharing the same location, with lesions between them that allow some kind of exchange between the characters; and then you realise that you and every other participant in Pages Fall [sic] is helping to shape the outcome of the story.[10]

2 Looking-glass city – a 'reader' of *These Pages Fall Like Ash* (2013) seeks Portus Abonae in and through Bristol. *Photo: Catherine Butler*

'The real voyage of discovery consists not in seeking new landscapes but in having new eyes' wrote Marcel Proust in a line quoted in *These Pages Fall Like Ash*.[11] The approach is very much in the tradition of Diana Wynne Jones's own work, and it is probably no coincidence that both Abba and Gaiman were admirers and close friends of hers. (Indeed, the character of Nick in *Deep Secret* is partly based on Gaiman.) In the rest of this essay I wish to consider not so much as what place meant to Diana Wynne Jones as a writer[12] as what her use of place has meant to me as one of her readers.

A Taxonomy of Place

Diana Wynne Jones (1934-2011) was one of the twentieth century's most inventive writers of fantasy and science fiction, a writer whose range and originality have given her a unique place among British novelists. In a career spanning four decades she influenced more than one generation of readers, including many (such as Neil Gaiman) who went on to become authors themselves. Although described above as a Bristol writer, Jones did not begin her association with the city and the southwest until she was in her early forties. Having led a peripatetic wartime childhood she grew up in the village of Thaxted in Essex before studying English Literature at Oxford, where, shortly after graduating in 1956, she married the mediaevalist John Burrow. The first twenty years of their marriage were spent in that city; but in 1976 they moved to Bristol, where they lived until Jones's death. There she produced several dozen novels, the best known being perhaps her Chrestomanci series (beginning with *Charmed Life* in 1977), and *Howl's Moving Castle* (1986), which went on to be made into a feature film by Hayao Miyazaki (2004). Most of her output was published for children, although she also wrote books under adult imprints, such as *Deep Secret*. In Jones's case, however, such distinctions meant relatively little: it is telling that *The Merlin Conspiracy* (2003), the sequel to *Deep Secret*, was published as a children's book – a fact indicative of the intergenerational nature of her work and readership.

Much speculative fiction is set in other worlds, either on other planets or perhaps in other universes altogether. This is true of some of Jones's books, but in many the setting appears to be the world as we know it. Even where that is not the case the mundane and fantasy worlds may still merge into each other, opening up the possibility of pilgrimage. In one of her own critical essays, Jones pointed out the extent to which J.R.R. Tolkien was indebted for the landscape of Middle-earth to the geographical and archaeological features around Oxford and the upper Thames valley:

> Here there are stuffy willow-choked flats, Wychwood, rivers like the Windrush and the Evenlode, the Rollright Stones, the longbarrow called Wayland's Smithy, ploughland and orchards round Didcot, the Seven Barrows, Thames water meadows, and the austere landscape of the chalk downs. And he used them all: there is even a real place called Buckland.[13]

Jones goes on to argue that the road from the Shire to Rivendell, followed first by Bilbo in Tolkien's *The Hobbit* (1937) and later by Frodo in *The Lord of the Rings* (1954-5), carries echoes of 'the old prehistoric road called the Ridgeway, which is probably the oldest road in Britain, leading from east to west [...] sometimes as a cart-track, sometimes as broad as a motorway, and at other times vanishing in a valley'.[14] What is true of Tolkien is true also of Jones's own fantasy settings. Her geographical inspirations range across Britain, but understandably they cluster in the places that she knew best. A long-term resident of Oxford, she drew as Tolkien had on the geography of that area – on Oxford itself in *A Tale of Time City* (1987) and on Otmoor in *Power of Three* (1976), as well as on the landscape around Wayland's Smithy and the Uffington White Horse for *The Merlin Conspiracy*. Since Jones lived in Bristol for thirty five years and wrote most of her books there it is not surprising that Bristol and the surrounding area also feature heavily in the topography of her books, although they appear in a variety of guises, partly reflecting the range of genres in which she worked. We shall begin by considering a selection of her novels to produce a taxonomy of the ways that Jones incorporates place in her fiction.

In some ways the most straightforward category is the explicit use of named locations. For example, Bristol features *in propria persona* in a number of Jones's books, notably *Deep Secret* and her young adult novel *Fire and Hemlock* (1985), both of which include important scenes at the Clifton Suspension Bridge. In *Fire and Hemlock* the teenaged heroine Polly, rejected by both her jealous mother and by her weak father, seriously considers throwing herself from the bridge, which she knows to be a popular suicide spot. In a passage partly inspired by the opening of T.S. Eliot's 'The Dry Salvages' (1941)[15] Jones writes:

> The bridge was a flat double strip under the cables, hung high, high up between two cliffs. Polly walked out to the middle and stopped. The wind took her hair there and hurled it about. She leaned both arms on the chubby metal fence at the edge and looked down, dizzyingly far, to the sinewy brown water of the Bristol Avon racing between the thick mud banks below. The wind hurled seagulls about in the air like wastepaper.[16]

Here is a very precise description of a very precise place. Anyone visiting Bristol would be able to follow Polly to this spot and look down at the same sinewy brown water, even if today they will not (like Polly) have to pay a two pence pedestrian toll to do so.

A different presentation of place can be found in *A Tale of Time City* (1987). In this novel, the eponymous Time City is a place that sits outside time, from which it is possible to visit any era. Time City's architecture and interminable round of ceremonies were inspired by Oxford,[17] but the novel includes an episode in which the child protagonists visit an unnamed West Country town at the time of the Second World War. This town has a Tor, where one of the Caskets of Time City's Guardians is hidden, and the children wish to retrieve it:

> They went up over the bulge in a floundering run, into sudden wide blue sky at the top of the hill. The space was quite small and flat. The tower was only some yards away and it was indeed a church tower without a church. There were two open church-like archways in it at the bottom.

Vivian could see sky right through it for a second, before Jonathan blocked her view by springing upright and sprinting for the tower.[18]

In this case, in contrast to *Fire and Hemlock*, the precise location is never named. However, for anyone familiar with the area, the description is exact and unmistakable: the children are on Glastonbury Tor. The realisation of this provides an experience distinct from the passive recognition of a named location, as in the case of the Suspension Bridge, but is of course available only to those readers who have the experience necessary to make the discovery.

A third category is exemplified by *The Merlin Conspiracy*. Most of this novel is set not in our world but in a magical analogue for Britain called Blest, which has much the same geography and includes versions of London, Salisbury and Stonehenge. At one point the protagonist, Roddy Hyde, visits an ancient, unnamed village, where in the stones of a ruined hut she encounters the spirit of a former inhabitant, a witch with a broken hip and an abundance of botanical lore, who proceeds to download her knowledge into Roddy's mind. This incident was inspired by a visit to the ancient Romano-British settlement of Chysauster in west Cornwall, where Jones had a very similar encounter, to the extent that she felt the pain in her own hip, and could not walk for some minutes. Roddy describes the village in these terms:

It was like an accidental garden strewn with heaps of regularly piled stones. Small rowans and hawthorns had grown up among the stones, along with heather and gorse, big bushes of broom and small shrubs of bilberry. [...] We sat down on the nearest sunny tumble of wall, just beside what looked like the ruins of a front door with very civilised steps leading up to it, where we ate an improbable quantity of sandwiches in peace and contentment filled with insect sounds.[19]

The description certainly corresponds to the reality of Chysauster as I saw it on a visit (or pilgrimage) in 2007 (*figure 3*). However, one difference between this example and that of Glastonbury Tor is that the Tor's unique features make it instantly recognisable, whereas there are numerous sites in the United Kingdom that resemble Roddy's description to some degree. The presence of Chysauster within *The Merlin Conspiracy* thus remains shadowy. In fact, I am aware of the Chysauster connection only because Jones told me about her experience there in conversation, a source of information unavailable to most readers. That knowledge has inevitably come to colour my sense both

3 Romano-British walls at Chysauster ancient village.
Photo: Catherine Butler

of the scene in *The Merlin Conspiracy* and of Chysauster, but to what extent is it reasonable to say in general terms that Chysauster is a feature of the book?

When I interviewed Jones in March 2001 I asked her about the role of locations in inspiring her work. At the time, Hayao Miyazaki was planning the animated version of her 1986 book *Howl's Moving Castle*, and her answer reflects this:

> Recently I was invaded by a Japanese film team, and they tried to make me identify the landscapes from *Howl's Moving Castle* (1986). (It was difficult because they had two interpreters, each interpreting differently all the time.) Eventually, after scratching my head and forcing my brain in wrong directions (as it seemed to me) I managed to work out that Exmoor played quite a part in it, and so did Lyme Regis and the coast around there, which is of course within reach of Bristol. But it wasn't there directly: I had to

4 Exmoor. *Photo: Michael Clark, 2010, published under the terms of Creative Commons attribution share-alike license, Version 2.5*

dig for it. I don't as a rule say: 'I will set this book in Bristol city centre.'[20]

Howl's Moving Castle is set not in Dorset or Somerset but in the fantasy realm of Ingary, a place where 'seven-league boots and cloaks of invisibility really exist'.[21] Nevertheless, armed with this hint it is of course possible to go back to the novel and read its hilly hinterland through the prism of Exmoor, and its seaside town of Porthaven through the prism of Lyme Regis. For example, in the following passage the protagonist Sophie is running to Porthaven harbour in order to watch Wizard Howl take part in a magical battle:

> Sophie and Michael joined the rush of braver people down the long sloping lanes to the dockside. There everyone seemed to think the best view was to be had along the curve of the harbour wall. Sophie hobbled to get out along it too, but there was no need to go beyond the shelter of the harbour master's hut.[22]

How useful is it, if at all, to read this passage in the light of the suggestion that Porthaven is inspired by Lyme Regis, which does indeed boast 'long sloping lanes' running down to the dockside? The 'curve of the harbour wall' in Porthaven may evoke Lyme's famous Cobb, which certainly curves – though no more so than dozens of similar walls in ports throughout the southwest. On the other hand, Jones's sense that retrieving the information involved forcing her 'brain in wrong directions' should give us pause, even if our priorities as readers do not entirely mirror hers as a writer. It may even be that foregrounding the Lyme connection will be detrimental to our sense of the integrity of Ingary as a fictional world. If we remember Lyme when we read of Porthaven, might we not find Jones's world being drowned out by interference from the Dorset town, or even by Lyme's previous fictional appearances in books such as Jane Austen's *Persuasion* (1818) and John Fowles's *The French Lieutenant's Woman* (1969)?

Having raised some doubts about the usefulness of reading in the light of real-world places, let us proceed to exacerbate them by considering one further example, Jones's 1984 novel, *Archer's Goon*. This book is set in an unnamed city or largish town in what appears to be contemporary England. Unknown to most of its citizens the town is in fact run from behind the scenes by seven megalomaniac siblings with superhuman powers, each of whom has been allotted one aspect of the town's activities to run, or as they say, 'farm'. So, Archer farms electricity, Hathaway farms transport, Torquil education, Dillian the police, and so on. *Archer's Goon* is, amongst many other things, a social satire that uses George Orwell's *Nineteen Eighty-Four* (1949) (the date of Jones's book is not coincidental) to produce a comic dystopia in which local government bureaucracy is the chosen method of oppression.[23]

When I first read *Archer's Goon* I found that several features of the town's geography reminded me of central Bristol. Many of the street names and buildings were familiar, if rather inexactly placed. The family of the protagonist, Howard Sykes, lives on Upper Park Street, and important scenes are played out at the Museum, the Town Hall, and near the Cathedral. Not only that, in the book the local polytechnic is sited nearby, and when Jones wrote *Archer's Goon* there was indeed a campus of Bristol Polytechnic in Unity Street, a road running off Park Street. Other streets mentioned in the novel, such as Corn Street and Union Street, are five minutes' walk away, as is (most tellingly) Zed Alley, down which Howard and his sister Awful are chased by Ginger Hind's gang:

So Awful turned aside and streaked off down Zed Alley, running in long,

5 'The first zig of the alley'.
Photo: Catherine Butler

pounding strides, with her head down and her arms working. Howard waited while her feet went splashing and stamping down the first zig of the alley. As he heard them go faint when she turned into the zag, he turned around, scowling against the rain, to face the boys.[24]

Bristol's Zed Alley, like its namesake in *Archer's Goon*, is shaped like the letter Z, and it appears to be a street name unique to the city (*figure 5*).

There are other Bristol connections, too. Jones reported that one incident in the book, in which the road outside Howard's house is repeatedly dug up by workmen as a form of municipal harassment, was inspired by an occasion when her own terrace in Bristol (fairly inaccessible at the best of times) was entirely surrounded by a trench dug by one of the utility companies, and it was necessary to ask the workmen to lay a plank across the resulting moat in order to leave the house.[25] Howard's father, a polytechnic lecturer called Quentin Sykes, was strongly rumoured to be based on Nick Otty, a lecturer at Bristol Polytechnic. Quentin's exasperated cry to a student – 'I don't want to know what the Structuralists think! I want to know what *you* think!'[26] – may have been a nod to the fact that Otty contributed a hostile structuralist reading of *The Lord of the Rings* to the same volume of essays in which Jones discussed Tolkien's use of Oxfordshire geography, a volume that had appeared just a year before the publication of *Archer's Goon*.

Despite Jones's warning that 'I don't as a rule say: "I will set this book in Bristol city centre"' I was happy with this private association of *Archer's Goon* with Bristol, and found that it enhanced my enjoyment of both book and city. However, on 5 July 2009, in the wake of a discussion at the Diana Wynne Jones conference held at the University of the West of England in Bristol that weekend,[27] Helen Harvey posted an alternative proposition to the Diana Wynne Jones Livejournal community, Homeworld8. Harvey suggested that the city of *Archer's Goon* was actually Oxford, citing numerous circumstantial parallels to justify her opinion. For example:

> The Sykes family live in 'Upper Park Street' (16), which, we later find out, has a corresponding 'Parks Street' (143), paralleling Parks Road/South Parks Road in Oxford.

> 'Corn Street' is Cornmarket Street. At one point, some characters go 'up Corn Street and along High Street' which matches exactly the geography of Oxford's Cornmarket in relation to the High Street.

> The poly is of course Oxford Brookes (a polytechnic at the time).[28]

Harvey's list of such points is lengthy, and while none is individually conclusive her argument is cumulatively quite persuasive. Harvey added that she had written a fan letter to Jones, laying out her theory, and that Jones had replied as follows:

> I found, soon after my marriage, that I had to go back and *live* in Oxford. We were there for the next 20 years. This is undoubtedly why, when I want to write about an anonymous mid-England town, I tend to base it on Oxford (minus colleges). *You are actually the only person to recognise the place.*[29]

Later, I told Jones about Harvey's Oxford post, and my own rival Bristol theory. The author replied diplomatically (but no doubt also truthfully) that both had contributed a part to *Archer's Goon*. And of course, why *not* draw on both? It is possible that one reason Jones habitually refrained from naming places in her books is that it allowed her the flexibility to reconfigure and combine them in ways that were useful to her as a writer, and meaningful to as large a pool of readers as possible. Even so, this example should caution us against relying on such associations too heavily or interpreting them too mechanistically.

Intertopicality

Our rough-and-ready taxonomy has so far yielded a sliding scale of specificity, ranging from locations that are mentioned by name, like the Clifton Suspension Bridge, through ones that are strongly indicated, like Glastonbury Tor, to more nebulous presences such as those of Chysauster, Exmoor and Lyme Regis. We could easily multiply these examples, and no doubt identify other positions on this spectrum in doing so, but we have established at any rate that this is a more complicated question than one of asserting in a binary manner that a given place is, or is not, 'in' the book. We have also seen that, whatever Jones's intentions, the 'game' of perceiving real places in fantasy landscapes (and *vice versa*) can be a significant part of the pleasure of reading her work, as it has been not only for me but also for Helen Harvey, and probably many others besides.

Nevertheless, these places are likely to be experienced in a variety of very different ways. The named locations may or may not be familiar to individual readers. Those readers may or may not have the resources or desire to visit them. They may or may not realise that a real place is being referred to at all. Several of my own clues come from a fannish obsessiveness, private conversations with the author, or the fact of having lived in Bristol for over two decades, all of which are atypical. While knowledge of this sort significantly informs some people's reading experience it is necessarily so variable between individuals that it may seem difficult to say something of general use and validity about it. There is also the danger that too tight a focus on the 'treasure hunt' aspect of locating texts within their landscape may prove reductive, obscuring other possible insights.

Jones had one additional motive for vagueness – or flexibility, if you prefer; namely, the fact that she did not wish her writing to exclude her readers. In an interview, she explained:

> It always seemed to me when I was a child reading books that people were much too prone to talk about little pieces of London that they knew, or

> obscure parts of Kent or Canterbury [...] and I felt terribly left out by this.
> It seemed to me a bad thing to do to children, to express a deep knowledge
> of a place they haven't a chance of going to see.[30]

In her novels Jones is a consistent champion of outsiders. Her protagonists
are frequently neglected or despised individuals who must learn to outgrow
the restrictive templates of understanding and behaviour ordained by those
in authority. She is keenly interested in the subtler mechanisms of oppression,
as they operate within families and elsewhere, and is sensitive to the ways in
which words and knowledge may be used as shibboleths to divide people into
insiders and outsiders. It is not surprising that she wished to avoid such strate-
gies in her own writing. Might familiarity with the places mentioned in fiction
serve this kind of exclusive role, however inadvertently?

There are thus a number of reasons to exercise caution in conferring a
central role in accounts of literary texts on readers' experience of physical
locations. Visiting such places is not an option open to all; knowledge of
them has the potential to be used as a tool of exclusion; and, of course, such
extra-textual encounters have traditionally been regarded as difficult to
integrate with the insights generated by traditional, text-focused forms of
criticism. Here, however, an analogy with intertextuality may be helpful. Many
novels and poems allude to other texts that their readers may or may not have
read, and these allusions inevitably inform the readings of those with the
requisite literary experience, while being opaque to those who lack it. To take
an example from Jones's own work, *Fire and Hemlock* (as mentioned before)
alludes to Eliot's *Four Quartets* (1943), as well as to many other texts, myths
and ballads.[31] Jones did not however see this as a strategy likely to exclude
those readers unfamiliar with Eliot's work. On the contrary, she suggested
that reading *Fire and Hemlock* might establish for such people a mental framework through which Eliot's poem could be better understood at some point
in the future:

> when they come to read *Four Quartets* later, if any of them do, it will chime
> somewhere. I think it's quite important to give children as many pegs to
> hang things on as is possible. This is the way you learn.[32]

Intertextuality is the never-ending conversation that literature has with itself,
and this preparation of the minds of readers for later literary experience is
one of the many functions that children's literature in particular has tradi-

tionally fulfilled. It sinks textual roots into other soils, offering a complex hybridization of experience, both now and in readings to come. Intertextuality also has a social function, and while this may be negative in effect – intertextual references may be used for the purposes of literary intimidation or one-upmanship – in its more benign aspect intertextuality offers readers the pleasure of recognition, and membership of a community with shared touchstones and experiences.

As with literary texts, so it is with the larger text of the world. Rather than intertextuality we might speak of intertopicality, as a way to describe the ways in which physical places, along with their history and associations, are bound to texts and to their readers' understanding of texts. It is of course possible to enjoy and understand *Archer's Goon*, *Fire and Hemlock* or *Deep Secret* without having visited Bristol, but if one is familiar with the city then one's experience of both it and the texts that make use of it will be enhanced – indeed, enchanted; and if one visits later, 'it will chime somewhere'. Intertextuality and intertopicality have in common the shock and pleasure of perceiving a phrase or place within two conflicting frames of reference simultaneously, of attempting to reconcile their differences, and of enjoying one's inability to do so. But intertopicality inevitably foregrounds the physical aspects of the encounter, the sights and sounds, the weather, the feeling of being out of breath from a long climb. These aspects of experience embed themselves differently in memory and in one's body, but are no less part of a reading life. Indeed, reading is always a physical activity as well an intellectual one.

These considerations apply to all fiction, but are perhaps particularly germane in the case of fantasy, because of fantasy's more explicit consideration of enchantment's relationship with the physical world. C. S. Lewis once wrote that a child 'does not despise real woods because he has read of enchanted woods: the reading makes all real woods a little enchanted'.[33] He proved his point by writing *The Lion, the Witch and the Wardrobe* (1950), since the publication of which wardrobes have ceased to be utilitarian pieces of bedroom furniture and have been invested with magical potential, as many thousands of Narnia-seeking children can attest. If wardrobes can be viewed as supernatural portals, it should not be impossible to find Bristolia within Bristol.

Folk long to go on pilgrimage. For some of Chaucer's Canterbury pilgrims, perhaps, the primary attraction of pilgrimage was a few weeks' holiday from pardoning, reeving, or wiving it wealthily in Bath. But others I think saw their journey as a flight not from reality but towards it. Similarly with fantasy fiction: it may look superficially like an escapist form and is frequently dismissed as such, but that is a mistake. One of the values of this kind of reading is that it takes advantage of the fact that stories can never be entirely contained. It offers a channel along which enchantment can wash back into the mundane, overwhelming the dry sea walls of deadened habit. It is thus that fantasy literature, and the work of Diana Wynne Jones in particular, can help us to recognize Bristol as an enchanted city.

Notes

Introduction Literary Bristol

1 Letter from Robert Southey to Joseph Cottle, February-March c.1796, *The Collected Letters of Robert Southey Part 1: 1791-1797* (2009), ed. Lynda Pratt, Romantic Circles, http://www.rc.umd.edu/editions/southey_letters, 4-5, accessed 24 Juy 2014.

2 This appears in Mary Robinson's 'Present State of the Manners, Society, etc. etc. of the Metropolis of England' (1800) and is quoted in Paula Byrne, *Perdita: The Life of Mary Robinson* (London: Harper Perennial, 2005), p.7.

3 Just before publication, Cottle sold the copyright to a London publisher, which led to a new title page being grafted onto the Bristol imprint. From 1800 onwards, Cottle concentrated on book-selling and printing rather than publishing. It is worth noting that the term 'bookseller' was synonymous with that of 'publisher' until the end of the eighteenth century when they became increasing separate roles.

4 See *The Longman Anthology of Gothic Verse*, ed. Caroline Franklin (Harlow: Pearson, 2011), p.300.

5 The word '*zombi*' [sic] first appears in English in 1819 in Robert Southey's *History of Brazil* (1810-9). See Markman Ellis, *The History of Gothic Fiction* (Edinburgh: Edinburgh University Press, 2000), p.212. Bristol was the first city to start the zombie chase game, 'Asylum: 2.8 Hours Later', which is a recreation of the zombie apocalypse and involves being chased around the city by actors made up as zombies.

6 Some of these women will be discussed in a forthcoming volume of this series, on women in Bristol by Madge Dresser.

7 See Madge Dresser, *Slavery Obscured: The Social History of the Slave Trade in Bristol* (Bristol: Redcliffe Press [2001], 2007), p.182.

8 The word was first used in German in 1869 by K. Kertbeny (the pseudonym of Karoly Maria Benkert). Alain Corbin has made the claim that it was first used in French in 1809 in an undocumented source, while the *Oxford English Dictionary* gives 1892 as the earliest printed source in English, which is C. G. Chaddock's translation of Richard von Krafft-Ebing's *Psychopathia Sexualis* (1886).

9 For an account of the Bristol connections of Caroline Oliphant and Lady Nairne, see the *Western Daily Press*, 7 March 1914, p.8. I am indebted to Steve Poole for this reference.

10 See Connie Ann Kirk, *J. K. Rowling: A Biography* (Westport, CT: Greenwood, 2003), pp.13-4.

11 Several web pages draw attention to some of the leading writers associated with Bristol, as in 'Literary Bristol', http://visitbristol.co.uk/about-bristol/all-about-bristol/literary-bristol, accessed 26 October 2014 and Bristol Literary Trail, http://www.walkingbritain.co.uk/walks/walks/walk_b/2214/, accessed 26 October 2014.

12 See *English Romantic Writers and the West Country*, ed. Nicholas Roe (Houndmills: Palgrave Macmillan, 2010) and *From Gothic to Romantic: Thomas Chatterton's Bristol*, ed. Alistair Heys (Bristol: Redcliffe Press, 2005).

13 These are *Richard the Redeless* about the recklessness of King Richard II and the later more satiric *Mum and the Sothsegger*, which refers to Henry IV.

14 As Peter Fleming has pointed out to me, the only surviving manuscript is written in a London dialect and there are no detailed references to Bristol, which might have indicated that it was written by a Bristolian.

15 This draws on research carried out by Melanie Ord for the Mapping Literary Bristol project.

16 Quoted in Kenneth Morgan, *Bristol and the Atlantic Trade in the Eighteenth Century* (Cambridge: Cambridge University Press, 2004), p.33.

17 Philippa Gregory, *A Respectable Trade* (London: Harper [1995], 1996), p.48. For this quotation I am indebted to Mariadele Boccardi, who has been researching Gregory for the Mapping Literary Bristol project. The novel is set in Queen Square where it was filmed for a TV mini-series in 1998. There is a Philippa Gregory walk in the footsteps of characters from the novel

and its TV adaptation.

18 In 1937, the poet John Betjeman declared in an article entitled 'Bristol: An Unspoiled City' that 'Bristol is still the most beautiful big city of England', *Coming Home: Anthology of Prose*, ed. Candida Lycett Green (London: Vintage, 1998), p.85. See the epigraph to this book.

19 See David Hussey, 'Leisure and Commerce: The Hotwell and the Port of Bristol, 1750-1850', *A City Built Upon the Water: Maritime Bristol 1750-1900*, ed. Steve Poole (Bristol: Redcliffe Press, 2013), p.41. The water was also pumped up to the Clifton Grand Spa and Hydropath Institution, now known as the Avon Gorge Hotel. There was also more than one spring hence the plural form of the name Hotwells. By the time of the middle of the eighteenth century, this had been discovered further down the river. See 'The Heyday of Hotwells', Bristol Past, http://www.buildinghistory.org/bristol/hotwells.shtml, accessed 26 October 2014. This other spring was believed to have cured John Wesley, the founder of Methodism, of tuberculosis.

20 William Whitehead, *An Hymn to the Nymph of Bristol Spring* (London: R. Dodsley, 1751), pp.5-6.

21 See *The Oxford Literary Guide to the British Isles*, eds Dorothy Eagle and Hilary Carnell (Oxford: Clarendon Press, 1997) p.37.

22 Frances Burney, *Evelina: or The History of a Young Lady's Entrance into the World*, ed. Edward A. Bloom (Oxford: Oxford University Press, 1970), p.268.

23 Quoted by Hussey, 'Leisure and Commerce', *A City Built Upon the Water*, ed. Poole, p.40.

24 Charles Dickens, *The Pickwick Papers*, ed. James Kinsley (Oxford: Clarendon Press, 1986), p.584.

25 This draws on Amy Firth's research on Edgeworth for the Mapping Literary Bristol project.

26 Maria Edgeworth, 'Angelina; or L'Amie Inconnue', *Moral Tales*, in *Works of Maria Edgeworth*, 13 vols (Boston: Samuel H. Parker, 1825), 9, p.262.

27 Susan Manly, 'Maria Edgworth (1768-1849)', Chawton House Library, http://www.chawton-house.org/wp-content/uploads/2012/06/Maria-Edgeworth.pdf, accessed 31 July 2014.

28 Richard Polwhele, *Poems*, 5 vols (London and Truro: J. Michell and co. for Messrs Rivingtons, 1810), 5, p.5.

29 See *The Oxford Literary Guide to the British Isles*, eds Eagle and Carnell, p.37.

30 The plan was rejected because of cost. In the summer of 1802, William Jessop devised a a scheme for the cut which was agreed and implemented, see Peter Malpass, 'The Bristol Dock Company and the Modernisation of the Port', ed. Poole, *A City Built upon the Water*, pp.122-5.

31 Frances Trollope, *Domestic Manners of the Americans*, ed. Elsie B. Michie (Oxford: Oxford University Press [1832], 2014), p.146.

32 See *Prose by Victorian Women: An Anthology*, ed. Andrea Broomfield and Sally Mitchell (New York: Garland, 1996), p.34.

33 Marguerite Steen wrote a biography of Bristol novelist Mary Robinson called *The Lost One* (1937).

34 Quoted in Barbara Taylor Paul-Emile, 'Samuel Taylor Coleridge as Abolitionist', *ARIEL: A Review of International English Literature*, 5:2 (April 1974), p.64.

35 Quoted in Chine Sonoi, 'Coleridge and the British Slave Trade', *The Coleridge Bulletin*, 27 (Summer 2006), p.32.

36 Quoted in Tim May, 'Coleridge's Slave Trade Lecture: Southey's Contribution and the Debt to Thomas Cooper', *Notes and Queries*, 55: 4 (December 2008), p.425.

37 See ibid., pp.426 and 428. E. H. Coleridge identifies the lecture as having been written partly by Southey and partly by Coleridge. See Robert Southey, *Selected Shorter Poems 1793-1810*, ed. Lynda Pratt, in *Robert Southey: Poetical Works 1793-1810* (gen. ed.), Lynda Pratt, 5 vols (London: Pickering and Chatto, 2004), 5, p.54.

38 Quoted in May, 'Coleridge and the British Slave Trade', p.425.

39 S. T. Coleridge, 'On the Slave Trade', *The Watchman*, ed. Lewis Patton (London: Routledge and Kegan Paul, 1970), p.137.

40 Quoted in Stuart Andrews, 'Coleridge, Bristol and Revolution', *The Coleridge Bulletin*, New Series, 7 (Spring 1996), 2-29.

41 Joseph Cottle, *Early Recollections; Chiefly Relating to the Late Samuel Taylor Coleridge, during his Long*

Residence in Bristol, 2 vols (London: Longman, Rees & Co. and Hamilton, Adams and Co., 1837), 1, p.111.

42 Her sisters, Mary , Betty and Sally More started a school initially in Trinity Street in 1758 before it moved to Park Street. Hannah and her sister Patty were pupils there and later became junior teachers.

43 See Mary Waldron, *Lactilla, Milkwoman of Clifton: The Life and Writings of Ann Yearsley, 1753-1806* (Athens, GA and London: University of Georgia Press, 1996), p.26.

44 'The History of Penguin Books', http://www.penguinfirsteditions.com/index.php?cat=history, accessed 30 July 2014.

45 In 2015, the 150th anniversary of the opening of the Clifton Suspension Bridge was celebrated in Isambard Kingdom Brunel's Passenger Shed with the show, *Walking the Chains*, written by A.C.H. Smith and performed in association with Bristol's Show of Strength Theatre Company and Circomedia.

46 Martin Sampson researched Alyson Hallett's work for the Mapping Literary Bristol project. For two years she was the Visiting Writer at the University of the West England, Bristol and in the spring of 2002 planted flower seeds in the garden at the St Matthias campus, which grew into 'WORD', and wrote poems on the windows of the library.

47 Carter also wrote *The Magic Toyshop* (1967) while she was living in Bristol.

48 This project, started in 2013, was supported by the REACT hub and developed at the Pervasive Media Studio in Bristol.

49 This suggestion was made during his talk, 'Place-Names and History in the Bristol Area', The Regional History Centre seminar series, M Shed, 20 March 2014.

50 See C.F.W. Dening, *Old Inns of Bristol* (Stroud: Tempus [1943], 2005), p.14.

51 See ibid., pp.58-9.

52 I am indebted to Richard Dury for information about the family holiday and for pointing me towards this archival material (HM 204, the Robert Louis Stevenson notebook) and to Gaye M. Richardson, Catalogue Librarian at the Huntington Library, California.

53 This was the initiative of Bristol Cultural Development Partnership.The director of BCDP had encountered a similar project – One Book, One Chicago – while on holiday when the city was involved in a mass reading of Harper Lee's *To Kill a Mocking Bird* (1960).

54 Defoe apparently denied ever having met Selkirk, dismissing him as an illiterate sailor. See Long John Silver Trust, *The Bristol Treasure Island Trail* (Hawkesbury Upton: Black Spot Publishing, 2005), pp.38-9. Stephen H. Gregg is not convinced by this denial or by claims that they ever met, as indicated in an email to Marie Mulvey-Roberts, 'Defoe and Selkirk', 18 June 2014.

55 See Nick Groom, 'The Death of Chatterton', *From Gothic to Romantic*, ed. Heys, p.123-4.

56 This is the title of the first book in this series, *A City Built upon the Water: Maritime Bristol 1750-1900,* ed. Poole.

Chapter One Gothic Bristol: City of Darkness and Light

1 Robert Lovell, 'Bristol: A Satire' (London: Printed for the Author, 1794), lines 35-8.

2 Quoted in Caroline Franklin, 'Monstrous Combinations of Horrors and Mockery'? Southey, Catholicism and the Gothic', *Romanticism*, 17:1 (2011), p.33.

3 The conference, Bristol: Romantic City, was held at Bristol University, 18-22 September 1998.

4 See chapter 7 of this book, Zoe Brennan's 'Angela Carter's "Bristol Trilogy": A Gothic perspective on Bristol's 1960s counterculture'.

5 Angela Carter, *The Infernal Desire Machines of Doctor Hoffman* (Harmondsworth: Penguin [1972], 1987), p.17.

6 Ibid., p.15. The effect of gun-running in Britain by those with a vested interest in slavery extended the American Civil War by two years. Recently the under-water wreck of a Confederate gun-running ship called *Matilda* was discovered in the Bristol Channel.

7 Quoted in Brian L. Harris, *Harris's Guide to Churches and Cathedrals: Discovering the Unique and Unusual in 500 Churches and Cathedrals* (London: Ebury Press, 2006), p.52.

8 Horace Walpole, letter to Horace Mann, 10 January 1750, *The Yale Edition of Horace Walpole's Correspondence*, eds W. S. Lewis *et al*, 48 vols (New Haven: Yale University Press, 1937-83), 20, p.111.

9 Thomas Chatterton, 'To Horace Walpole', *Thomas Chatterton*, ed. Grevel Lindop (Oxford: Carcanet Press, 1972), p.27, lines 8-9 and 14-17.

10 Alistair Heys, 'Visionary and Counterfeit', *From Gothic to Romantic: Thomas Chatterton's Bristol*, ed. Alistair Heys (Bristol: Redcliffe Press, 2005), p.92.

11 See ibid., p.7.

12 Chatterton, 'Chatterton's Last Verses', *Thomas Chatterton*, ed. Lindop, p.94, lines 1-4 and 11-12.

13 I am grateful to Madge Dresser for this information which was included in the final lecture at the Chapel Lecture Theatre at St Matthias on 1 Jun 2014, which she delivered to mark the closing of the campus.

14 Quoted in John Ruskin, *The Stones of Venice* (1851-3), ed. J. G. Links (Cambridge, MA: Da Capo [1960], 2003), p.10. I am indebted to William Greenslade for drawing my attention to the connection between the two dates.

15 Rosemary Hill, *God's Architect: Pugin and the Building of Romantic Britain* (London: Allen Lane, 2007), p. lxxxviii.

16 See Marc Reboul, 'Charles Kingsley: The Rector in the City', *Victorian Writers and the City*, eds Jean Paul Hulin and Pierre Coustillas (Lille: Universite de Lille, 1980), p.50.

17 Ruskin, *The Stones of Venice*, p.166.

18 Mary Robinson, *Perdita: The Memoirs of Mary Robinson*, ed. M. J. Levy (London: Peter Owen [1801], 1994), p.18.

19 Ibid., p.18.

20 Ibid., p.47.

21 Ibid., p.17.

22 Ibid., pp.45-6.

23 Ibid., p.91.

24 Other novels include *Hubert de Severac* (1796) and *The Natural Daughter* (1799).

25 See Paula Byrne, *Perdita: The Life of Mary Robinson* (London: Harper Perennial, 2005), pp.299 and 293.

26 See Stuart Curran, 'Mary Robinson and the New Lyric', special issue on Mary Robinson, ed. Jacqueline Labbe, *Women's Writing*, 9:1 (2002), p.22.

27 The title page states that book is printed by Biggs and Co. Bristol. The abbreviation 'co.' usually denotes a company though in this case it could be referring to Cottle who was Nathaniel Biggs' only business partner at that time.

28 Another example of Robinson's Gothic verse is 'Ode to Despair' (1806). See *The Poetical Works of Mary Robinson*, ed. Caroline Franklin, 3 vols (London and Bristol: Routledge/Thoemmes, 1996), 1, pp. xix and 117.

29 *Mary Robinson: Selected Poems*, ed. Judith Pascoe (Peterborough: Broadview Press, 2000), p.287, lines 531-5.

30 See Mary Robinson [Anne Frances Randall], 'A Letter to the Women of England, on the Injustice of Mental Subordination' (1799), in *The Radicals: Revolutionary Women* in *Perspectives on the History of British Feminism*, 6 vols, ed. Marie Mulvey-Roberts and Tamae Mizuta (London and Bristol: Routledge /Thoemmes, 1994).

31 See *Robinson*, ed. Pascoe, pp.28-9 and 33.

32 Robinson, *Perdita*, p.148.

33 See *Robinson*, ed. Pascoe, p.53.

34 See Abbot E. Smith, *Colonists in Bondage: White Servitude and Convict Labour in America 1607-1776* (Chapel Hill, NC: University of North Carolina Press, 1947), p.209.

35 Robinson, *Perdita*, ed. Levy, pp.91 and 21.

36 See 'Historical Gothic in Varieties of Female Gothic,' 6 vols (London: Pickering and Chatto, 2002), ed. Gary Kelly London: Pickering and Chatto, 2002, 4, pp.xxii-iv.

37 I owe this point to Nick Groom. See *The Broadview Anthology of Literature of the Revolutionary*

Period 1770-1832, ed. D.L. Macdonald and Anne McWhir (Peterborough: Broadview, 2009), p.583.

38 See Diego Saglia, 'Sophia Lee (1750-1824)', *British Women Playwrights around 1800*, 1 December 1999, http://www.etang.umontreal.ca/bwp1800/essays/saglia_queen_lee.html, accessed 6 June 2014.

39 Both sisters were buried in the churchyard of St Andrews on Clifton Hill which was bombed during World War II.

40 This is from Elizabeth Tomlins' novel, *The Victim of Fancy* (1787), quoted in Sophie Lee, *The Recess; or, A Tale of Other Times*, ed. April Alliston (Lexington, KY: The University Press of Kentucky [1783], 2000), p.x.

41 Byrne, *Perdita*, p.298.

42 'Lesley *is* a noble name', Austen had asserted, quoted by Janine Barchas, *Matters of Fact in Jane Austen: History, Location,* and *Celebrity* (Baltimore, MD: Johns Hopkins University Press, 2012), p.16.

43 Quoted in Jane Austen, *Lesley Castle*, ed. Jan Fergus *et al* (Edmonton: Juvenilia Press, 1998), p.ix.

44 See David Nokes, *Jane Austen: A Life* (London: Fourth Estate, 1997), p.104.

45 Austen, *Lesley Castle*, ed. Fergus, p.18. The spelling of Lutterell is inconsistent.

46 Ibid., p.16.

47 That Burke was also the first person to Gothicise India in the Houses of Parliament was pointed out to me by Michael Franklin. Burke gave talks in the Prince Street Assembly Rooms in Bristol, see Bruce Tyldesley, 'The Clifton Spa Pump Room', http://www.thespasdirectory.com/profilego.asp?ref=2841383C, accessed 31 July 2014.

48 Patricia Meyer Spacks, *Novel Beginnings: Experiments in Eighteenth-Century English Fiction* (New Haven: Yale University Press, 2006), p.203.

49 *A Choice of Southey's Verse*, ed. Geoffrey Grigson (London: Faber and Faber, 1970), p.16.

50 See Caroline Franklin, 'Monstrous Combinations of Horrors and Mockery', p.27.

51 See *The Longman Anthology of Gothic Verse*, ed. Caroline Franklin (Harlow: Pearson Education, 2011), p.300.

52 See Franklin, '"Monstrous Combinations of Horrors and Mockery"', pp.25 and 31.

53 Ibid., p.31.

54 The title in some editions is simply 'Cornelius Agrippa'.

55 Matthew Gregory Lewis, *Tales of Wonder*, ed. Douglas H. Thomson (Peterborough: Broadview, [1801], 2010), p.236.

56 For a discussion of the mystery surrounding the withdrawal of the poems, see Lewis, *Tales of Wonder*, ed. Thomson, pp.232-7.

57 See ibid., p.232.

58 Robert Southey, 'Ode to Horror', *Selected Shorter Poems 1793-1810*, ed. Lynda Pratt, *Robert Southey: Poetical Works 1793-1810* (gen. ed.), Lynda Pratt, 5 vols (London: Pickering and Chatto, 2004), 5, p.102, lines 1-6.

59 Ibid., p.104, lines 66-72.

60 Franklin, 'Monstrous Combinations of Horrors and Mockery', p.25.

61 Robert Southey, 'The Sailor who had served in the Slave Trade', *Shorter Poems*, ed. Pratt, p.291, lines 73-84.

62 Robinson attended the school at 43 Park Street, half way up the hill, run by Hannah More's sisters. In a letter of 14 July 1786 published in the *Morning Post*, she claimed that she had been taught by More herself. See *Robinson*, ed. Pascoe, p.23.

63 Ann Yearsley, 'A Poem on the Inhumanity of the Slave-Trade', *Poetry and Letters*, in *The Collected Works of Ann Yearsley*, ed. Kerri Andrews, 3 vols (London: Pickering and Chatto, 2014), 1, p.109, lines 1-3.

64 See Byrne, *Perdita*, p.7.

65 Quoted in Madge Dresser, *Slavery Obscured: The Social History of the Slave Trade in Bristol* (Bristol: Redcliffe Press [2001], 2007), p.96.

66 Robert Southey, *Letters from England by Don Manuel Alvarez Espriella*, 2nd edition, 3 vols (London: Longman, Hurst, Rees and Orme, 1808), 3, p.343. The latter quotation refers to the removal of rocks from the side of the River Avon presumably for building which, according to Southey,

was destroying the natural beauty of the scenery.

67 Quoted in Dresser, *Slavery Obscured* , p.96. The original is in italics.

68 Quoted in Byrne, *Perdita*, p.7.

69 Lovell, 'Bristol: A Satire', lines 9-12.

70 Southey, *Letters from England*, 3, p.333. This travelogue was read by Mary Shelley in 1815.

71 During the eighteenth century, the Bristol medicinal waters became 'a hotbed of quackery' which was promoted as a cure for tuberculosis. See Roy Porter, *Doctor of Society: Thomas Beddoes and the Sick Trade in Late-Enlightenment England* (London: Routledge, 1992) p.133.

72 Ibid., p.132.

73 Southey, *Letters from England*, 3, pp.343-5.

74 Southey, 'The Old Woman of Berkeley', Lewis, *Tales of Wonder*, ed. Thomson, p.164, lines 29-40.

75 Southey, 'The Cross Roads', *Selected Shorter Poems*, ed. Pratt, 5, p.288, lines 41-5. During his early years, Southey spent time at the house of his maternal grandfather, Edward Hill, in Bedminster.

76 Quoted by Diane Long Hoeveler, 'Victorian Gothic Drama', *The Victorian Gothic: An Edinburgh Companion*, eds Andrew Smith and William Hughes (Edinburgh: Edinburgh University Press, 2012), p.68.

77 Quoted in David Stafford, *The Silent Game: The Real World Of Imaginary Spies* (Toronto: Lester and Orpen Dennys, 1988), p.115.

78 See William Vivian Butler, *The Durable Desperadoes* (London: Macmillan, 1973), p.181.

79 Sydney Horler, *The Vampire* (New York: Bookfinger [1935], 1974), p.v.

80 Ibid., p.142.

81 Ibid., p.284.

82 Sydney Horler, 'The Vampire: Ten Minutes of Horror' in *The Screaming Skull and other Stories* (London: Hodder and Stoughton, 1930), pp.143-4.

83 Interiors were filmed at the Paint Works on Bath Road, Bristol.

84 It appears that she left Torquay with Shelley at the end of June 1815 and stayed in Bristol during the period of his absence. A small red journal from May 1815 to June 1816, which is now missing, covered the period of Mary's visit to Bristol and the genesis of *Frankenstein*.

85 Victor Frankenstein and Shelley shared an interest in science and magic and there is certainly common ground to be found between the Romantic scientist and the Romantic poet.

86 *The Letters of Mary Wollstonecraft Shelley*, ed. Betty T. Bennett, 3 vols (Baltimore: Johns Hopkins University Press, 1980), 1: *'A part of the elect'*, p.15.

87 See Daisy Hay, *Young Romantics: The Shelleys, Byron and Other Tangled Lives* (London: Bloomsbury, 2010), p.308.

88 See Janet Todd, *Death and the Maidens: Fanny Wollstonecraft and the Shelley Circle* (London: Profile Books, 2007), p.167.

89 Janet Todd suggests that the reason for Claire's departure to Lynmouth, which had been financed by Shelley and included the period when Mary was in Clifton, might have been to conceal a pregnancy. See ibid, p.167. There were also rumours that Claire gave birth to Shelley's child in Naples on 27 December 1818. She was in the city at that time and reported to be ill. Shelley registered the birth of a child named Elena Adelaide Shelley for that date with the Neapolitan authorities.

90 This is recorded in Claire Clairmont's journal and is quoted by Deirdre Coleman, 'Claire Clairmont and Mary Shelley: Identification and Rivalry within the "tribe of the Otaheite philosophers"', *Women's Writing*, special issue on Mary Shelley, ed. Marie Mulvey-Roberts and Janet Todd, 6:3 (1999), p.312.

91 See Hay, *Young Romantics* p.308.

92 *The Letters of Mary Wollstonecraft Shelley*, ed. Bennett, 1, p.15. Clara Mary Jane Clairmont, more commonly known as Claire, was called Clary at this time.

93 Piozzi died at 10 Sion Row, Clifton in 1821.

94 Mary Shelley, *Frankenstein or The Modern Prometheus*, ed. Maurice Hindle (London: Penguin [1818], 2007), p.79.

95 See Todd, *Death and the Maidens*, p.229.

96 See Dorian Gerhold, *Bristol's Stage Coaches* (Salisbury: The Hobnob Press, 2012), pp.92-3.

97 See Todd, *Death and the Maidens*, p.229 and plate 18.

98 Quoted in ibid., p.229.

99 Ibid., p.229.

100 See Byrne, *Perdita*, p.286.

101 Quoted in Todd, *Death and the Maidens*, p.229.

102 Quoted in ibid, p.254.

103 Quoted in ibid., p.xi.

104 Quoted in ibid., p.234.

105 Quoted in ibid., p.239.

106 Quoted in ibid., pp.238-9.

107 Quoted in ibid., p.3.

108 Quoted in Emily W. Sunstein, *Mary Shelley: Romance and Reality* (Baltimore, MD: Johns Hopkins University Press, 1989) p.127.

109 In 1815 Mary Shelley read Matthew Lewis's book *Tales of Wonder*, which contains a substantial number of Southey's poems including 'Cornelius Agrippa's Bloody Book'. It was first published anonymously in Bristol in the *Annual Anthology* and Douglass H. Thomson has suggested that it might have influenced Mary Shelley's short story 'The Mortal Immortal' (1833), see Lewis, *Tales of Wonder*, ed. Thomson, p.185.

110 See Mary Shelley, *Frankenstein or The Modern Prometheus The 1818 Edition*, ed. Marilyn Butler, (Oxford: Oxford University Press, 1994), pp.xxviii-ix.

111 See E.J. Clery, *Women's Gothic: From Clara Reeve to Mary Shelley* (Tavistock: Northcote House, 2004), p.47.

112 See Miranda Seymour, *Mary Shelley* (London: Picador, 2001), pp.138-9. Seymour notes that slaves were still working in some private houses in Britain as late as 1843, despite the Emancipation Act of 1833

113 I owe this point to Madge Dresser.

114 Quoted in Chris Baldick, *In Frankenstein's Shadow: Myth, Monstrosity, and Nineteenth-century Writing* (Oxford: Clarendon Press, 1987), p.60.

115 Mary Shelley, letter to Teresa Guiccioli, 20 August, 1827, *The Letters of Mary Wollstonecraft Shelley*, ed. Bennett, 1, p.417. Translated by Ricki Herzfeld for Betty Bennett.

116 For a fuller discussion, see chapter 2 in Marie Mulvey-Roberts, *Dangerous Bodies: Historicising the Gothic Corporeal* (Manchester: Manchester University Press, 2016).

117 Shelley, *Frankenstein*, ed. Hindle, p.55

118 Strictly speaking this is not a folly, which is purely ornamental, since it is habitable.

119 See Dresser, *Slavery Obscured*, p.114.

120 Henry Jones, *Clifton: A Poem in Two Cantos* (Bristol: E. Farley and Co., 1767), http://ota.ox.ac.uk/text/3611.html, accessed 1 July 2014.

121 See Dresser, *Slavery Obscured*, pp.114-5 and 126 for archival sources.

122 See Thomas Keymer, '*Northanger Abbey* and *Sense and Sensibility*', *The Cambridge Companion to Jane Austen*, 2nd edition, ed. Edward Copeland and Julia McMaster (Cambridge: Cambridge University Press, 2011), p.30.

123 He also built Beckford's Tower, situated just outside Bath.

124 Thomas Hardy, *Jude the Obscure*, ed. Dennis Taylor (London: Penguin [1895], 1998), p.136.

125 See John Ruskin, 'Mr. Ruskin's Influence: A Defence', *The Complete Works of John Ruskin*, eds E.T. Cook and Alexander Wedderburn, 39 vols (London: George Allen, 1903-12), 10, p.459.

126 Horace Walpole, *Anecdotes of Painting in England* (Twickenham: Thomas Farmer at Strawberry Hill, 1762), p.108.

127 One of the contributors to this book, Catherine Butler, writes novels with a Gothic inflection for young people.

Chapter Two Bristol's Romantic Poets: Robert Southey and Samuel Taylor Coleridge

1   Robert Southey to Grosvenor Bedford, 12 June 1794, in Lynda Pratt, Tim Fulford, and Ian Packer (gen. eds), *The Collected Letters of Robert Southey* (henceforth *CLRS*), Romantic Circles Electronic Edition, Letter 94; S.T. Coleridge to Robert Southey, 6 July 1794, in.*The Collected Letters of Samuel Taylor Coleridge*, ed. E.L. Griggs, 6 vols (Oxford: Clarendon Press, 1956-71; henceforth *CLSTC*), 1, pp.83-4.

2   Southey to Grosvenor Bedford, c.1 October 1795, *CLRS*, Letter 135; *CLSTC*, 1, p.171.

3   S.T. Coleridge, *Poetical Works*, ed. J.C.C. Mays, in Kathleen Coburn and Bart Winer (gen. eds), *The Collected Works of Samuel Taylor Coleridge*, 16, Bollingen Series 75, 3 vols in 6 parts (Princeton: Princeton University Press, 2001), 1.1, pp.261-2, lines 9-17. This text of 'Reflections' is that of Coleridge's *Poems* (1797). Subsequent line references will be included parenthetically in the text.

4   This was how Joseph Cottle, Coleridge's publisher, described the location of the poet's cottage in *Reminiscences of Samuel Taylor Coleridge and Robert Southey* (1847; repr. Highgate: Lime Tree Bower Press, 1970), p.41. For this reason it seems unlikely that the house in Old Church Road in the town centre, long identified as Coleridge's, actually has anything to do with him.

5   It is customary to state that the faint city-spires belong to Bristol: see, for example, Berta Lawrence, *Coleridge and Wordsworth in Somerset* (Newton Abbot: David & Charles, 1970), p.76. Lawrence claims that the 'Mount' in question is Dial Hill. However, it was and is impossible to see Bristol from any of the hills mentioned above; if Coleridge saw a Bristol city-spire, it was in his mind's eye.

6   Cottle, *Reminiscences*, pp.64-5.

7   Tom Mayberry, *Coleridge & Wordsworth in the West Country* (Stroud: Alan Sutton, 1992), p.57.

8   Richard Warner, *Excursions from Bath* (Bath: R. Cruttwell, 1801), p.277.

9   Robert Lovell, *Bristol: A Satire* (London: Printed for the Author, 1794), lines 50 and 114. Subsequent line references are incorporated parenthetically in the text.

10 J.C. Ibbetson, *A Picturesque Guide to Bath, Bristol, Hot-wells, the River Avon, and the Adjacent Country; Illustrated with a Set of Views, Taken in the Summer of 1792* (London: Hookham and Carpenter, 1793), p.157.

11 John Evans, *The Picture of Bristol; or a Guide to Objects of Curiosity and Interest, in Bristol, Clifton, the Hotwells, and their Vicinity, including Biographical Notices of Eminent Natives* (Bristol: W. Sheppard, 1814), pp.103-4.

12 Joseph Cottle, *Early Recollections; Chiefly Relating to the Late Samuel Taylor Coleridge, during his Long Residence in Bristol*, 2 vols (London: Longman, Rees & Co. and Hamilton, Adams & Co., 1837), 1, pp.ix-x.

13 See Catharine Edwards, 'The Roads to Rome', *Imagining Rome: British Artists and Rome in the Nineteenth Century* ed. Michael Liversidge and Catharine Edwards (London: Merrell Holberton, 1996), pp.8-19.

14 Richard Cronin, 'Joseph Cottle and West Country Romanticism', *English Romantic Writers and the West Country*, ed. Nicholas Roe (Basingstoke: Palgrave Macmillan, 2010), pp.67 and 71.

15 Peter Kitson, 'Coleridge's Bristol and West Country Radicalism', *English Romantic Writers and the West Country*, ed. Roe, p.115.

16 *CLSTC*, 1, p.152.

17 Coleridge, *Poetical Works*, 1.1, pp.203-4, lines 1-16. The unusual spelling ('brouze') and grammatical solecisms ('it's') here are Coleridge's.

18 E. Shiercliff, *The Bristol and Hotwell Guide* (Bristol: Printed for the Author, 1789), p.78.

19 Evans, *Picture of Bristol*, p.137.

20 Coleridge, *Poetical Works*, 1.1, p.143, lines 92, 103 and 98. May's detailed account of this poem's complex textual history makes clear that these lines date from September-October 1794.

21 David Simpson, 'Locating Southey', *Eighteenth-Century Studies*, 41:4 (2008), p.566.

22 Mark Storey, *Robert Southey: A Life* (Oxford: Oxford University Press, 1997), p.129.

23 Southey to Thomas Southey, 8 September 1803, *CLRS*, Letter 837.

24 Bodleian Libraries, University of Oxford, MS. Eng. Poet. e.10.

25 Although a monument to Chatterton's memory was proposed in 1792, it was not until 1839 that a statue of the poet was finally erected on a tall column outside St Mary Redcliffe. This monument, subsequently moved to a different part of the churchyard, suffered severe weather damage over time and was eventually demolished in 1967. A new statue of a seated Chatterton was installed in Millennium Square in 2000. See Douglas Merritt and Francis W. Greenacre with Katharine Eustace, *Public Sculpture of Bristol* (Liverpool: Liverpool University Press, 2011), pp.151-2.

26 *Poems by Robert Southey. Second Edition* (Bristol: Joseph Cottle, and London: Robinsons, 1797; hereafter *Poems* (1797)), p.124, lines 7 and 14, and p.126, line 4.

27 Southey to Thomas Southey, 2-3 February 1800, *CLRS*, Letter 484; *The Annual Anthology*, 2 vols (Bristol and London: Longman and Rees, 1800), 2, p.157, lines 2, 4, 6, 10 and 14. This sonnet first appeared on 26 August 1799 in *The Morning Post*, where Porlock was renamed 'Mornock', but was revised for publication in the *Annual Anthology*.

28 *Poems* (1797), pp.133-4, lines 1-20.

29 *Southey's Common-Place Book*, ed. J.W. Warter, 4 vols (London: Longman, Brown, Green, and Longman, 1849-50), 4, pp.195-6.

30 This name was current in the early nineteenth century, as was the alternative 'Ghyston Cave'. Sometimes the cave is simply referred to as the site of a former chapel dedicated to St Vincent.

31 I am grateful to Karen MacDonald, who helped coordinate the exhibition, 'Turner: Water-colours from the West', at Bristol Museum and Art Gallery in May-July 2014, for information on the location of Turner's cave.

32 Geoffrey Hartman, 'Wordsworth, Inscriptions, and Romantic Nature Poetry', in *Beyond Formalism: Literary Essays 1958-1970* (New Haven: Yale University Press, 1970), pp.207-8 and 211-2.

33 Hartman, 'Wordsworth, Inscriptions', p.208.

34 Dean MacCannell, *The Tourist: A New Theory of the Leisure Class* (New York: Schocken, 1976), pp.41-2.

35 *Poems* (1797), pp.135-6, lines 8-16. Subsequent line references are included parenthetically in the text.

36 Nicholas Roe, *The Politics of Nature: William Wordsworth and Some Contemporaries* (Basingstoke: Macmillan, 1992), p.132.

37 *The Morning Post*, 12 October 1798, lines 1-2. Subsequent line references are incorporated parenthetically in the text.

38 Lynda Pratt, 'Southey's West Country', *English Romantic Writers and the West Country*, ed. Roe, p.209. I am greatly indebted to Pratt's fine essay in my exploration of Southey's dealings with Bristol and its environs.

39 *Southey's Common-Place Book*, ed. Warter, 4, p.193.

40 Malcolm Andrews, 'The Metropolitan Picturesque', *The Politics of the Picturesque: Literature, Landscape and Aesthetics since 1770*, eds Stephen Copley and Peter Garside (Cambridge: Cambridge University Press, 1994), pp.283-5.

41 Ibbetson, *Picturesque Guide*, p.184.

42 G.W. Manby, *Fugitive Sketches of the History and Natural Beauties of Clifton, Hotwells, and Vicinity* (Bristol: Norton & Son, 1802), pp.32, 36-7.

43 R. Southey, *Letters from England* (1807), ed. J. Simmons (London: Cresset Press, 1951), pp.479-80.

44 D. Huston, *The New Clifton and Bristol Guide. Being a Series of Poetical Epistles Written by Simkin Blunderhead* [. . .] *to his Distant Friends* (Bristol: Printed by the Author, 1826), p.9.

45 Southey to Grosvenor Bedford, 25 September-14 October 1796, *CLRS*, Letter 178.

46 Southey to Thomas Davis Lamb, c.31 July 1792, *CLRS*, Letter 20.

47 See *Edinburgh Review*, 1:1 (1802), pp.77-8.

Chapter Three In Her Place: Ann Yearsley or 'The Bristol Milkwoman'

1 Ann Yearsley, 'Lines Addressed to the Revd Mr Leeves on his Visiting Stella to Cowslip Green', 'Poetry and Letters in The Collected Works of Ann Yearsley', ed. Kerri Andrews, 3 vols (London: Pickering and Chatto, 2014), 1, p.1, lines 1-8.

2 See Anne Stott, *Hannah More: the First Victorian* (Oxford: Oxford University Press, 2003), p.70.

3 Yearsley, 'Lines Addressed to the Revd Mr Leeves on his Visiting Stella to Cowslip Green', p.2, lines 43-55.

4 Ibid., lines 38-9.

5 Mina Gorji, *John Clare and the Place of Poetry* (Liverpool: Liverpool University Press, 2008), p.15.

6 Bridget Keegan, *British Labouring-Class Nature Poetry, 1730-1837* (Basingstoke and New York: Palgrave Macmillan, 2008), p.2.

7 It should be mentioned here that there has been considerable controversy around Yearsley's societal place. Her biographer Mary Waldron resists the notion that she should be seen as a member of the labouring-class on the grounds that she ran a milk-selling business, thus making her a tradeswoman who had married into the yeomanry. Representations of Yearsley by Hannah More as 'poor' and 'humble' served the purpose of making Yearsley a suitable subject for the benevolence of the subscribers More was amassing, but are not necessarily indicative of Yearsley's real class status. Matters are further complicated, however, by Yearsley's use, after the failure of her relationship with More, of the sobriquet 'Milkwoman of Clifton' or 'Milkwoman of Bristol', descriptions of her first used by More. In short, Yearsley's class status, her own attitudes to that status, and contemporary and recent responses to that status, are extremely vexed.

8 Keegan, *British Labouring-Class Nature Poetry*, p.69.

9 Ibid., pp.65-6.

10 Sir John Denham, *Cooper's Hill* (London: Humphrey Moseley, 1655), pp.1-2.

11 John Dyer, 'Grongar Hill', *Poems* (London: R. and J. Dodsley, 1761), p.11.

12 Alexander Pope, *Windsor-Forest* (London: Bernard Lintot, 1720), p.20.

13 John Barrell, *The Idea of Landscape and the Sense of Place 1730-1840: An Approach to the Poetry of John Clare* (Cambridge: Cambridge University Press, 1972), p.22.

14 Ibid., p.22.

15 Ibid., p.6.

16 Ibid., p.7.

17 Yearsley, 'Clifton Hill', *The Collected Works of Ann Yearsley*, ed. Andrews, 1, p.37, lines 11-26.

18 Tim Fulford, *Landscape, Liberty and Authority: Poetry, Criticism and Politics from Thomson to Wordsworth* (Cambridge and New York: Cambridge University Press, 1996), p.3.

19 Keegan, *British Labouring-Class Nature Poetry*, p.67.

20 Yearsley, 'Clifton Hill', pp.37-8, lines 45-52.

21 Fulford, *Landscape, Liberty and Authority*, p.3.

22 Denham, 'Cooper's Hill', p.2.

23 Dyer, 'Grongar Hill', p.10.

24 James Thomson, *Winter: a Poem* (London: J. Millan, 1726), p.34.

25 Yearsley, 'Clifton Hill', p.39, lines 100-9.

26 Denham, 'Cooper's Hill', p.12.

27 My thanks to my colleague Erica Fudge for sharing with me her expertise on animal literature.

28 Keegan, *British Labouring-Class Nature Poetry*, p.67.

29 Yearsley, 'Clifton Hill', pp.40-1, lines 166-178.

30 Pope, *Windsor-Forest*, p.7.

31 Yearsley, 'Clifton Hill', p.40, lines 156-65.

32 Ibid., p.41, line 181.

33 Yearsley, 'Clifton Hill', p.40, lines 146-55.

34 Dyer, 'Grongar Hill', pp.13-4.

35 Donna Landry, *The Muses of Resistance: Labouring Class Women's Poetry in Britain, 1739-1796* (Cambridge: Cambridge University Press, 1990), p.131.

36 Keegan, *British Labouring-Class Nature Poetry*, p.65.

37 Frontispiece to *Poems on Various Subjects* (London: G.G.J. and J. Robinson, 1787).

38 Mary Waldron, *Lactilla, Milkwoman of Clifton: The Life and Writings of Ann Yearsley, 1753-1806* (Athens, GA: Georgia University Press, 1996), p.113.

39 Ann Yearsley, 'A Poem on the Inhumanity of the Slave Trade. Humbly Inscribed to the Right Honourable and Right Reverend Frederick, Earl of Bristol, Bishop of Derry &c.', in *The Collected Works of Ann Yearsley*, ed. Andrews, 1, p.109.

40 Yearsley, *A Poem on the Inhumanity of the Slave Trade*, pp.109-10, lines 1-17.

41 See 'Stanzas, Written by Mrs. Yearsley, on her Leaving London', *The Collected Works of Ann Yearsley*, 1, pp.102-5. The poem was first published in August 1787 in the *European Magazine*.

42 Ann Yearsley, 'To the Bristol Marine Society', *The Collected Works of Ann Yearsley*, 1, p.55, lines 10-7.

43 Yearsley, 'To the Bristol Marine Society', p.57, lines 91-3.

44 Ibid., pp.57-8, lines 108-17.

45 *Felix Farley's Bristol Journal*, 5 October 1793.

46 Ibid.

47 Mark Harrison, *Crowds and History: Mass Phenomena in English Towns, 1790–1835* (Cambridge: Cambridge University Press, 1988), p.281.

48 Ann Yearsley, 'Advertisement' to "Bristol Elegy"', *The Collected Works of Ann Yearsley*, ed. Andrews, 1, p.225.

49 Waldron, *Lactilla, Milkwoman of Clifton*, p.263.

50 Ibid., p.263.

51 Yearsley, 'Bristol Elegy', p.225, lines 1-16.

52 'Elegy', *Oxford English Dictionary* Online. December 2013. Oxford University Press. http://www.oed.com/view/Entry/60350?redirectedFrom=elegy, accessed February 24, 2014.

53 Yearsley, *A Poem on the Inhumanity of the Slave Trade*, p.120, lines 424-5.

Chapter Four John Gregory, St Mary Redcliffe and the Memorialising of Thomas Chatterton

1 E.H.W. Meyerstein, *A Life of Thomas Chatterton* (London: Ingpen and Grant, 1930), p.31.

2 Ibid. For a fuller list of literary responses, see my 'Rowley's Ghost: A Checklist of Creative Works Inspired by Thomas Chatterton's Life and Writings', *Thomas Chatterton and Romantic Culture*, ed. Nick Groom (Basingstoke: Macmillan, 1999), pp.262-92.

3 David Fairer, *Organising Poetry: The Coleridge Circle, 1790-1798* (Oxford: Oxford University Press, 2009), p.139.

4 Nick Groom, *The Forger's Shadow: How Forgery Changed the Course of Literature* (London: Picador, 2002) and '"With certain grand Cottleisms": Joseph Cottle, Robert Southey and the 1803 *Works of Thomas Chatterton*', *Romanticism*, 15: 3 (2009), 225-38; Maria Grazia Lolla, '"Truth Sacrifising [sic] to the Muses": The Rowley Controversy and the Genesis of the Romantic Chatterton' and David Fairer, 'Chatterton's Poetic Afterlife, 1770-1794: A Context for Coleridge's *Monody*' both in *Thomas Chatterton and Romantic Culture*, ed. Groom, pp.151-71 and 228-52; Daniel Cook, *Thomas Chatterton and Neglected Genius, 1760-1830* (Basingstoke: Palgrave Macmillan, 2013).

5 S.T. Coleridge, 'Monody on the Death of Chatterton', *The Oxford Authors: Samuel Taylor Coleridge*, ed. H.J. Jackson (Oxford: Oxford University Press, 1985), p.5, line 155, William Wordsworth, 'French Revolution', *Poetical Works*, ed. Thomas Hutchinson, rev. Ernest de Selincourt (Oxford: Oxford University Press, 1978), p.165, line 5.

6 On 'forgery' see Nick Groom, 'Forgery or Plagiarism? Unravelling Chatterton's Rowley', *Angelaki*, 1:2 (Winter 1993/94), pp.41-54, 'Thomas Chatterton Was a Forger', *Yearbook of English Studies*, 28 (1998), pp.276-91, and *The Forger's Shadow*, esp. pp.67-102 and 140-80; Ivan Phillips, 'A Clash of Harmony: Forgery as Politics in the Work of Thomas Chatterton', *Critical Survey*, 24: 3 (2012), pp.23-47. On 'suicide' see Richard Holmes, 'Thomas Chatterton: The Case Re-opened', *Cornhill Magazine*, 178 (1970), pp.201-51; Nick Groom, 'The Death of Chatterton', in *From Gothic to Romantic: Thomas Chatterton's Bristol*, ed. Alistair Heys (Bristol: Redcliffe Press, 2005), pp.116-25.

7 Principal sources consulted on John Gregory are his five main published volumes, plus the John Gregory Papers, Special Collections Department, Bristol University Library, ref. DM1741; an album of memorabilia, Local Studies Department, Bristol Public Library, ref. 21416; the papers of Gregory's friend and fellow shoemaker-poet John Wall, Bristol Record Office, ref. 37886;

W.H. Kearley Wright, *West Country Poets: Their Lives and Works* (London: Elliot Stock, 1896), pp.211-14; *A Souvenir of John Gregory*, ed. Gerrard Sables (Bristol: Fiducia Press, 2007); Iain Rowley, 'Gregory, John (1831-1922)', in *Labouring-class Poets Online*, ed. John Goodridge, http://laboringclasspoetsonline.omeka.net/. Accessed 15 February 2014. Other specialist sources are cited below.

8   Laycock sold 14,000 copies of his sheet poems; see his *Selected Poems*, ed. Glyn Hughes (Sunderland: Ceolfrith Press, 1981), p.13.

9   John Davis, *The Life of Thomas Chatterton* (London: Thomas Tegg, 1806), pp.10-11.

10   Ibid., pp.33-4.

11   *Song Streams* (Bristol: published by the author, 1877), pp.108-10; lines are here numbered as a single poem.

12   Groom notes in passing that the church's north porch 'harbours the remains of a shrine, once favoured by pilgrims and especially sailors', *The Forger's Shadow*, p.6.

13   *The Complete Works of Thomas Chatterton, A Bicentenary Edition*, ed. Donald S. Taylor in association with Benjamin B. Hoover (Oxford: Clarendon Press, 1971), 1, pp.644-6.

14   Gregory uses the term elsewhere, for example in his poem 'Grandfather Hoare, the Good Shoemaker' ('pilgrims, worn and wan', *Idyls of Labour*, p.118).

15   Michael Quinton Smith, *St Mary Redcliffe: An Architectural History* (Bristol: Redcliffe Press, 1995), p.30.

16   Groom, '"Al under the Wyllowe tree": Chatterton and the Ecology of the West Country', in *English Romantic Writers and the West Country*, ed. Nicholas Roe (Basingstoke: Palgrave Macmillan, 2010), p.37.

17   'Concerning Chatterton', *Bristol Observer*, 25 January 1908, also separately printed.

18   See also 'Love Sowing', which begins, 'We call this world a vale of tears', Gregory, *Murmurs and Melodies* (Bristol: J. W. Arrowsmith; London: Simpkin, Marshall & Co, [1884]), p.93.

19   'On oure Ladies Churche', *Complete Works*, 1, p.53. In 'The Storie of Wyllyam Canynge' Rowley apostrophises the church as 'Oh Worke of hande of Heav'n / Whare Canynge sheweth as an Instrumente', *Complete Works*, 1, p.247.

20   Gregory begins the poem 'A Joy of the Spring Time' with 'See! to this temple which we call our world', Gregory, *Murmurs and Melodies*, p.110.

21   Thanks to Rory Waterman for this observation.

22   Simon Schama, *Landscape and Memory* (London: HarperCollins, 1995), pp.228-32; Smith, *St Mary Redcliffe*, p.68.

23   He also liked to climb 'the towers of the church', see Meyerstein, *A Life of Thomas Chatterton*, p.26.

24   Nick Groom, *The Gothic: A Very Short Introduction* (Oxford: Oxford University Press, 2012), p.21.

25   Smith, *St Mary Redcliffe*, p.149; Smith describes the 'reassembling of ancient glass' in one of the transept windows.

26   Michael Liversedge, 'Romantic Redcliffe: Image and Imagination', in Heys, *From Gothic to Romantic*, p.53.

27   Gregory, 'God is a Spirit', *Murmurs and Melodies*, pp.19-20.

28   Joseph Skipsey, *Selected Poems*, ed. Chris Harrison, William Daniel McCumiskey and R.K.R. Thornton, second edition (Newcastle upon Tyne: Rectory Press, 2014), p.15.

29   George Hare Leonard, *Some Memories of John Gregory* (Bristol: *Bristol Times and Mirror*, 1922), p.7.

30   Ibid., pp.7-8.

31   Smith, *St Mary Redcliffe*, p.151.

32   Gregory, *Murmurs and Melodies*, p.203.

33   Unidentified press cutting, cropped above the byline 'By J. Gregory', dated 14 November 1884; Gregory Papers (DM1471), Bristol University Library, Special Collections.

34   'Saint Crispin's Bell', lines 1-9, Gregory, *Murmurs and Melodies*, p.64. St Crispin is the patron saint of shoemakers.

35   Sally Mullen, 'The Bristol Socialist Society, and John Wall the Shoemaker Poet (1885-1914)', in *Bristol's Other History*, ed. Ian Bild (Bristol: Bristol Broadsides, 1983), p.42. On music in the

socialist movement see Chris Waters, *British Socialists and the Politics of Popular Culture, 1884-1914* (Manchester: Manchester University Press, 1990), pp.97-130.

36 There are two postcard photographs of the Sunday Schools in the John Wall Collection, Bristol Record Office, ref. 37886/1/5 (figure 3).

37 Following 'Sonnets on Chatterton's Church' in *Song Streams* is another poem about a beloved 'Mary', one of several Gregory poems about lost children, 'How Mary died', p.110.

38 Gerrard Sables, 'John Gregory, William Morris, and the Bristol Socialist Society', *William Morris Society in the United States Newsletter* (January 2010), pp.7-8.

39 Al Alvarez, *The Savage God: A Study in Suicide* (New York: Random House, 1972), p.198. The fuller context for the expression is '[T]he boy's only patrimony was a pile of old parchments his father had taken from the Muniment Room of the church, where they had been left scattered on the floor.'

40 Groom, 'The Death of Chatterton', pp.118-20.

41 'A Cloud with a Door in It', lines 18-23, Gregory, *Murmurs and Melodies*, p.7.

42 Louise J. Kaplan, *The Family Romance of the Imposter Poet Thomas Chatterton* (New York: Atheneum, 1988), pp.30-2 and 263-4; Groom, *The Forger's Shadow*, pp.6-7.

43 Meyerstein, *A Life of Thomas Chatterton*, pp.443-5; Groom, *The Forger's Shadow*, pp.4-5.

44 Groom, *The Forger's Shadow*, p.155 and 'Love and Madness: Southey Editing Chatterton', *Robert Southey and the Contexts of English Romanticism*, ed. Lynda Pratt (Aldershot: Ashgate, 2006), pp.19-35.

45 *St Mary Redcliffe Bristol* (London: Pitkin Pictorials, 1971), p.3.

46 Groom, *The Forger's Shadow*, p.7.

47 Quoted by Smith, *St Mary Redcliffe*, p.160.

48 See the stories in the *Bristol Post* for 30 August 2011 and 6 January 2014, http://www.bristol-post.co.uk. For a sense of how some young Bristolians feel about the poet's house see http://ursulawrites.blogspot.co.uk/2011/07/few-days-ago-im-walking-into-town-to-go.html. Accessed 5 March 2014.

49 S. B[ale], Obituary of John Gregory in *Justice* (June 1922), press cutting in Bristol Central Library, ref. 21416.

50 See Julie Crane, '"Wandering between Two Worlds": The Victorian Afterlife of Thomas Chatterton', *Romantic Echoes in the Victorian Era*, ed. Andrew Radford and Mark Sandy (Aldershot: Ashgate, 2008), pp.27-37.

Chapter Five E.H. Young, Popular Novelist and the Literary Geography of Bristol

1 Andreas Huyssen, 'Geographies of Modernism in a Globalizing World', *Geographies of Modernism: Literatures, Cultures, Spaces*, eds Peter Brooker and Andrew Thacker (London and New York: Routledge), p.7.

2 E.H. Young, *Jenny Wren* (London: Virago [1932], 1985), p.5.

3 The phrase 'literary geography', coined by Franco Moretti in *An Atlas of the European Novel* (London: Verso, 1998), p.8, is cited by Andrew Thacker, *Moving through Modernity: Space and Geography in Modernism* (Manchester and New York: Manchester University Press, 2003), p.2.

4 E.H. Young, *Miss Mole* (London: Virago [1930], 1984), p.74.

5 Walter Benjamin, *The Arcades Project* (Cambridge, Mass.: The Belknap Press of Harvard University Press, 1999), p.10.

6 Rachele Dini, *Walter Benjamin: Arcades Project* (London: Mouseion, September 2015).

7 E.H. Young, *Celia* (London: Virago [1937], 1990), p.90.

8 See Chiara Briganti and Kathy Mezei's *Domestic Modernism, The Interwar Novel, and E.H. Young* (Aldershot: Ashgate, 2006) for a discussion of this phenomenon. By 'domestic modernism' we mean the valorisation of the home, the household, the everyday, and domesticity in the work of a striking number of women writers who flourished during the interwar years.

9 '[...] we have tried to define the river and harbour less as place restricted by discourses of "trade" and commerce, and rather more as a social and cultural environment, "tidescape" and throroughfare whose impact upon the quotidian life of the city was both essential and

multifarious', Steve Poole, 'Introduction: Built on the Water,' in *A City Built Upon the Water: Maritime Bristol*, ed. Steve Poole (Bristol: Redcliffe Press, 2013), p.8.

10 E.H. Young, *Celia*, p.16.

11 E.H. Young, *William* (London: Virago [1925], 1988), p.5.

12 See Maggie Lane, 'E.H. Young and Bristol' in '*A Great Adventure Enlivened by Countless Minor Episodes': The Life and Work of Emily Hilda Young: The First International E. H. Young Conference,* ed. Stella Deen (Privately printed, 2000), pp.1-7. The conference took place at Bristol Grammar School.

13 E.H. Young as E.H. Daniell, 'Reminiscences', *The Climbers' Club Journal*, 6 (1935), pp.25-9, and 27. We thank Maggie Lane for giving us a copy of this article.

14 'If London had its Dulwich, Richmond and Edgware, the same single-class exclusiveness was to be found in Bristol's Clifton, Cotham and Redland', John Burnett, *A Social History of Housing: 1815-1985,* (London: Methuen, 1986) p.193.

15 Stanley J. Kunitz and Howard Haycraft, eds, *Twentieth Century Authors: A Biographical Dictionary of Modern Literature* (New York: H. W. Wilson, 1942), p.1564.

16 We thank Mr Michael Booker for this information.

17 The other nine were André Maurois, *Ariel* (1924); Dorothy Sayers, *The Unpleasantness at the Bellona Club* (1928); Compton Mackenzie, *Carnival* (1912); Ernest Hemingway, *Farewell to Arms* (1929); Mary Webb, *Gone to Earth* (1917); Susan Ertz, *Madame Claire* (1923); Agatha Christie, *The Mysterious Affair at Styles* (1920); Eric Linklater, *Poet's Pub* (1929) and Beverley Nichols, *Twenty-Five* (1926).

18 Stella Deen, 'Emily Hilda Young's *Miss Mole*: Female Modernity and the Insufficiencies of the Domestic Novel', *Women's Studies: An Interdisciplinary Journal*, 30:3 (June 2001), pp.351-68; '"So Minute and Yet So Alive": Domestic Modernity in E.H. Young's *William*', *Tulsa Studies in Women's Literature,* 22:1 (Spring 2003), pp.99-120; '"There is No Ordinary Life": Privacy and Domesticity in E.H. Young's *Celia* and Elizabeth Bowen's *The Death of the Heart*', in *Challenging Modernism: New Readings in Literature and Culture, 1914-1945*, ed. Stella Deen (Burlington, VT: Ashgate, 2002), pp.97-114; Meike Fritz, *The Apostle of Quiet People: Die Schriftstellerin E. H. Young und ihre Romane als Beispiel populärer Frauenliteratur der englischen Mittelschicht in der ersten Hälfte des 20 Jahrhunderts* (Frankfurt am Main: Peter Lang, 2002); Diana Wallace, *Sisters and Rivals in British Women's Fiction, 1914-1939* (New York: St. Martin's Press, 1999); Kathy Mezei and Chiara Briganti, 'E.H. Young', *The Cambridge Guide to Women's Writing in English*, ed. Lorna Sage (Cambridge: Cambridge University Press, 1999), p.686; '"She Must be a Very Good Novelist": Re-reading E.H. Young (1880-1949),' *English Studies in Canada* 27 (2001), pp.303-31; Chiara Briganti and Kathy Mezei, *Domestic Modernism, The Interwar Novel, and E.H. Young* (Aldershot: Ashgate, 2006) and Maggie Lane, in '*E.H. Young and Bristol: A Great Adventure Enlivened by Countless Minor Episodes.*'

19 Ralph B. Henderson, 'E.H. Young, Her Muse, Her Method, and Her Message,' ts. 9 pp, n.d. Young Papers. Courtesy of William Saunders, London, U.K, p.8.

20 E.H. Young, *William*, p.195.

21 Young., p.28.

22 Ibid., p.30.

23 Ibid., p.7.

24 Ibid., p.5.

25 Ibid., p.7.

26 Ibid., p.17.

27 Ibid., p.40.

28 Ibid., p.167.

29 E.H. Young, *Miss Mole*, pp.10 and 9.

30 Ibid., p.44.

31 Ibid., p.45.

32 Ibid., p.282.

33 Georg Simmel, 'Bridge and Door', p.6.

34 E.H. Young, *Jenny Wren*, p.129.

35 Simmel, 'Bridge and Door'

36 Ibid., p.14.

37 Ibid., p.5.

38 Ibid., p.9.

39 Ibid., p.155.

40 Ibid., p.149.

41 E.H. Young, *The Curate's Wife* (London: Virago [1934], 1985), p.8.

42 Ibid., p.14.

43 Ibid., p.33.

44 Ibid., p.33.

45 Ibid., p.209.

46 Ibid., p.105.

47 Ibid., p.225.

48 Young, *Cecilia*, p.253.

49 Ibid., p.9.

50 E.H. Young, *Chatterton Square* (London: Virago [1947], 1987), p.5.

51 Ibid., p.5.

52 Ibid., p.9.

53 Ibid., p.12.

54 Ibid., p.327.

55 Ibid., p.347.

56 Ibid., p.361.

Chapter Six The Bristol New Wave: Radical Drama 1957-1968

1   *Bristol Evening Post*. October 1963. Wood sent me the clipping of this article personally and I have been unable, as yet, to trace further details.

2   Card from Charles Wood to Dawn Fowler, 7 August 2005. Orton and Wood shared the same agent, Margaret Ramsey.

3   John Boorman, *Adventures of a Suburban Boy* (London: Faber and Faber, 2003), pp.112-3.

4   Richard Findlater, *Banned! A Review of Theatrical Censorship in Britain* (London: Macgibbon and Kee, 1967), p.178.

5   Peter Nichols, *Feeling You're Behind* (Middlesex: Penguin, 1984), p.214.

6   Charles Wood, email to Dawn Fowler, 5 March 2005.

7   Charles Wood, transcript of interview with Dawn Fowler, 30 March 2005, p.15.

8   Charles Wood, email to Dawn Fowler, 24 February 2005.

9   A.C.H. Smith, *WordSmith: A Memoir* (Bristol: Redcliffe Press Ltd, 2012), pp.76-7.

10 Paul Delaney, 'Exit Tomáš Sträussler, enter Sir Tom Stoppard', *The Cambridge Companion to Tom Stoppard*, ed. Katherine Kelly (Cambridge: Cambridge University Press, 2001, p.27.

11 Smith, *Wordsmith*, p.72.

12 Ibid., pp.79-80.

13 For more details, see Tom Stoppard, 'My Love Affair with Newspapers', *British Journalism Review*, 16:4, 2005, 19-29.

14 Kenneth Tynan, *Profiles* (London: Nick Hern Books, New ed. 2007), p.304.

15 Michael Billington, *State of the Nation: British Theatre Since 1945* (London: Faber and Faber, 2007), p.65.

16 John Russell Taylor, *Anger and After: A Guide to the New British Drama* (Middlesex: Penguin, 1963), p.286.

17 Quoted in Billington, *State of the Nation*, p.67.

18 Harold Pinter, *The Room* and *The Dumb Waiter* (London: Faber and Faber, 1991), p.26.

19 Ibid., p.30.

20 Billington, *State of the Nation*, p.72.

21 Charles Wood, transcript of interview with Dawn Fowler, 30 March 2005, p.11.

22 Ibid., p.6.

23 Charles Wood, list of works with notes, document sent to Dawn Fowler, June 2004, p.1.

24 Arnold p.Hinchliffe, *British Theatre 1950-70* (Oxford: Basil Blackwell, 1974), p.164.

25 Dromgoole went on to produce over 60 films, television series and episodes of British drama. He is the father of the theatre director Dominic Dromgoole.

26 Charles Wood, *Cockade: Prisoner and Escort, John Thomas, Spare*, in *New English Dramatists 8* (London: Penguin, 1965), p.33.

27 Edward Mason, 'Watch this New Writer' 1963, Samuel Story Archives, 'The Charles Wood Papers'.

28 Letter from Dennis V. Lavington to The Head Producer, TWW, 7 April 1964.

29 Letter from A. Hellingway to Charles Wood, 9 April 1964.

30 Oscar Lewenstein, *Kicking Against the Pricks* (London: Nick Hern Books, 1994), p.118.

31 Smith, *Wordsmith*, p.158.

32 Letter from Margaret Ramsey to Wood, 29 July 1963. Samuel Story Archives, CW/2/27/2/2.

33 Memorandum from Kenneth Tynan to the National Theatre Board, 11 February 1965. Samuel Story Archives, CW/2/27/2/6.

34 An example is Alan Moorehead's *The Desert War: The North Africa Campaign 1940-1943* (1965) which was an influence on the play.

35 Ronald Bryden, 16 November 1967, n.p.Samuel Storey Archives: CW/2/27/3/4.

36 Charles Wood, transcript of interview with Dawn Fowler, March 30 2005, p.12.

37 Ibid., p.11.

38 Charles Wood, *Plays Two: 'H', Jingo and Dingo* (London: Oberon, 1999), p.309.

39 Ibid., p.306.

40 Ibid., 'Introduction to Plays Two', p.7.

41 Ibid., p.289.

42 Derek Weekes, 'A Survey of Charles Wood's plays for Stage and Screen, with Particular Reference to the Treatment of War in *Dingo, H* and the Assorted Films', 1982. Samuel Storey Archives: CW/2/118/1, p.69.

43 Wood, 1999, p.304.

44 Ibid., p.305.

45 Ibid., p.7.

46 Nichols, 1984, pp.214-5.

47 Bristol Festival of Ideas Programme for 'Bristol Films of the 1960s and 1970s', May 2012.

Chapter Seven Angela Carter's 'Bristol Trilogy': A Gothic Perspective on Bristol's 1960s Counterculture

1 See Patricia Juliana Smith, 'All You Need is Love: Angela Carter's Novel of Sixties Sex and Sensibility', *The Review of Contemporary Fiction*, 14:3 (Fall 1994), pp.24-9 and Marc O 'Day, 'Mutability is Having a Field Day': The Sixties Aura of Angela Carter's Bristol Trilogy', ed. Lorna Sage, *Flesh and The Mirror: Essays on the Art of Angela Carter* (London: Virago [1994], 2007), pp.24-59. Although not conceived by Carter as a three-part series, I am convinced by O'Day that they share many of the same concerns.

2 Nowhere in the trilogy is Bristol explicitly named. However, the individual locations are recognisable and Carter later confirmed that she set them in the city in which she was living at the time. See John Haffenden, *Novelists in Interview* (New York: Methuen Press, 1985), pp.76-96.

3 Ibid., p.80.

4 For an earlier biographical approach to the writer, see Sarah Gamble, *Angela Carter: A Literary Life* (Basingstoke: Palgrave Macmillan, 2006). Edmund Gordon's biography of Carter is scheduled for publication in 2016 by Chatto & Windus.

5 Quoted in Sarah Gamble, ed. *The Fiction of Angela Carter: A Reader's Guide to Essential Criticism* (Basingstoke: Palgrave Macmillan, 2001), p.10.

6   This slogan was popularised in 1967 by Timothy Leary, a vocal advocate of psychedelic drug experimentation.

7   Haffenden, *Novelists in Interview*, p.80.

8   Lorna Sage. 'A Brief Biography of Angela Carter', ecmd.nju.edu.cn/UploadFile/25/12359/11carterbio.doc, accessed January 2014.

9   O'Day, 'Mutability is Having a Field Day', p.28.

10 Ibid., p.28.

11 Anon, 'Mod to Suedehead', Style Forum, http://www.styleforum.net/t/89027/mod-to-suede-head, accessed January 2014.

12 Quoted in Sage, 'A Brief Biography'.

13 Angela Carter, *Several Perceptions* (London: Virago [1968], 1997), p.5.

14 That is not to suggest that there were not more life-affirming philosophies around in the 1960s but that they do not make their way into the trilogy, apart from in a piecemeal way at the end of *Several Perceptions*.

15 Carter quoted in Alison Lee, *Angela Carter* (London: Prentice Hall, 1997), p.23. Notice that she uses a locational metaphor, of a demolition site, to help capture her feelings and it is this technique I discuss later in the chapter.

16 See Madge Dresser, *Black and White on the Buses: The 1963 Colour Bar Dispute in Bristol* (Bristol: Bristol Broadsides, 1986).

17 Carter, *Several Perceptions,* p.6.

18 Ibid., p.60.

19 Angela Carter, *Shadow Dance* (London: Virago Press [1966], 1994), p.13.

20 Sarah Gamble, *Angela Carter: Writing From the Front Line* (Edinburgh: Edinburgh University Press, 1997), p.54.

21 Ibid., p.54.

22 Angela Carter, 'Notes from the Front Line' in *Shaking a Leg: Collected Writings*, ed. Jenny Uglow, (Harmondsworth: Penguin, 1997), p.38.

23 Quoted in Lee, *Angela Carter,* p.27.

24 Ibid., p.28.

25 These are the sort of female figures we find in her re-working of fairy-tales *The Bloody Chamber* (1979) or Carter's last novel *Wise Children* (1991).

26 Kelly Hurley, 'British Gothic Fiction, 1885-1930', Jerrold E. Hogle, ed. *The Cambridge Companion to Gothic Fiction* (Cambridge: Cambridge University Press, 2002), p.194.

27 Emily Alder, 'The Urban Gothic', eds William Hughes, David Punter, and Andrew Smith, *The Encyclopedia of The Gothic*, 2 vols (London: Wiley-Blackwell, 2013), 2, p.703.

28 Carter, *Shadow Dance*, pp.11-2.

29 Quoted in Gamble, ed. *The Fiction of Angela Carter,* p.21.

30 Carter, *Several Perceptions*, p.88.

31 David Punter, 'The Uncanny', eds Catherine Spooner and Emma McEvoy,*The Routledge Companion to Gothic* (London: Routledge 2007), p.130.

32 Sigmund Freud, 'The Uncanny', James Strachey, ed. in *The Standard Edition of the Complete Psychological Works of Sigmund Freud*, 24 vols (London: The Hogarth Press, 1955), XVII, pp.218-52.

33 Anon., 'Bomb Census Bristol: The Blitz In Brislington', *Culture*, 24, http://www.culture24.org.uk/places-to-go/south-west/bristol, accessed January 2014.

34 Paul Townsend, 'Bristol at war 1939-1941', Brizzle Born and Bred, accessed January 2014, http://www.flickr.com/photos/20654194@N07/. I cannot recommend this site run by a local historian highly enough. It is particularly useful for accessing first-hand accounts of people who knew Bristol during the 1960s.

35 Bryan Little, *The Story of Bristol: from the Medieval Period to the Present Day* (Bristol: Redcliffe Press, 1991), p.95.

36 There was one exception, the Mecca centre to which I return.

37 Little, *The Story of Bristol*, p.95.

38 Carter, *Shadow Dance,* p.86.

39 Ibid., pp.88-9. Steptoe is a rag and bone man who runs the business with his son in a British TV sitcom first broadcast from 1962-1974.

40 Ibid., pp.89-90.

41 O'Day, 'Mutability is Having a Field Day', p.39.

42 Carter, *Shadow Dance,* p.35.

43 Ibid., p.68.

44 Ibid., p.40.

45 Ibid., p.40.

46 Ibid., pp.23-4.

47 Ibid., p.25.

48 Ibid., p.25.

49 O'Day, 'Mutability is Having a Field Day', p.41.

50 Carter, *Several Perceptions,* p.3.

51 Ibid., pp.9-10.

52 See David Hussey, 'Leisure and Commerce: The Hotwell and The Port of Bristol, 1750-1850', ed. Steve Poole *A City Built Upon the Water,* (Bristol: Redcliffe Press, 2013), pp.44-8.

53 Carter, *Several Perceptions,* p.10.

54 Gamble, *Writing From the Front Line,* p.62 . Viv's mum Mrs Boulder gets her beau back in *Several Perceptions* and one of the 'Struldbrugs' who crosses paths with Honeybuzzard survives to Morris' delight in *Shadow Dance.*

55 Carter, *Several Perceptions,* p.14.

56 Ibid., p.18.

57 Ibid., p.127.

58 Ibid., pp.128- 9.

59 Ibid., p.146.

60 Gamble, *The Fiction of Angela Carter,* p.31.

61 Angela Carter, *Love* (London: Picador [1971], 1988), p.14.

62 Ibid., pp.6-7.

63 Ibid., p.1.

64 Ibid., p.1

65 Ibid., p.2.

66 Ibid., p.2.

67 Ibid., p.1.

68 Paul Townsend '"Mecca", Brizzle Born and Bred', http://www.flickr.com/photos/20654194@N07/, accessed January 2014.

69 Carter, *Love,* p.78.

70 Ibid., p.76.

71 Ibid., p.106.

72 Ibid., p.79.

73 Ibid., p.79.

74 Ibid., p.80.

75 Carter, *Shadow Dance,* p.86. Because of his sociopathic tendencies, it does not seem likely that the reader is expected to agree with his opinions.

76 Ibid., pp.54-5.

77 Ibid., p.29.

78 Ibid., pp.29-30.

79 Ibid., p.30.

80 Jonathan Swift, *Gulliver's Travels* (Harmondsworth: Penguin [1726], 1997). The Struldbrugs are discussed in book 3, chapter 10.

81 Carter, *Several Perceptions,* p.23.

82 Ibid., p.23.

83 Ibid., p.23.

84 Ibid., p.10.

85 Carter, 'Elizabeth Wilson: Adorned in Dreams', in *Shaking a Leg*, ed. Uglow, p.138.

86 I see this collection of essays as part of a larger movement that is interested in regional literature and so challenging London-centricity.

87 Alder, 'Urban Gothic', 2, p.705 and Robert Mighall, 'Gothic Cities', *The Routledge Companion to Gothic*, pp.54-62.

88 Haffenden, *Novelists in Interview*, p.80.

89 Quoted in O'Day, 'Mutability is Having a Field Day', p.26.

90 Gamble, *Writing from the Front Line,* p.54.

91 For a comic representation of Bristol's counterculture see Mike Manson's novel *Where's My Money?* (Bristol: Tangent Books, 2008). Set slightly later than the trilogy in 1976 it focuses on the adventures of an unlikely dole clerk, the recently-graduated Max.

92 Gamble, *Writing from the Front Line*, p.8.

Chapter Eight Enchanting the City: Diana Wynne Jones and Bristol

1 Charles Butler, *Four British Fantasists: Place and Culture in the Children's Fantasies of Penelope Lively, Alan Garner, Susan Cooper, and Diana Wynne Jones* (Lanham MD: Scarecrow Press/Children's Literature Association, 2006).

2 Jane Bennett, *The Enchantment of Modern Life: Attachments, Crossings, and Ethics* (Princeton and Woodstock: Princeton University Press, 2001), p.4.

3 Diana Wynne Jones, *Deep Secret* (New York: Tor [1997], 2000), p.76.

4 Ibid., p.76.

5 Ibid., pp.76-7.

6 Ibid., p.80.

7 Ibid., p.81.

8 Tom Abba and Duncan Speakman, *These Pages Fall Like Ash: A Volume of Circumstance* (2013), http://wearecircumstance.com/these-pages-fall-like-ash.html, accessed 14 February 2014.

9 Portus Abonae was also the name of the Roman settlement at what is now known as Sea Mills.

10 Sarah Ditum, 'Urban novelties: How Bristol itself became a short story' *New Statesman* 8 May 2013, http://www.newstatesman.com/sci-tech/2013/05/urban-novelties-how-bristol-itself-became-short-story, accessed 8 February 2014.

11 Abba and Speakman, *These Pages Fall Like Ash* [n.p.].

12 This is a subject covered at length in my *Four British Fantasists, passim*.

13 Diana Wynne Jones, 'The Shape of the Narrative in *The Lord of the Rings*', in *J.R.R. Tolkien: This Far Land*, edited by Robert Giddings (London: Vision, 1983) p.89.

14 Jones, 'The Shape of the Narrative', p.89.

15 Eliot's *Four Quartets* is one of several structuring intertexts in this complex novel. For more on these, see Diana Wynne Jones, 'The Heroic Ideal – A Personal Odyssey', *The Lion and the Unicorn*, 13:1 (1989), pp.129-40.

16 Diana Wynne Jones, *Fire and Hemlock* (London: HarperCollins [1985], 2000), p.225.

17 See Judith Ridge, 'Diana Wynne Jones 1992 Interview', http://www.misrule.com.au/dwj92_6.html, accessed 9 February 2014.

18 Diana Wynne Jones, *A Tale of Time City* (London: HarperCollins [1987], 2000), p.117.

19 Diana Wynne Jones, *The Merlin Conspiracy* (New York: Greenwillow, 2003), p.123.

20 Butler, Charles, 'Interview with Diana Wynne Jones', *Diana Wynne Jones: An Exciting and Exacting Wisdom*, eds Teya Rosenberg *et al* (New York: Peter Lang, 2002), p.163.

21 Diana Wynne Jones, *Howl's Moving Castle* (London: HarperCollins [1986], 2000), p.9.

22 Jones, *Howl's Moving Castle*, p.215.

23 For a detailed discussion of the relationship between Jones' and Orwell's novels, see Kyra Jucovy, 'Little Sister Is Watching You: *Archer's Goon* and *1984*', *Journal of the Fantastic in the Arts*, 21:2 (2010), pp.271-89.

24 Diana Wynne Jones, *Archer's Goon* (London: HarperCollins [1984], 2000), p.85.

25 Diana Wynne Jones, letter to Suzanne Rahn (14 May 1991), quoted in Suzanne Rahn, *Rediscoveries in Children's Literature* (New York and London: Garland Publishing, 1995), p.171.

26 Jones, *Archer's Goon*, p.10.

27 For more about this events, see Alison Flood, 'A fantastic weekend with Diana Wynne Jones', 9 July 2009, http://www.theguardian.com/books/booksblog/2009/jul/09/fantastic-diana-wynne-jones, accessed 13 February 2014.

28 Helen Harvey, '*Archer's Goon* and the Oxford Theory', Homeworld8 http://dianawynnejones.livejournal.com/154227.html, accessed 13 February 2014.

29 Ibid.

30 Butler, 'Interview with Diana Wynne Jones', pp.163-64.

31 For Jones's own discussion of the intertexts she used in writing *Fire and Hemlock*, see Wynne Jones, 'The Heroic Ideal – A Personal Odyssey', pp.129-40.

32 Butler, 'Interview with Diana Wynne Jones', p.172.

33 C.S. Lewis, 'On Three Ways of Writing for Children' (1952), in Sheila Egoff, G.T. Stubbs and L.F. Ashley, eds, *Only Connect: Readings on Children's Literature* (Toronto, New York and Oxford: Oxford University Press, 1969), p.215.

The Authors

Kerri Andrews is Senior Lecturer in English Studies at the University of Strathclyde. She is the editor of *The Collected Works of Ann Yearsley* (2014), and the author of *Ann Yearsley and Hannah More, Patronage and Poetry* (2013). She has published extensively on Ann Yearsley's works, as well as on the poetry of Hannah More and Charlotte Smith.

Zoe Brennan is Senior Lecturer in English Literature at the University of the West of England, Bristol. Her research interests include the representation of ageing in fiction, contemporary women writers and the female Gothic. She is author of two literary critical books: *The Older Woman in Recent Fiction* (2004) and *Bronte's Jane Eyre: A Reader's Guide* (2010). She would like to add that she considers herself 'local-ish' to Bristol. Born and bred in the West Country, she spent some rowdy youthful nights at 'Lakota' and 'The Fleece and Firkin'.

Chiara Briganti is a former Professor of English and Women's and Gender Studies at Carleton College, Minnesota. She is a Research Fellow in the Department of English Literature at King's College London. Her areas of research are the late Victorian period and modernity, particularly in relation to urban culture, political writing, material culture, and domestic space. With Kathy Mezei she has published *The Domestic Space Reader* (2012), and *Domestic Modernism, the Interwar Novel, and E.H. Young* (2006).

Catherine Butler is Senior Lecturer in English Literature at Cardiff University. She is the author of *Four British Fantasists* (2006) and (with Hallie O'Donovan) of *Reading History in Children's Books* (2012) as well as of numerous articles and chapters on the subject of fantasy, and is the editor of several critical collections. Catherine is also a fantasy author for children and young adults, her most recent book being the edited collection, *Twisted Winter* (2013). She is Associate Editor of the journal *Children's Literature in Education*.

Dawn Fowler is Senior Lecturer in Drama at the University of the West of England, Bristol where she leads the modules, The Radical Self and Applied Theatre. Her research interests include regional theatre, war, atrocity and conflict on stage, late twentieth- and early twenty-first century British and Irish Drama and marginalised performance histories. She has published on the Scottish playwright and director David Greig and the Bristol dramatist Charles Wood, whom she is currently researching, along with languages of terrorism in performance, suffragettes on stage, dramatic representations of humanitarianism and theatre as political protest.

John Goodridge is Professor of English at Nottingham Trent University. He has edited and published widely, usually in the field of eighteenth- and nineteenth-century poetry. Publications include *Rural Life in Eighteenth-Century English Poetry* (1994) and *John Clare and Community* (2013). He is working on a co-authored study of *Labour in Labouring-Class*

Poetry for Palgrave and an edited volume, *A History of British Working-Class Writing* for Cambridge. Professor Goodridge is a Fellow of the English Association, Vice-President of the John Clare Society, academic advisor to the Robert Bloomfield Society and co-founder of the Thomas Chatterton Society.

Robin Jarvis is Professor of English Literature at the University of the West of England, Bristol. He is the author of *Wordsworth, Milton and the Theory of Poetic Relations* (1991), *Romantic Writing and Pedestrian Travel* (1997), *The Romantic Period: The Intellectual and Cultural Context of English Literature 1789-1830* (2004), *Romantic Readers and Transatlantic Travel: Expeditions and Tours in North America*, 1760-1840 (2012), and numerous journal articles and book chapters on topics in Romantic literature and travel writing studies.

Kathy Mezei is Professor Emeritus, Department of Humanities, Simon Fraser University, Vancouver, Canada. Her research interests include Canadian literature, translation studies, modern British women writers, and domestic space. She is the author, along with Chiara Briganti, of *The Domestic Space Reader* (2012), and a study of E.H. Young and the domestic novel called *Domestic Modernism, the Interwar Novel, and E.H. Young* (2006).

Marie Mulvey-Roberts is Associate Professor in English Literature and Reader in Literary Studies at the University of the West of England, Bristol. She is the founder of the Mapping Literary Bristol Project and is the editor-in-chief of *Women's Writing*. She is the editor of *The Handbook to the Gothic* (2009) and co-editor of *Gothic Fiction* (2002-3) and author of *British Poets and Secret Societies* (1986 rpt 2014), *Gothic Immortals* (1990) and *Dangerous Bodies: Historicising the Gothic Corporeal* (2016). She has lived in Bristol more than anywhere else and loves the city.

Index bold denotes illustration